0X(10/08)7/11

FIRST STRIKE

TWA FLIGHT 800 AND THE ATTACK ON AMERICA

JACK CASHILL
AND
JAMES SANDERS

WND BOOKS
A DIVISION OF THOMAS NELSON, INC.

Dedicated to the memory of Commander William S. Donaldson

Published in Nashville, Tennessee, by Thomas Nelson, Inc.

ISBN 0-7852-6354-3 (hardcover)

Printed in the United States of America

CONTENTS

Preface: Understandings   v

1. First Impressions   1

2. Lost Opportunities   13

3. False Dialectic   31

4. Dog Days   51

5. Red Herring   67

6. Decent Interval   83

7. Hangar Man   99

8. Damage Control   120

9. The Big Lie   142

10. Black Boxes   160

11. Exploding Hypotheses   176

12. Show Trial   199

13. Imaginary Flagpoles   220

14. First Strike   234

Notes   259

Acknowledgments   275

About the Authors   277

About WND Books   278

UNDERSTANDINGS

> *The case of TWA 800 served as a turning point because of Washington's deter-*
> *mination and to a great extent ability to suppress terrorist explanations and*
> *"float" mechanical failure theories. To avoid such suppression after future*
> *strikes, terrorism-sponsoring states would raise the ante so that the West cannot*
> *ignore them.*
>
> —YOSSEF BODANSKY, DIRECTOR OF THE CONGRESSIONAL TASK
>   FORCE ON TERRORISM AND UNCONVENTIONAL WARFARE, 1999

Perhaps on his deathbed former president Bill Clinton will tell *Washington Post* reporter Bob Woodward exactly what did transpire in those first few hours and days after TWA Flight 800 exploded off the coast of Long Island on July 17, 1996.

Perhaps in the interim someone of significance in the American military will come forward and tell what happened in those crucial seconds before the explosion and those crucial minutes afterwards. Perhaps, too, someone in the al-Qaida network will reveal what happened in the weeks and hours leading up to the tragic event.

But at this juncture, none of these possibilities seem likely. The task is left to us to tell the story of what happened on and after that fateful day without the help of the only people who truly know. We acknowledge that limitation from the outset.

This challenge is not unlike writing a book on the murder of Nicole Brown and Ron Goldman without the help of O. J. Simpson and the friends who abetted him. To make the challenge more daunting, imagine if Johnny Cochran and the defense team controlled all the evidence in the case and exploited a willing media, even a corrupt Justice Department, to condemn as a "conspiracy theorist" or worse anyone who dared to dissent. Imagine, too, that this condemnation turned to scorn and scorn to public ridicule after a jury of peers attested to Simpson's innocence.

In both cases, however, there is no denying the truth. The circumstantial evidence is overwhelming. The thrust of the story is irrefutable. The principals, even if they were willing, could only add or subtract details. Given the limitations, however, we will take great care throughout this book to distinguish what we know from what we believe. Conjecture will always be qualified.

We will leave the tales of heroic work at sea and tragedy at home to others. There is no denying the magnitude of either. The shame of it all is that the former was squandered and the latter exploited. We will reveal instead, as well as the evidence permits, how and why agents of the government transformed the most public destruction of an airliner in American history—second only to the 9/11 terrorist attacks—into an unsolved mystery.

In her book on this case, *Deadly Departure,* CNN reporter Christine Negroni laments that advocates of a cover-up still do not accept that "bungling, benign or otherwise," explains the contradictions and misdirection endemic in the investigation.[1] We do not deny the bungling. If anything, it provided a fortunate screen for those who would subvert the search for truth. But in far too many instances the misdirection is purposeful, and we will show with a high degree of confidence where those misdirections occurred.

A second book that has proved useful is Associated Press reporter Patricia Milton's *In the Blink of an Eye.* According to Milton, the book "resulted from the willingness of the FBI to open itself up to a journalist."[2] It does not disappoint. The book reads like an FBI defense brief. In both books, high-level government agents "open up" to reporters because they know in advance that the reporters will not look beyond the obvious, will not even challenge the contradictions that stare them in the face.

Negroni and Milton each had major publishers for their TWA 800 books, big-time talk-show bookings, and respectful reviews in the *New York Times*. Like virtually all TWA 800 stories from the major media, these books hewed to the government line with a passion and pride that would make Edward R. Murrow squirm in his grave. Said the *New York Times* review in perfunctory praise of Milton's *In the Blink of an Eye*, it "avoids the pitfalls of conspiracy mongering."[3]

From the perspective of the major media, to seek the truth about the Clinton administration *was* to monger conspiracy. They would leave that unpleasant task to the alternative media and blind themselves to all evidence short of the DNA. Indeed, in their cynicism and passivity, it was they, Bill Clinton's media friends, who undid his presidency. Had they ever shamed him into honoring his office, he might have become the president they once thought he could be.

CHAPTER 1

FIRST IMPRESSIONS

Only those who live by the sea know how mesmerizing the sea can be. For no easily explained reason, they watch it ceaselessly, observe every nuance, and share their observations with others who care as they do.

On Long Island's south shore, on a sweet summer eve like that of July 17, 1996, the temperature a perfect seventy-one degrees, the sky serene and fair, they would all be out watching. They would be watching from their boats, from the beaches, from the decks of their summer rentals. Not that they expected to see anything unusual. No, life in America that summer appeared as soft as the evening itself, as soft and stressless perhaps as it had ever been before or ever would be again.

"The fact is," President Clinton had told America's governors just the day before, "our economy is now the soundest it's been in a genera-tion."[1] The American people did not seem to begrudge him his bragging rights. A poll that same week showed him leading the Republican's aging warrior, Bob Dole, by a staggering twenty percentage points. Barring the unforeseen, indeed the catastrophic, Clinton would cakewalk to reelection in November.

To be sure, there was some trouble around the world, but not enough to disturb anyone's summer, contained as it was in places few in America cared much about—the Balkans, the Middle East, Africa, Russia.

Closer to home, Islamic terrorist Ramzi Yousef was standing trial in New York for his role in the Bojinka plot, an attempt to blow up eleven American airliners in one day over the Pacific.[2] To most observers, however, the plot seemed fanciful, preposterous even. One element of Bojinka—the transformation of a small plane into a flying bomb to attack American targets—borrowed a page from Yousef's most notorious crime: the truck bombing of the World Trade Center in 1993. He would soon enough stand trial for that outrage as well.

Of more immediate concern was the terrorist bombing of Khobar Towers, an American barracks in Saudi Arabia. That attack, just three weeks earlier, had killed nineteen American servicemen. The president had responded with tough talk. "The cowards who committed this murderous act must not go unpunished," he declared. "Let me say again: We will pursue this. America takes care of our own. Those who did it must not go unpunished."[3] Adviser Dick Morris ran a quick poll for the relentlessly political president and found that Americans approved of his handling of the bombing 73 to 20 percent. Only 18 percent held Clinton responsible.[4] Words would suffice. Besides, Saudi Arabia was eight time zones away. And New Yorkers had a hard time worrying about events in New Jersey, let alone in the Middle East, especially with the Yankees heating up, the Atlanta Olympics around the corner, and a sweet summer night like this one at hand.

At 8:30 that evening, a minute before sunset, Lisa Perry enjoyed the view from her elevated deck on Fire Island, twenty-two feet above the beach. For no good reason, she was looking eastward towards the Hamptons. Paul Angelides, having finished dinner, walked through the sliding doors to the deck of his summer rental on the beach in Westhampton. Richard Goss and his friends relaxed on the deck of a nearby yacht club.

Also in Westhampton, Mike Wire took a breather from the switch gear room on Beach Lane Bridge, where he had been working all day, and leaned out over the rail with his eye on the dunes and beach. Joseph Delgado had just completed a few laps at a school track in Westhampton, and he was looking south. National Guard pilots Maj. Fritz Meyer and Capt. Chris Baur likewise looked south as they maneuvered their HH-60 military helicopter in for a landing at Gabreski Field a few miles away. And twenty-two thousand feet overhead, Dwight Brumley, a retired twenty-five-year United States Navy master chief, relaxed on US Air 217 as it headed north to Providence, Rhode Island.

The clear weather pattern held sway at least as far west as Montoursville, Pennsylvania, a good three-hour drive from New York City. Don Nibert had a little more daylight there and was using it to pick berries at his small orchard. He was finishing a job his sixteen-year-old daughter, Cheryl, had started. Her hands still stained from the picking, she and fifteen of her fellow French club members and five of their chaperones had left the local high school early that afternoon on a bus bound for JFK airport in New York. Don had promised Cheryl that he would finish the work she had contracted to do and wished her bon voyage.

At 8:30 P.M. Cheryl and her friends were comfortably strapped in to their seats on TWA 800, a workhorse 747 wide-body, flying parallel to the Long Island coast and a few miles south. The plane had left the runway at 8:19, made a wide turn to the south, and then turned back east. It ascended slowly to more than thirteen thousand feet and held there to let Dwight Brumley's plane, US Air 217, pass comfortably overhead.

Cheryl was one of 230 people on board, 53 of them TWA employees—19 crewmembers and the rest just catching the six-hour ride to Paris. The pilot was Capt. Ralph Kevorkian of Garden Grove, California, an Air Force veteran who had been with TWA since 1965. Although this was his first flight as captain, Kevorkian had logged more than five thousand hours in a 747 either as cocaptain or crew. He had a perfect safety record, as did his cocaptain, Steve Snyder, an experienced TWA pilot who also served as Kevorkian's instructor.

On this peaceful eve, so free of stress for so many people, no one along the Long Island shore then could have imagined that they were just a minute away from witnessing the biggest news story of 1996 and the greatest untold story of our time—one whose suppression would shape the course of American history.

SOMETIMES the old saws make sense. Appearances *can* deceive. The evening of July 17 was not as peaceful as it appeared to be. Not nearly so. The signs of unease were everywhere, some literally beneath the surface. It's just that few were prepared to interpret them.

Dean Steward observed one such sign earlier in the day at Gilgo State Park, where he and his friend Susan Smith were enjoying a day off. They had arrived at this park on Long Island's south shore, Steward recalls, at about 1 P.M. About two hours later Smith walked back to the car to retrieve a Frisbee.

When she returned to the beach, Steward alerted her to a navy ship about three miles offshore, moving slowly westward towards New York City.

Steward pointed out the rake of the bow and the staggered sets of jet-black exhaust from the stacks. From what he could see, Steward thought the ship to be a cruiser, one equipped with a sophisticated Aegis missile-guidance system. The telltale sign was the bulky forward superstructure that houses the system. Says Steward, "I'm 90 percent sure it was U.S. and 100 percent sure it was a warship."[5]

Steward did not think much of the sighting at the time, other than that it gave him a chance to show off his military knowledge. The thirty-four-year-old Steward had spent eight years in the U.S. Navy, including two tours on carriers as a bombardier-navigator flying A-6 Intruders. As to Smith, she offered a more knowing ear than the average date. She herself was a pilot for a Dulles-based commuter airline.

About three hours later on that same day, and about twelve or so miles east of Gilgo State Park, at Fire Island, Lisa Perry and her friend Alice Rowe saw what may have been the same ship or one quite similar. They remembered the time because they had returned to the beach after a quick dinner so the kids could play in the tidal pools. The women noticed the ship just outside the sandbar toward the west. The bow was high, and it cut smoothly into the water. The combination of the ship's size and proximity to shore held their attention. They watched as it moved directly from the west at a moderate pace, the opposite direction of the ship Steward and Smith had seen. "Not fast," says Perry, "but not slowly."[6]

Once in front of them, they could see that it was "a military fighting ship," battleship gray with the characteristic ID numbers on the front. "There was a lot of equipment on board," says Perry, "such as the big globe, which we assumed must be radar, and military gunnery." The ship was so large and close that the women could barely capture its profile in one glance. Although they each had spent many years at Long Island beaches, neither Perry nor Rowe had ever observed a ship of that size so close to shore.

What Perry and Rowe had seen at Fire Island and Steward and Smith had seen at Gilgo State Park were two signs out of many that July 17 was in no way ordinary. On that fateful day, in fact, the United States military was on its highest state of home-front alert since the Cuban Missile crisis. Yossef Bodansky, director of the Congressional Task Force on Terrorism and Unconventional Warfare, described two of the communications that ratcheted up the tension. The first was an editorial in the respected London-based paper *al-Quds al-Arabi* that "outlined the logic for escalating the armed terrorist struggle against the United States." The editorial made a compelling case that the truck bombing of the Khobar Towers in Saudi Arabia three weeks earlier and the recent fatal stabbing of a female American Embassy official in Cairo were the beginning of a larger terrorist campaign. "Thus," concluded the editorial, "we would not be surprised if such attacks on the Americans continue on a large scale in the future."[7] The editor, according to Bodansky, was a close friend of Osama bin Laden, then little known in the West beyond intelligence circles.

The second communication came in the form of a fax sent to *Al-Hayah* in London, the most prestigious Arabic language newspaper. It arrived shortly before noon, Washington time, on July 17. Sent by the Islamic Change Movement—the jihad wing in the Arabian Peninsula—the warning came one day after the group had taken responsibility for the destruction of Khobar Towers.[8] It was as serious as a truck bomb:

> The mujahideen will give their harshest reply to the threats of the foolish U.S. President. Everybody will be surprised by the magnitude of the reply, the date and time of which will be determined by the mujahideen. The invaders must be prepared to leave, either dead or alive. Their time is at the morning-dawn. Is not the morning-dawn near?[9]

As the sun was about to rise on the Arabian Peninsula, it was about to set on Long Island. At 8:31 Dwight Brumley, whose long Navy career included special expertise in electronic warfare, put down the book he was reading and glanced out the window of US Air 217. Night had already fallen to the east, the direction in which he looked.

"I NOTICED off the right side what appeared to be a small private airplane that was flying pretty much at a course right at the US Air flight," Brumley recounts. "I followed it until the fuselage and the inboard wing cut off my field of view. My first thought—that was awfully close!"[10] Brumley estimates that the plane passed a mere three or four hundred feet beneath him.

About fifteen seconds after the small plane had passed, Brumley noticed "what appeared to be some kind of a flare," but he realized quickly that this bright, burning object ascending off the ocean was no flare. "It was definitely moving pretty much parallel to the US Air flight, and it was moving at least as fast, perhaps even faster."

As the flarelike object raced north—and as Flight 800 ascended slowly and innocently eastward along the Long Island coast—Mike Wire, a millwright from Philadelphia working on a Westhampton bridge, saw a streak of light rise up from behind a Westhampton house and zigzag south-southeast away from shore at about a forty-degree angle, leaving a white smoke trail behind it.[11]

Richard Goss, upon seeing the same object, turned to his friends at the yacht club and said, "Hey, look at the fireworks." Everybody turned to look, and they all watched it climb. "It was bright, very bright," says Goss, "and, you know, that almost bright pink, you know, and orange glow around it and it traveled up."[12]

Vacationer Lisa Perry, on her Fire Island deck, watched an object shoot up over the dunes of Fire Island. "It was shiny, like a new dime," says Perry. "It looked like a plane without wings. It had no windows. It was as if there was a flame at the back of it, like a Bunsen burner. It was like a silver bullet."[13] The object was heading east-southeast towards the Hamptons.

As Paul Angelides walked out onto his Westhampton deck, he picked up the same object now high in the sky. From his angle, it appeared to be a "red phosphorescent object . . . leaving a white smoke trail."[14] At first he thought the object a distress flare, but he soon realized it was too large and moving too fast. Spellbound, he followed the object as it moved out over the ocean in the direction of the horizon.

Goss followed it too. "It seemed to go away in the distance towards the south, and that's when I saw it veer left, which would bring it out east. It was a sharp left."

From a Westhampton school parking lot, Joseph Delgado saw the same streak Brumley viewed, the one heading north towards shore and slightly west. As he told the FBI, he saw an object like "a firework" ascend almost vertically. The object had a "bright white light with a reddish-pink aura surrounding it." The tail, gray in color, "moved in a squiggly pattern." From Delgado's perspective, the object "arced off to the right in a southwesterly direction."[15]

At 8:31, FAA radar operators out of Islip saw an unknown object appear on-screen and head towards Flight 800. At the same moment FAA radar picked up something else unusual—a ship of good size nearly right under Flight 800's airborne position.

The two National Guard pilots in their nearby helicopter now picked up the streaks high in the sky. Capt. Chris Baur saw the streak Brumley had first observed. "Almost due south, there was a hard white light, like burning pyrotechnics, in level flight. I was trying to figure out what it was. It was the wrong color for flares. It struck an object coming from the right and made it explode."[16] Maj. Fritz Meyer, a winner of the Distinguished Flying Cross for his service over Vietnam, saw the southbound missile clearest. "It was definitely a rocket motor," says Meyer.[17]

Delgado saw a second object "glitter" in the sky and the first object move up towards it. He thought at first it was "going to slightly miss" the glittering object, TWA 800, but it appeared to make "a dramatic correction at the last second." Then Delgado saw a "white puff."

"From my vantage point," says Goss, "there was a direct explosion that followed, and then after that there was a second explosion that was off to the east a little farther that was much larger."

Meyer saw a bright white light also. "What I saw explode was definitely ordnance," he said. "The initiating event was a high-velocity explosion, not fuel. It was ordnance."

"I then saw a series of flashes, one in the sky and another closer to the horizon. I remember straining to see what was happening," says Paul Angelides. "There was a dot on the horizon near the action, which I perceived as a boat."

"About two seconds later," claimed Meyer, "lower, I saw one or two yellow explosions, from that the fireball, third. The first two high-velocity, the last low-velocity petrochemical explosion."

"Then a moment later there was another explosion and the plane broke jaggedly in the sky," says Lisa Perry. "The nose is continuing to go forward; the left wing is gliding off in its own direction, drifting in an arc gracefully down; the right wing and passenger window are doing the same in their direction out to the right; and the tail with its fireball leaps up and then promptly into the water below. The sounds were a huge BOOM!—then another BOOM!"

"You could feel the concussion like a shock wave," reports Mike Wire of the initial blast. Indeed, it shook the bridge on which he was standing in Westhampton, even at ten miles distance.

"The sounds shook the house," remembers Angelides. "My wife, who was on the bathroom floor drying our son from his bath, felt the floor shaking as she heard the noise and I heard her cry out, 'What is going on?'"

And then confusion—a hellish, horrific confusion. "There seemed to be a lot of chaos out there," says Angelides. Now he, Wire, Perry, Meyer, Baur,

Goss, Delgado, and Brumley watched as the plane's fuel tanks exploded, and Flight 800 morphed into what Delgado described as a "firebox" and others described as a "fireball."

"It got much larger, maybe four or five times as large," says Brumley, who was watching the explosion from overhead. "It was the same explosion. It just got bigger. My first thought was, *Boy, what was that?*"

"When that airplane blew up it immediately began falling," adds Major Meyer. "It came right out of the sky. From the first moment, it was going down."

Brumley saw the burning debris hit the water and turned to summon a flight attendant. As he did, a passenger in the seat behind him, James Nugent, cried out, "Did you see that too?"[18] Brumley and the others were hardly alone in what they had seen. On that soft summer eve, thousands were watching the sea and the sky. More than seven hundred of them would share their stories with the FBI.

AT this very moment, far from the chaos off Long Island, deep within his idyllic orchard farm outside Montoursville, Don Nibert heard a voice behind him. He could not mistake the southern Ohio, northern Kentucky accent anywhere. It was his mother's. "Don, Cheryl is okay," the voice whispered. "She is with me. You even sent her with raspberry stains on her hands." Don was startled. His mother had been dead for years. At the same moment, his wife, Donna, complained of an unexpected, almost crippling pain in her hip.[19]

Uneasy about the experience, Don brought Donna back to the house. Moments later the phone rang. Don answered it. A mother of another child had called in panic. She told him there was a crash out of JFK and wanted to know the flight number of their kids' plane. Don replied that the flight was to have left JFK an hour earlier, but he sensed otherwise. "I recalled what my mother told me," he says, "and I knew it was our plane." He checked the ticket receipts only for confirmation.

In Glendale, California, Flora Headley watched the news accounts in horror. The plane that had gone down was piloted by her son, Capt. Ralph Kevorkian. "Don't worry, Grandma," her nine-year-old grandson said, trying desperately to comfort her and himself. "Dad, can fly through anything."

"You don't understand," she remembers saying. "This was a missile."[20]

The FAA sensed the worst also. At the New York Air Route Traffic Control Center, which is responsible for flights within a sixty-mile radius of

JFK, two veteran controllers observed an object arching and intersecting with TWA 800 just as it exploded. They immediately reported what they saw. A manager from that center rushed the radar data to the FAA technical center in Atlantic City for further analysis.[21] In Atlantic City a playback of the data was recorded on videotape and plotted on paper. From there, it was faxed to FAA headquarters in Washington and rushed directly to the White House Situation Room. It was in this situation room, "in the aftermath of the TWA Flight 800 *bombing* [emphasis added]," as former Clinton aide George Stephanopoulos inadvertently told Peter Jennings on that fateful September 11, that all key parties converged.[22]

Richard Clarke, the designated chairman of the Coordinating Security Group on terrorism (CSG), had called the meeting. It began at about 10 P.M. that evening. Gathered in the room were some forty representatives of the agencies involved. Teleconferencing in on the room's eight monitors were terrorist experts from around the nation. Represented either in person or on screen were the Pentagon, the FBI, the FAA, the Secret Service, the CIA, the State Department, the Justice Department and the Joint Chiefs of Staff, and the White House. The National Transportation Safty Board (NTSB) was not present.[23]

There is no reason to doubt that Clarke called the meeting in anything but good faith and that it was executed in the same spirit. The presumption reigned during the meeting that the destruction of the plane had been a terrorist act. Years later, Clarke casually acknowledged "the widespread speculation within the CSG that [TWA 800] had been shot down by a shoulder-fired missile from the shore."[24] Those gathered had received the heads-up from the FAA on the radar data. They were aware of reports that streaks of light had been seen in the sky heading towards the plane prior to the explosion. They knew that the plane had vanished without a word of distress from the pilots, a fact that suggested terrorism as well.

Adm. Paul Busick reassured the group that the downing was not the result of so-called "friendly fire." Busick had thought that there were Department of Defense assets in the area. But when he inquired of the National Military Command Center if there were any assets nearby "with missile shooting capability," he "was told there was not."[25]

The FAA made clear that, at this point, there was no effective deterrence if terrorists were planning to take out additional planes. The attendees realized that two days before the Olympics and a month before the political conventions, a terrorist scenario had the potential to virtually shut down the airline industry and cripple the economy.

In New York City, James Kallstrom had been working the phones an hour before Clarke could convene his meeting. The gruff, squat fifty-three-year-old had assumed the directorship of the FBI's New York office a year earlier, and that night he wasted no time gearing up the Bureau's efforts. Long before the next morning, Kallstrom had concluded that the downing of the plane was an "act of war," a sentiment shared in Washington.[26] His calls to the NTSB only validated his opinion. Its officials had never heard of a mechanically induced explosion that was not preceded by a distress call.[27] As with Clarke, there is no reason to doubt the sincerity of Kallstrom's efforts at this point in the investigation.

If Kallstrom's office was a picture of focused energy, the scene at the National Transportation Safety Board office in Washington was one of futility. At midnight, as a small group huddled in Chairman Jim Hall's office, the Board's PR honcho, Peter Goelz, was screaming into the telephone demanding that an adequately rested crew be found for the sixteen-passenger Gulfstream that the FAA kept for just such emergencies. A victim of the safety regulations his agency helped promulgate, Goelz would not be able to find one until morning, ten hours after the plane went down.

Founded in 1967 as an independent entity, the NTSB was responsible for the investigation of all major civilian transportation accidents in the United States. Over its first thirty years the agency performed admirably, identifying the cause of all but a few of the roughly two hundred major aviation accidents in that period and suggesting future remedies.

But in 1996, the NTSB was not the agency it seemed to be or once was. Three years prior, President Clinton used his first appointment to name Jim Hall to the Board. Hall's connections were his best credentials, arguably his only ones. He had served on the staffs of Sen. Al Gore, Sr. and Sen. Edmund Muskie and had been a top aide to Sen. Harlan Matthews of Tennessee. A sign of the times, Hall replaced a pilot and aviation lawyer who also had a master's degree in aeronautical engineering from Princeton University. Upon his nomination, a *Washington Post* columnist archly described Hall as "a politically connected white male Democrat whose only transportation experience apparently is a driver's license."[28] Less than a year after his appointment, for all the wrong reasons, Clinton would name the ineffectual Hall chairman.

As to Peter Goelz, he had honed his transportation skills lobbying for the riverboat gambling interests in Missouri. His involvement in that dubious venture cost him the job for which he really pined: commissioner of the

Indian Gaming Commission. The NTSB posting, in fact, represented something of a consolation prize. A decent consolation at that. In just a few years, long before the TWA 800 investigation ended, Goelz would be named the managing director. From the perspective of the White House, Goelz and Hall were both reliable.

The most interesting man at the NTSB meeting arrived late. His name was Robert Francis, a tall, balding patrician from Massachusetts who served the Board as its vice chairman. Francis was Clinton's second appointment. He had spent the previous nine years running the FAA's Paris office, a job with more perks than prestige. There, as the story goes, he had made the acquaintance of one of the Democratic Party's ultimate power brokers, Pamela Harriman, Clinton's ambassador to France. It would seem that her patronage secured for Francis his posting at the NTSB in 1995.[29] In that, the most desperately political year of Clinton's career, all serious appointments were political.

According to the official story, Francis was the NTSB board member on call for this disaster. Curiously, however, he had also been the board member on call for the ValueJet crash in Florida just three months earlier and from which he had just returned after an exhausting stint as the public face of that investigation, a job for which he had no conspicuous gift.

It would be wrong to read too much into the NTSB's failure to find a crew that evening, even as Coast Guard officials left from the same hangar hours earlier with ample room for passengers. The late departure seems less the result of conspiracy than incompetence. What does raise eyebrows, however, is this: When Al Dickinson, NTSB's investigator in charge, did finally arrive at the East Moriches Coast Guard station in Long Island early the next morning, he found, much to his surprise, the elusive Bob Francis already in a meeting with James Kallstrom. If anyone should have been in that meeting, it was Dickinson. Francis's role was largely ceremonial. Apparently, however, Kallstrom had arranged to meet Francis at the Long Island airport and helicoptered him to East Moriches.[30]

As Patricia Milton notes, "Bob Francis felt responsible only to the person who had appointed him: the president of the United States."[31] Given his sources, Kallstrom knew and appreciated the fact that "Francis had ready access to the highest circles of the Clinton administration." Although Francis was not in charge of the NTSB investigation and said as much on the record, Kallstrom dealt with him as though he were. "I don't care what the book says," Kallstrom would acknowledge. "Francis was in charge."[32]

OF all the meetings taking place that night and early morning—the CSG meeting in the situation room, the NTSB meeting in Washington, the FBI meeting in New York—the only single meeting that really mattered is all but lost to history. This is the meeting that took place in the family quarters of the White House.

We know how exclusive the meeting was by who wasn't there at the hour of decision-making. When Kallstrom called Louis Freeh at 3 A.M., he found him home asleep, a detail that speaks volumes about Freeh's relationship to the White House. When Clinton called National Security Adviser Tony Lake at the same hour with a critical announcement, Lake was in his office downstairs at the White House. This was a meeting too private even for him.[33]

It seems likely that satellite imagery would have been restricted to the upstairs meeting and the handful of people present. Clinton surely knew what the military knew. He had appointed the new chairman of the Joint Chiefs, Gen. John Shalikashvili. Neither the general nor the military would have dared to keep such explosive information to themselves, nor would they have shared it in the situation room. Clinton would have also had the FAA radar data and updated reports from witnesses on the scene.

Recently, the Joint Chiefs had drawn up "contingency plans" for a severe retaliatory response to any act of state-sponsored terrorism. The state in question was Iran. The leaders of the Islamic Change Movement had participated in a June 1996 terrorist-planning meeting held in Tehran, and it was intelligence emanating from this conclave that helped trigger the high state of alert. America seemed to be on the verge of war.

By 3 A.M., Clinton had gathered enough information to call Lake with the following message: "Dust off the contingency plans."[34] But right now, especially on these terms, war was the last thing Clinton needed or wanted.

CHAPTER 2

LOST OPPORTUNITIES

Had the year been 1997 or had anyone but Bill Clinton been president, it is likely that the American people would have known the truth about TWA 800 within twenty-four hours of the crash. But the year was 1996, a presidential election year. Bill Clinton was the incumbent running for a second term. And the White House, indeed the nation, was moved by his one, almost primal urge.

"All that mattered was his survival," Clinton aide George Stephanopoulos writes of his former boss. "Everyone else had to fall in line: his staff, his cabinet, the country, even his wife."[1] Stephanopoulos speaks here of another circumstance. In fact, in his memoirs, *All Too Human*, Stephanopoulos devotes not a word to TWA 800, an event too large to be slighted by chance, given his deep involvement. But to understand this event and all its ramifications, one must first accept the logic that guided the investigation, and that is, as Stephanopoulos suggests, the logic of survival.

In another time, survival might have dictated a retaliatory response, the contingency plan now "dusted off." A president's star, after all, is rarely dimmed by decisive action. But as the president mulled his options during the early morning hours of July 18, he understood something few others ever would: The events off the coast of Long Island were not neat, not at all. They would take a good deal of explaining. And these explanations might very well expose his own Achilles' heel: his uncertain grip on the role of commander in chief. This was a chance he did not want to take.

ONLY a John Le Carré would put the refined, ineffable Robert Francis in the living quarters of the White House with Clinton that anxious early morning of July 18. In real life, his presence there does not seem likely. And yet it seems altogether likely that the White House communicated with Francis almost immediately, made sure he was the NTSB representative on the scene, made sure perhaps that he got to East Moriches before anyone else. The White House would tell him no more than he had to know, but the marching orders he received, unlike Anthony Lake's, had no hint of fife and drum about them. While Lake was being led to believe that terrorist missiles had taken down Flight 800, Francis was being told something different, something less.

There is only one message from the White House that makes sense of all the actions that follow, and it goes something like this: "Terrorists are ultimately responsible for the downing of TWA 800. We cannot respond for sure until we know exactly who they are. Until then, we cannot even let them or the American people know that we are aware it was a terrorist act. To accomplish this, we have to remove all talk of 'missiles' and all evidence of the same, at least for now." Francis was a good soldier. In the next months, the word *missile* would not freely pass his lips.

The president's public message on July 18 reinforced his private one. "We do not know what caused this tragedy," he protested, perhaps too much. "I want to say that again: We do not know as of this moment what caused this tragedy." He then cautioned the American people against "jumping to any conclusions."[2]

The White House likely gave Francis one other assignment—to keep his eyes on the FBI, to shadow Kallstrom, and to report back. All that we have to confirm this order is Francis's behavior from the moment he arrived in Long Island, but there is almost no other way to explain it.

The White House did not much trust the ineffectual Louis Freeh and had no reason to trust James Kallstrom either. At the same time, however, the White House had little to fear from the FBI. The agency had no experience with airline crashes and had been badly compromised by several scandals of its own making. For its part, the Department of Justice (DOJ) had been politicized as never before in its history. From the top down, it was now Hillary Clinton's show. She had hard-core loyalists placed throughout the department.[3] If need be, the White House could always reel Kallstrom in through the DOJ. Besides, the FBI's penchant for secrecy might just serve the White House well.

If the plan sounds well conceived, it wasn't. Like much of White House strategizing, it was improvised, chaotic, even desperate. About twelve hours after TWA Flight 800 went down, a military officer, off the record, attested to this chaos. He told a very tired FOX News senior reporter on Long Island that "a major screw-up" had occurred and that the "White House" had ordered the military to "stand down" for forty-eight hours until policy decisions were reached.[4] This did not surprise the FOX journalist. For hours the previous evening, FOX News had been involved in a bidding war for a videotape of the 747 being destroyed by what appeared to be missile fire. When the electronic bidding war reached $50,000, FOX was eliminated from the process.

The high bidder seems to have been NBC. Reportedly, late on the night of the crash, editors at MSNBC had the tape on their monitors when "three men in suits" came to their editing suites, removed the tape, and threatened the editors to within an inch of their lives if they ever revealed its contents. The threats worked all too well. The editors will not speak on record to this day.[5]

What exact "policy decisions" the White House reached in those first twenty-four hours may never be known. The administration evoked "national security" considerations to protect critical information. Over the years, however, the outline and intent of the administration's strategy have become clearer.

In the beginning, with all their talk of this "painstaking process," Clinton and his innermost circle were stalling for time, probably just hoping to push everything back until after November 4, Election Day. They might have gotten away with this stall and still revealed the truth. In those first few months, most believed that the government was merely being prudent by refusing a rush to judgment.

Clinton must have sensed that the major media would allow him to buy time. For the last eighteen months they had been the rock on which he had built his comeback, even dubbed by them to be "The Comeback Kid." To be sure, they had favored his 1992 election—a now-famous Roper poll of 139 bureau chiefs and Washington correspondents revealed a stunning 89 to

7 percent preference for Clinton over the incumbent Bush—but for all of that, they rode him hard those first two years.

What solidified the media's support was the shocking sweep of the Gingrich-led Republicans in the 1994 congressional election. "Imagine a nation full of uncontrolled two-year-old rage," lamented ABC news anchor Peter Jennings a week after the election. "The voters had a temper tantrum last week."[6]

This stepped-up partisanship became evident at Oklahoma City. As soon as Timothy McVeigh was apprehended—just three months after Gingrich assumed power—the major media seized on this homegrown terrorist as the inevitable consequence of the "Republican revolution" and its primary organ, "hate radio."[7]

As to President Clinton, he never looked back. He proved masterly at manipulating the victims' families and massaging his own ratings. With the media's help he climbed above 50 percent public approval at Oklahoma City for the first time in ages and never fell below again. The Republican revolution was buried in the rubble, and a politically revived Bill Clinton understood how and why. To be sure, the TWA 800 controversy would not have the partisan tinge of an Oklahoma City, a Travelgate, a Whitewater, let alone the impeachment. It is just that in the months leading up to this desperately critical election, with the nation's future at stake, no newsroom more influential than the Riverside, California, *Press-Enterprise* would dare to look beneath the surface, dare to challenge even the most transparent deceptions.

AT their first meeting in East Moriches, on the morning of July 18, it is unlikely that Robert Francis discussed White House strategy with James Kallstrom. If anything, he might have shared concern that the investigation be tightly controlled for reasons of national security, that all information suggesting a missile attack be kept at least temporarily under wraps. In return, as Kallstrom would soon discover, Francis would keep the NTSB out of the FBI's way.

The law favored the NTSB, empowered as it is by Congress to direct an investigation after a civilian transportation disaster. Typically, the Safety Board takes control of the wreckage. In crashes at sea, the NTSB summons the United States Navy for assistance. In this case, the NTSB failed to honor its legal obligations. At that first meeting, Francis yielded the NTSB's lead agency status and agreed instead to a partnership with the FBI in which the

NTSB would be subordinate in every meaningful way. If the evidence were to suggest a criminal act, the FBI could take full control at any time. And in those early hours an FBI takeover seemed imminent. As one federal official told the *Times* that first morning, "It doesn't look good," with the clear implication of terrorism.[8]

But a criminal act would demand explanation and retaliation, neither of which much interested Clinton. A formal takeover could not happen and would not. So the FBI just took over informally, an arguably illegal maneuver that had the full blessing of the Justice Department.

As the plan was conceived, the FBI would interview the eyewitnesses, triage the wreckage, and monitor the autopsies, a rich source of likely criminal evidence. As to the NTSB, Patricia Milton notes ingenuously, it "would set up its own system to scrutinize plane parts after the FBI had done its job of checking for explosive residue or signs of a bomb or missile."[9] Indeed, were some evil genius devising a mechanism for a cover-up, he could not have imagined something quite this neat and easy. The independent agents of the NTSB—the pilots, mechanics, and engineers who join NTSB teams only at the time of a crash—would be denied any meaningful role in ascertaining the cause of the crash, despite their superior knowledge. They would see only what the FBI wanted them to see.

The deal was sealed while the Coast Guard and officers from the large and sophisticated Suffolk County Police Department as well as scores of recreational boaters were braving the seas to search for survivors. Ultimately, the deal would undercut their gallant efforts and accommodate the corruption of the entire investigation.

The mood of that first twenty-four hours was well captured by Kallstrom's number two man, Lewis Schiliro, who arrived on-scene the night of the crash:

> Upon arrival, additional reports came in that changed the nature of our mission, including that there had been a large explosion and fireball, that all communications from the plane had been normal, that no distress calls had been issued, and that numerous eyewitnesses reported seeing flarelike objects and other events in the sky. It is against this background . . . at the same time that one of the world's foremost terrorists was on trial in Federal court charged with an audacious conspiracy to attack American airliners—that the FBI launched its criminal investigation of the TWA Flight 800 tragedy.[10]

The surest sign of Kallstrom's sincerity early in the investigation and of his inflated self-esteem throughout was his vain attempt to question the military. On July 18, as Kallstrom related to Patricia Milton, he became aware that a Navy P-3 Orion had been flying almost directly above the disaster when it occurred.

The P-3 is a long-range, antisubmarine warfare patrol aircraft with advanced submarine detection and avionics equipment. It is a good-sized plane, 110 feet long with a 95-foot wingspan and four 4,300-horsepower turbo prop engines. In the Balkans, P-3s proved their ability to spot ships carrying contraband both at coastal sites and in transit, downlink these images to the battle group, and give the group commander an unprecedented real-time or delayed view of the situation.

Despite assurances from Gen. John Shalikashvili that friendly fire had not downed the plane, Kallstrom determined that the P-3 crew should be interviewed. At first, crew members told the FBI that they were flying a routine mission that night from Brunswick, Maine, to the coast off Lakehurst, New Jersey. There they were to rendezvous with a submarine for a training exercise. Despite their proximity to the explosion and their sophisticated electronic gear, crew members told the FBI that they saw nothing unusual and learned of the crash only when other pilots reported it.[11]

Throughout the eighteenth, however, Kallstrom became more aware of the sightings of streaks in the sky and ordered his agents to reinterview the crew. On the morning of the nineteenth, they did just that, but this time the crew proved uncooperative. "Are you saying I'm lying?" Capt. Ray Ott responded brusquely to the agents. "Are you questioning my patriotism here?"[12] Ott then informed the FBI agents that his mission had been classified and that he could not and would not discuss it until he had been ordered to do so.

Furious, Kallstrom contacted Adm. William "Bud" Flanagan. The admiral told Kallstrom, "They've given you all the information relevant to your search, sir. Anything else is outside what you need to know."[13] Not one to be deterred, Kallstrom kicked up a fuss until his agents were allowed access to the crew and their mission.

What the agents were told on their third interview with the P-3 crew was that the plane was capable of carrying air-to-air missiles but was unarmed on the night in question. Its mission that night was to drop listening devices into the water off the coast of New Jersey in order to find the submarine USS *Trepang*.[14]

According to the crew, the plane was flying at twenty-two thousand feet about one mile away and heading south when the first explosion occurred. When the crew members learned of the blast, they promptly circled back over the area for half an hour and offered to help. When the Coast Guard finally waved them off, Milton casually reports that the crew then "flew on to complete their mission," dropping the listening devices in an area eighty miles south of the crash site, there locating the *Trepang*, before returning to Brunswick at 2 A.M.[15]

There is no reason to doubt the accuracy of Milton's report. The FBI was told that this sophisticated surveillance plane failed to capture the midair explosion of a huge commercial airliner one mile away. The agents were also asked to believe that the plane would run a routine exercise off the New Jersey coast against the "background" Schiliro described to the Senate—that is, of a likely terrorist missile attack. That the agents were satisfied with the story, however, is a testament to either their complicity or their incompetence. The military was involved in the CSG meetings at the White House during the whole time of the exercise. It would surely have commissioned every available asset to search for the terrorists, and no asset was more available or more valuable than the P-3. The story rings false in every detail.

Before the third interview, the FBI had learned something else about the P-3. Its transponder, the homing device that enables radar to track the plane, was off during the flight. Captain Ott reassured the FBI that it had been erratic for months and that it had simply failed. NTSB witness group chairman Norm Wiemeyer later interviewed the crew and would report that the transponder broke "en rout [sic] prior to the TWA event."[16]

The P-3 crew did, in fact, alert FAA Air Traffic Control in Boston that the transponder was off. Milton cites this communication as proof that the transponder was silent by accident.[17] But if the P-3 were trying to avoid detection during this high state of military alert, it was not the FAA it was trying to avoid but rather, as will be explained later, a potential terrorist. Given the mission of the P-3 and its sophistication, one has to wonder whether its transponder was not purposefully "erratic." In time, this transponder "failure" would prove convenient for a number of reasons.

Norm Wiemeyer of the NTSB learned something else in his interview with the P-3 crew. The crew told him that on the night of July 17, the P-3 and the *Trepang* performed their training exercise "a minimum of 200 miles south of the site of the loss."[18] That the site of this exercise was moved a good one hundred miles south for this later interview does not seem accidental or even unique. Indeed, from the beginning, there had been conspicuous misdirection and misinformation on the Navy's part.

KALLSTROM, on day one, had asked the Navy for a list of all its assets within two hundred miles of the crash site. The Navy responded with a list that included only the P-3, a salvage ship, a cargo plane on routine maneuvers, and various helicopters that had assisted in the rescue operation, including the National Guard helicopter piloted by Maj. Fritz Meyer and Capt. Chris Baur.

While waiting for the list, however, Kallstrom had learned of a "gray warship" off the coast of Long Island, spotted by two flight attendants an hour before the crash. This was likely the same ship seen by Lisa Perry an hour earlier and Dean Steward a few hours before that. Not finding this ship on the list, Kallstrom called Admiral Flanagan's office back and only then learned of the USS *Normandy*'s presence in the area.

"Why didn't you tell us about the *Normandy*?" Kallstrom reportedly bellowed. The answer he got back was that he had "not asked."[19]

A Ticonderoga-class cruiser, the *Normandy* had launched Tomahawk missiles both in the Gulf War and against hostile air-defense sites in northern Bosnia-Herzegovina. Milton reports that FBI agents, once made aware of the ship, "verified the precise location of the *Normandy* by military logs, radar maps and satellite data." They confirmed that at 8:31 P.M. the *Normandy* was positioned, as the Navy claimed, "181 miles southwest of the crash site, at latitude 37 degrees, 32.8 minutes north, longitude 74 degrees, 0.92 minutes west, off the Manasquan inlet in New Jersey."[20]

Milton obviously failed to check the coordinates the FBI had given her; if she had, she'd have noticed being given two separate locations for the vessel. The coordinates place the ship not off the coast of New Jersey but one hundred miles or so farther south off the southern tip of the Maryland-Virginia peninsula, about 181 miles from the crash site. The Manasquan inlet is less than one hundred miles from the site of the crash, and any place east of the inlet into the Atlantic is closer still. The only question here is, who was trying to deceive whom?

Although capable of going faster, the normal cruising speed for a ship of this class is about 30 knots, or 34.5 miles per hour. The ship the flight attendants had seen at about 7:30 P.M. or that Lisa Perry had seen an hour earlier might have made it to Manasquan, but the ship could not have made it 181 miles south to Virginia by 8:31 P.M. Indeed, had the ship turned south just when Dean Steward had seen it at 3 P.M., it would have just about made it to that point.

In a private meeting with the victims' family members soon after the crash, Adm. Edward Kristensen confirmed to Don Nibert that "the closest naval asset was 185 miles away off the coast of Virginia."[21] As late as November 1996, Admiral Kristensen would be quoted as saying publicly that the P-3 and the *Normandy*, 185 miles south, were "the only two assets that the Navy had operating off of the East Coast . . . in the vicinity or close to the TWA 800 crash site."[22] This 185-miles figure became the accepted distance for the *Trepang* and the *Normandy*. In its third interview with the NTSB, the P-3 crew likely attempted to honor this 185-mile zone in pushing its exercise with the *Trepang* one hundred miles to the south. Based on this information, Admiral Flanagan satisfied himself that "no American warship or submarine could have downed the plane."[23]

From day one, at the highest levels of information sharing, the investigation had been corrupted. The Navy either lied about the location of the *Normandy* or tried to pass off a second and even a third ship as the *Normandy*. That the FBI failed to catch these systematic discrepancies when they became obvious is a sign that it, too, had been compromised, either by deception or incompetence.

This misdirection, however, was not the military's idea. The consistent nature of its early resistance, from General Shalikashvili to Admirals Busick to Flanagan to Kristensen to the P-3 crew, strongly suggests that the command came from the top. Again, all the White House had to give as justification is "national security"—more specifically, "It is imperative that the American people not be put on war footing until a perpetrator can be positively identified."[24]

Soon enough Don Nibert would learn that the Navy's claimed nonpresence "proved not to be true."[25] This and other deceptions would turn him from a grieving parent into an angry one. He would become one of many citizens in and out of the government to lose faith in the formal investigation and to seek the truth where he could find it.

Nibert and the others would not get much help from the major media. The *New York Times*, clearly the lead news source on the case, did not investigate the role of the military in the downing of TWA 800. Not one paragraph. When the story changed, the *Times* failed to notice it. By March 12, 1997, the *Times* was reporting matter-of-factly that "a Navy P-3 plane and a submarine were near the flight path on a practice mission."[26] But the *Times* made no allusion to any discrepancies in earlier reports from the military.

By the time of the FBI's November 1997 conference, announcing its "disengagement" from the case, Kallstrom was identifying the USS *Normandy* and now *three* submarines—the USS *Trepang*, the USS *Albuquerque*, and the USS *Wyoming*—as being in the "immediate vicinity" of the crash site.[27]

How immediate? When asked about three vessels within six miles of that site by Reed Irvine of Accuracy in Media in September of 1998, Kallstrom answered, "We all know what those were. In fact, I spoke about those publicly. They were Navy vessels that were on classified maneuvers."[28]

FAA radar had captured four unidentified tracks "consistent with the speed of a boat" within three to six miles of Flight 800's course at the time of its midair breakup. The fact that three of the radar tracks disappeared right after TWA 800 crashed argues strongly that these were the submarines Kallstrom had identified and that they submerged almost immediately.

One "surface vessel" less than three miles from the crash scene headed away from the area at thirty knots. In response to questions from a congressional subcommittee, the FBI's number two man on the investigation, Lewis Schiliro, claimed that "the FBI first noted the presence" of this ship in January 1997, an astonishing five months after the disaster. Although the FBI was allegedly unable to identify this ship, Schiliro added the meaningless disclaimer that "based on our investigative efforts, we are confident it was not a military vessel."[29]

According to the FBI, this surface vessel had a "speed between 25 and 35 knots, is believed to be at least 25–30 feet in length, approximately 2.9 nautical miles from the position of Flight 800 at the time of the initial explosion."[30] Radar, however, is unable to judge the length of the ship. That detail was added to suggest a pleasure craft and not a Navy ship, whose length might be measured in the hundreds of feet. In any case, the ship was fleeing the scene. When questioned by Irvine, Kallstrom, still being elusive, identified this vessel as "a helicopter."

By the time of its final press conference, the FBI knew that all the stories the Navy had previously offered about the *Normandy* being the closest asset of consequence at 181 miles away were patently false. At this juncture, all information about any aspect of the case from any source should have been considered suspect.

"We left no stone unturned," Kallstrom famously claimed when the FBI withdrew from the case. "In fact, we looked under every rock multiple times."[31] But Kallstrom never bothered to explain these numerous discrepancies or shifting stories. What stuns the casual observer, in retrospect, is that no member of the major media even caught them.

THE P-3's transponder was not the only thing to break or go missing in those first few weeks. More troubling still is the fate of the FAA radar tape that alarmed Washington on the night of July 17. Indeed, when Ron Schleede of the NTSB first saw the data, he exclaimed, "Holy Christ, this looks bad." He added later, "It showed this track that suggested something fast made the turn and took the airplane."[32]

The tape passed through so many hands that its existence quickly became known to the media. On July 18, unnamed "government officials"—most likely the FBI—told the *New York Times* that air traffic controllers had "picked up a mysterious radar blip that appeared to move rapidly toward the plane just before the explosion." The officials did admit that "they could not definitively evaluate what caused the radar signal," but they did *not* imply that something was amiss with the data.[33]

These officials and the *Times* unequivocally linked the radar to the eyewitness sightings and the sightings to a missile attack. According to the *Times'* sources, "The eyewitnesses had described a bright light, like a flash, moving toward the plane just before the initial explosion, and that the flash had been followed by a huge blast—a chain of events consistent with a missile impact and the blast produced by an aircraft heavily laden with fuel."[34] This was the last day these officials were open with the media about the possibility of a missile strike. The story was reported on July 19. The words *radar* and *eyewitness* would all but disappear from the *Times'* reporting after that.

By July 19, the government had gotten its story straight. Christine Negroni reports that throughout the eighteenth the FAA "conducted more sophisticated analysis of the initial radar data." They also evaluated tapes from other radar centers in the New York area. Negroni adds that eventually the FAA and the NTSB "tossed off the anomalies in the radar as insignificant."[35]

Despite Negroni's reassurance, this data was not being "tossed off" at the FAA. As would happen throughout the investigation, certain stalwart individuals would resist the enormous pressure to toe the official line. Retired United Airlines pilot Dick Russell received a copy of the tape from one of them. "When the tape appeared, I looked at it and said, 'My gosh, what am I seeing here?'" says Russell. Troubled by what he observed, Russell took the copies to at least a few experts, and they confirmed his suspicions. "This was not an anomaly," Russell insists to this day. "It moved in a direct path, and that is a good indication there was something there."[36]

"It was a radar ghost," writes Negroni, "a ghost that came back to haunt the investigation again and again."[37] On this latter point, she could not be more right.

And here is where the P-3's broken transponder comes in handy. On March 21, 1997, *Newsday* reported that "a streak on a radar track that was purported to be a missile heading toward TWA Flight 800 was actually a Navy plane flying with a defective transponder."[38] This revelation came a day after officials of the FBI, Navy, and National Transportation Safety Board briefed the House Subcommittee on Aviation behind closed doors on the investigation. *Newsday* cites a congressional source and senior government officials for the news "that an unidentified blip on a radar tape was a Navy plane." *Newsday* also cited Kallstrom's appearance the day before at the International Airport Chamber of Commerce in which he, too, implicated the P-3, stating that a malfunctioning transponder shows an airplane's track as a solid line: "If you're a school kid, you could say it looks like a missile, or a cigar, or a pencil."

At the FBI's press conference in November 1997, Kallstrom would change the story once again. Now, the unidentified streak was no longer the P-3. "Analysis by experts," said Kallstrom, "determined that the object was not a missile, since it was positively identified. Object was a Ghost of Jet Express 18 which was at a different location."[39] At the time, according to NTSB reports, that "different location" was sixteen miles to the north.[40]

By 1999, Patricia Milton was referring to the radar mystery as a "computer glitch" or, more specifically, "a failure of the computers' software."[41] At the NTSB's final hearing in August 2000, Charles Pereira identified these blips as aircraft "being reflected off some building structure," but adds the revealing qualifier: "if these were false primary radar returns."[42]

In fact, the authorities never could agree on a credible explanation of what the radar showed. The damage, however, had been done three years earlier when it was decided what the radar could *not* show.

On the night of July 18 the State Department also got in line. Its officials dismissed a report on ABC News that a specific warning about the flight had been sent by the Islamic Change Movement, the organization that had claimed responsibility for the attacks on American servicemen in Saudi Arabia. This warning, cited earlier—"Their time is at the morning-dawn. Is not the morning-dawn near?"—was dismissed by State Department spokesman Glyn Davies. "While it's up to those leading the investigation to make a judgment on what this means," said Davies unconvincingly, "we think that this is a common type of political tract circulated commonly in the Middle East, and that the only connection is a vague chronological one—that this thing surfaced at this dreadful time."[43]

By the end of day two, July 18, 1996, all relevant arms of government—the FBI, the NTSB, the FAA, the State Department, and the military among them—had gotten the message: A missile strike was not to be talked about. To make the message work, all visual indications of a missile had to be suppressed. Were the radar the only such indicator to be declared irrelevant, the story of the "computer glitch" or "ghost" would be more credible. But it was only one "glitch" out of many.

THE data to be gleaned from America's satellites have proved even more elusive than from the radar. In 1996, the United States had two KH-11 satellites in polar orbit with extraordinary powers of resolution. The precision of such imagery cannot be doubted. On October 4, 2001, Defense Department satellites equipped with infrared sensors captured a Ukrainian missile striking a Russian airliner thirty thousand feet above the Black Sea. Our government informed Russia immediately. After initial denials, the Ukrainians admitted the tragic error.

The evidence is overwhelming that U.S. satellites did record the events of July 17, 1996. What remains in dispute, however, is what exactly the satellites recorded. On July 22, 1996, the *London Times* reported that "the satellite pictures show an object racing up to the TWA jet, passing it, then changing course and smashing into it."[44] This may be true, but the sourcing is indirect and unverifiable.

For no good reason, the major American media chose not to pursue this obvious line of inquiry. In the twenty-five most relevant *New York Times* articles of the investigation's first two months, amid the twenty-thousand-plus words dedicated to the story, there is not one single reference to a satellite. Patricia Milton and Christine Negroni, both of whom had excellent access to the leadership of the investigation, shed almost no light on the issue. Negroni avoids the topic altogether. Milton makes a few references but refuses to go where the story leads.

As Milton relates, the FBI gathered experts from all relevant branches of government on Saturday, July 20, at the FAA headquarters in Washington to review what was known about the crash. It was not a meeting at the highest levels and thus seems to have been held in good faith by those attending. The consensus among them was that a missile had downed the plane.[45] Participants learned from unnamed "intelligence officers" that "classified satellite imagery had disclosed a probable fishing boat traveling up and down the Long Island coast from July 16 to July 19."[46] This boat would prove to be something of a red herring, at least in Milton's retelling, one of many to follow. But even if it were a fishing boat, its identification as such confirms that there was satellite coverage in that area. Such a satellite could not have missed the U.S. Navy warship traveling up and down the same coast for at least four hours on the afternoon and evening of July 17. This information, however, was obviously not shared with those who did not "need to know."

These same intelligence officers proved coyer about the possibility of a missile strike on TWA 800. When the FBI agent in charge of this same meeting, George Andrew, asked whether U.S. weather or spy satellites had picked up any missilelike streaks that same night, the officers told him that they did not know "but promised to find out."[47]

Early in the investigation, the FBI's James Kallstrom sought out information on every satellite, American or otherwise, that might have recorded the events of that evening. More than once in pep talks at the Calverton hangar, he called them "our friends in the sky" and suggested that they held the answers to the investigation's seeming problems. Milton assures us that "the FBI soon had access to all U.S. satellites," but the very word *soon* suggests the emptiness of the assurance.[48]

If the Department of Defense knew immediately about the Ukrainian missile, they must have known immediately about the fate of TWA 800, especially on a clear evening in a period of such high alert. This information would have been shared with President Clinton on the night of July 17. The White House would have allowed Kallstrom to see only what it chose to show. Indeed, there is something more than a little sad about Kallstrom's blind doggedness at this stage of the investigation. For whatever promise the satellites once held for the FBI, the word *satellite* was not mentioned once at its comprehensive, final press conference in November 1997.

Keenly sensitive to public relations, the Clinton administration gave family members like Don Nibert a good deal of attention and access. A professor at a Pennsylvania University, Nibert asked a lot of questions. "I learned that they had three satellites that would have coverage of the site near the

8:30 time period," Nibert observes wryly. "All failed." Nibert asked John Clark of the NTSB what were the odds that one satellite should fail and how astronomical must the odds be for all three to fail at the same time. Clark responded that this information was considered classified.[49]

Despite what Nibert was told, all the satellites did not fail. If neither the FBI nor the NTSB had much of a line on satellite imagery, the CIA surely did. In November of 1997, at the climax of the FBI's final press conference, the spy agency unveiled a fifteen-minute video designed to assure the public that the eyewitnesses saw nothing of consequence. In the course of this video, the narrator casually acknowledges that the plane's final, consuming fireball was "corroborated by infrared sensors aboard a U.S. satellite which detected a large heat source."[50] In fact, the video shows an animated image of the presumed satellite at least twice.

Beyond the CIA's notorious video, the government has not been eager to share any information from the satellites. At the NTSB's final two-day hearings in August 2000, the word *satellite* was not mentioned. Despite repeated requests through the Freedom of Information Act, the data remain classified to this day.

THERE were at least two other highly credible visual images as well. On that fateful evening of July 17, Linda Kabot attended a fund-raising event on behalf of Vincent Cannuscio, the Republican Town Supervisor of Southampton. As Cannuscio's secretary, she was assigned to take photos of the guests assembled on the deck at Docker's, an East Quogue restaurant. One of the photos captured above the head of the guests was what the *New York Times* accurately described as a "cylindrical object with one end aglow." The object, continued the *Times*, "is in a roughly horizontal position, although its left end is tilted downward. Its right end seems to be brightly lighted."[51] When the Kabots alerted the FBI, its agents quickly took custody of the photos and the negatives.

No one doubts the authenticity of the photo or the motives of the Kabots, Linda and her husband, Lance, a schoolteacher. On the day that the *New York Times* covered the Kabot story, August 26, the missile theory was still alive. In fact, according to the *Times*, chemical residue that had been recently discovered "bolsters the theories of a missile or bomb, and deflates the third theory of mechanical failure."[52] After this brief flurry of attention, the major media lost interest in the Kabots and their photo. As Milton

relates, the photo "turned out to be a bust." "After two weeks," she continues, "analysis by the FBI and the CIA concluded that Kabot's camera was
facing north-northeast."[53] What Milton overlooks is that the Kabots knew
the camera was pointing in the opposite direction of the explosion fifteen
miles away and told the media and the FBI as much when they first handed
over the photos.

At the November 1997 press conference, the FBI raised the subject of
the Kabot photo merely to dismiss it. According to the FBI, analysis by the
CIA National Imagery and Mapping Administration revealed only that there
was an object in the photo, that the object was "not a missile," and that the
object "appears to be an aircraft" but cannot be identified because of
problems gauging distance, time, and detail.[54]

Milton adds that the object showed only "two of the necessary three signatures of a missile." These are the "white dot" that suggests a burning propellant and a "dark streak" that would be the missile itself. The missing
signature in the photo is the exhaust trail.[55]

Of note, those who saw the original photo almost inevitably described
the object in question as "cylindrical." The FBI, however, would not even
share the original with the NTSB. As the image was copied and recopied, the
"cylindrical object" of three years earlier became a "dark streak" and its "one
end aglow" a "white dot."[56]

What did Linda Kabot actually photograph? Milton offers the official
explanation: Radar captured eight or nine planes flying through the area at
the time, and "almost certainly the streak in Kabot's snapshot was from one
of them."[57] Left unsaid is just how many "signatures" a cylindrical object
with one end aglow shares with an airplane.

Interestingly, Milton does not raise the issue of a "drone" as the FBI did
at its press conference. The FBI of course dismissed the possibility, citing as
reason for its dismissal only the following: "No drone exercises conducted
near Long Island July 17, 1996."[58] Yet a drone—or unmanned aerial vehicle
(UAV)—would seem to be a good first guess, not a last. On a night of the
highest military alert like July 17, it would make perfect sense to deploy a
UAV like the now well-known Predator. The Predator, which was in service
over Bosnia as early as 1995, can linger for over twenty-four hours at alti-
tudes up to twenty-six thousand feet with a range in excess of two thousand
miles. It can also communicate with other members of a command group.

The FBI ruled out a drone not because it lacked the appropriate "signatures," but because the military said there were no drone exercises in the area

on the night of July 17. The military, however, had previously told the FBI that there were no warships or submarines in the area, and by this date, the FBI would have long since known that claim to be false.

The second visual reference that merits discussion is a photo taken by Heidi Krieger. Krieger was out in the Atlantic that evening photographing her father's boat as his boat ran parallel to hers. She was shooting out towards the sea, towards the horizon. Just moments after taking her last photo, she saw a flash and then a fireball in the sky. She watched dumbfounded as the pieces of wreckage wafted toward the water and disappeared. It was only when she returned to her car that she learned that a Boeing 747 had gone down over the Atlantic near the Moriches inlet.

When she viewed the photos, she discovered a squiggly white line in the sky that could easily be interpreted as an exhaust trail of a missile seeking its target. She called the FBI hot line over the objections of her husband who, like countless others, did not want to get involved.

As with the Kabot photo, the FBI promptly flew Krieger's photo to the FBI lab in Washington where it was "microscopically analyzed." There, Milton assures us, "Investigators literally wiped away the 'missile' during a conventional cleaning of the film. It was just a speck of dirt."[59] At its final press conference, however, the FBI was a bit more careful with its language. It described the image as a "streak in the sky" and commented only that the FBI lab had "determined there was debris on the film surface," not that the streak was caused by the debris.[60]

Milton's account matters because she is telling the FBI's story for public consumption. She has apparently not seen the Krieger photo, as she describes the image in question as "a slim, long object flying along the horizon just above land," a description that is wrong in every detail.[61] To the uninitiated, however, such an object could be more easily confused with a "speck of dirt" than could a white squiggly line. And so the Krieger photo quietly disappeared into history.

A QUICK review of the potential visual references at this stage in the investigation:

- The video of a missile striking the plane for which FOX News allegedly bid $50,000 and which an MSNBC team reportedly was in the process of editing is never again seen.

- The P-3 crew sees or hears nothing, and its sophisticated surveillance equipment captures no images despite its location about one mile from the explosion.

- The FAA radar data rushed to Washington reveals only an "anomaly," the result of a "computer glitch."

- The P-3's transponder "breaks" so that its position cannot be fixed.

- The satellites are said to be either malfunctioning or irrelevant; their images remain classified to this day.

- The Kabot photo proves to be a "bust," the image in question probably just a plane.

- The Krieger photo reveals not a missile-exhaust trail but "a speck of dirt."

Of interest, the government can produce no image of a 747 coming apart in flight due to a fuel-air explosion. Neither the satellites, nor the radar, nor the P-3, nor a casual photographer captures this phenomenon. All that those involved can do is make real evidence go away.

CHAPTER 3

FALSE DIALECTIC

On the afternoon of July 18, the day after the crash, Maj. Fritz Meyer of the New York Air National Guard, 106th Aerospace Rescue Group, joined a group of his colleagues for a press conference at the base auditorium. Little did Meyer know that by merely telling the truth, and insisting on it afterwards, he would be defamed by people he had never met in ways he could never have imagined.

Meyer, a seasoned and still-tough-looking aviator in his mid-fifties, had just come through an emotionally exhausting night. He and the two-man crew of his Blackhawk helicopter had been practicing instrument approaches at the nearby Gabreski Field. At about 8:30 that evening, with his copilot flying an approach, Meyer pressed his face up against the windscreen to scan for a Cessna said to be in the area. It was then that he saw a red-orange streak of light in the sky flash very rapidly from west to east for about three to five seconds.[1]

From ten miles away, as Meyer saw the streak, it "was moving in a gradually descending arc" that resembled "the path of a shooting star." There was a break, where it seemed to stop, and then for an instant Meyer saw nothing. "And then suddenly," says Meyer, "I saw an explosion, high-velocity explosion, military ordnance, looked like flak in the sky." No more than two seconds later, farther to the left but down, he saw a flash once again, a "high-velocity explosion, brilliant white light."[2]

His copilot, Capt. Chris Baur, saw "an object that came from the left. And it appeared to be like—like a white-hot. Like a pyrotechnic." The "incendiary device" Baur saw was moving from east to west when "it made the object on the right explode."[3]

"Is that pyro?" asked Baur, himself an experienced former Army helicopter pilot.

"No pyro I've ever seen," answered Meyer, and Meyer had seen a lot. They and their flight engineer, Dennis Richardson, all saw what came next: "a huge, slowly forming, low-velocity explosion fireball" that descended almost gracefully to the sea.[4]

Although known locally as an attorney and a "weekend warrior," Meyer had quite a history. He had become a naval aviator more than thirty years earlier. His specialty was combat search and rescue, a skill honed through four years in Southeast Asia, two of them in Vietnam. His job there had been to rescue downed American pilots from the North. He did it often enough and well enough to win a Distinguished Flying Cross.

Flying a helicopter at 120 knots through North Vietnam's infamous iron triangle gave Meyer all the experience he ever wanted or needed with military ordnance. "You see a lot of flak," said Meyer, "and I did. I saw a bunch of it. I know what it looks like."

Upon seeing the explosion, Meyer's crew called the tower to say they were going to investigate. They arrived so quickly, in fact, that they had to back off to let the lighter, floating debris fall in front of them. What they found stunned them—a lake of fire, probably three acres in size, burning with flames fifty feet high. There they undertook a methodical, if vain, search for survivors that lasted more than three hours. Their fuel exhausted, they flew back to shore. As they headed back, Meyer watched the lights of several hundred private boats stream out to sea to help, a sight that reminded him why he was "very proud to be from Long Island."

This experience is what the press wanted to hear about that afternoon of July 18. Meyer was joined at the briefing by his fellow crew members, the crew of a C-130 National Guard transport also airborne at the time of the explosion, and two parajumper rescue men who had seen a light in the sky. Before the event began, the public affairs officer from Meyer's unit issued three caveats: no speculation, no opinions, and no discussion of the condition of the bodies.

Meyer, like the others, paid heed. He offered only the most restrained and discreet observations. "I saw something that looked to me like a shooting star," he noted, carefully refraining from any speculation as to what he did see.

But by late in the day on the eighteenth, all relevant brass seemed to know that there was to be no talk of missiles. Meyer found out the hard way. Not too long after the press briefing, a colleague yelled over at Meyer, "Hey, I just saw you on television. Peter Jennings says you said it was a missile." Meyer soon got an urgent call from the adjutant general of the New York State National Guard, wanting to know why he had violated orders.

"General, the entire press conference was videotaped," Meyer responded. "Look at the videotape. I never said it was a missile."

It didn't matter. The media had reported it as such. Meyer was given the task of relaying to the press the complicated message that he never said he saw a missile. At the East Moriches Coast Guard station the very next day, the nineteenth, Meyer gave in excess of forty interviews to media crews in which he repeated his message as ordered. By and large the media misreported the new angle, in Meyer's words, as "pilot on the scene says it was not a missile." Burned by the experience and fully expecting the NTSB to do its job, Meyer ceased to give interviews. But it was in a sense too late. He had become a public symbol of eyewitness uncertainty. To make this impression stick, certain agents of the government were prepared to defame anyone who witnessed the event and insisted on the truth, even if he did have a Distinguished Flying Cross.

EYEWITNESSES were a problem from day one. There were so many of them, and too many of them were too credible. The plane, after all, had gone down off the coast of the Hamptons. People had witnessed the events from their boats, from their yacht clubs, from the decks of their posh summer homes. They could not be easily dismissed, Meyer least of all—an attorney, an aviator, a good-looking man's man with an easy air of bravado.

The strategy for dealing with the witnesses seems less a plan than an improvisation, but it would prove to be a stunning success. It began with a crude assumption of power by the FBI and its lead man on the investigation, James Kallstrom. It was abetted by the seemingly inexplicable submission of the NTSB.

On July 19, NTSB investigator Bruce Magladry formed a witness group that included representatives from TWA, the FAA, and ALPA, the Air Line

Pilots Association. This was standard procedure. The group was prepared to begin work on July 20.

On the very day the group was formed, however, FBI agent Robert Knapp told Magladry that the FBI would not share any information outside the NTSB. This meant that parties like TWA and ALPA could not be involved at all. In addition, as the NTSB's Witness Group Summary notes blandly, "Mr. Magladry was informed that he would not be permitted to conduct any interviews because the FBI did not want conflicting information."[5]

The FBI had no authority to do this. The disaster had not been declared a crime scene. More than once NTSB Chairman Jim Hall would admit that this power play was improper, if not illegal. "Again, I would like to emphasize," he said at the August 2000 NTSB hearings, "normal procedures were not followed, and we are addressing that."[6]

Kallstrom claims that the NTSB's Robert Francis had authorized the FBI takeover. "I said to Bob the first day," Kallstrom told Christine Negroni, "they were invited to go on any interview they wanted, but they had no one to go."[7] Francis insists that he never gave Kallstrom the go-ahead, but his protest rings hollow. Al Dickinson and others at the NTSB argue that Francis was urging the NTSB "not to cause any issues" with the FBI from day one.[8]

Evidence strongly suggests that the White House had given its blessing to the FBI takeover, and Francis was quietly accommodating the move. On July 21, at an NTSB progress meeting, Assistant United States Attorney Valerie Caproni bluntly told Magladry that "no interviews were to be conducted by the NTSB." In a demeaning bit of compromise, Caproni allowed that the NTSB could review FBI-supplied documents, "provided no notes were taken and no copies made."[9]

This was not what the law had intended. Title 49, section 1131(a)(2) reads as follows: "An investigation by the Board . . . has priority over any investigation by another department, agency or instrumentality of the United States Government." The "Board" in question is the National Transportation Safety Board. In other words, a "parallel" FBI investigation is inferior to the NTSB investigation. "The Board shall provide for appropriate participation," not the FBI, Justice Department, or the White House. The NTSB was created as an independent agency and was made the superior investigating agency at all crash scenes regardless of the cause. The reason was simple. Congress hoped it would be possible to create an entity within the federal bureaucracy that could not be corrupted by the political process. It failed in this effort.

Caproni, as an attorney and officer of the court, knew that the FBI was the subordinate agency. She knew that the NTSB could not legally be restricted in its pursuit of information. In spite of the law, she put the full weight of Justice and FBI behind her presence at the meeting with the NTSB witness group. The team was ordered to cease and desist.

On July 22, the FBI agreed that the NTSB could conduct interviews, but only under the direction and in the company of the FBI, with all information being kept private and no notes being taken. According to Magladry, "This caused him concern" because the NTSB, unlike the FBI, has a mandate to make its information part of the public record.[10] On July 24, Magladry and the NTSB finally just gave in and ceased all immediate plans to interview witnesses. They would not form a witness group until November 12.

Under oath before a Senate subcommittee in 1999, Lewis Schiliro, the number two man in the FBI's New York office, would remember this experience differently:

> The FBI had no problem in sharing investigative results with NTSB and the morning after the crash, we offered to have NTSB personnel participate in all our interviews. Overall, the cooperation between the FBI and the NTSB was excellent at every level.[11]

Schiliro did make one observation during this hearing that has the air of truth about it. As Schiliro related, the FBI was much more open with the Defense Intelligence Agency's Missile and Space Intelligence Center (MISIC) than it was with the NTSB. According to Schiliro, MISIC analysts arrived on the scene in Long Island just two days after the crash and interviewed and reinterviewed some of the eyewitnesses. Their expertise was in the area of shoulder-launched, surface-to-air missiles, known as MANPADS. "They reported to us," Schiliro told the senators, "that many of the descriptions given by eyewitnesses were very consistent with the characteristics of the flight of such missiles."[12]

These analysts left a very light public footprint. In the FBI's final comprehensive report, they barely merited a footnote. One can read every one of the FBI witness reports without getting any sense of their involvement. Although the work of the MISIC analysts was documented, and some of these documents have leaked out, the body of their work remains classified to this day.

Although the NTSB would not fade away quite so cleanly, its temporary withdrawal left full control of all witness testimony to the FBI. Despite the FBI's lack of aviation experience, its agents shut the NTSB out even when they interviewed the ground and maintenance workers at JFK. The FBI did not compensate with finesse for what they lacked in knowledge. "We feel that our expertise was unwelcome and not wanted by the FBI," wrote the International Association of Machinists and Aerospace Workers (IAMAW) in its final summary. "The threats made during the first two weeks of the investigation were unwarranted and unforgettable."[13] IAMAW's take on FBI involvement isn't unique. "They took over like a bull in a china shop," says ALPA investigator Jim Speer, who was on the scene from day two. "They didn't know the nose from the tail, a wheel from a bomb about accident investigating."[14]

For all its lack of diplomacy, the FBI did make a diligent effort to seek out eyewitness testimony. Kallstrom would claim some fifteen hundred interviews by late August, and half of these were with eyewitnesses. Despite their efforts, however, the agents accomplished little. They took cursory notes, used no instruments to fix bearing lines, and, unless accompanied by MISIC analysts or officers from the Suffolk County Police Department, failed to capture even the most basic positional data.

Although the witnesses from the Air National Guard unit may not have agreed on what they saw, as Christine Negroni admits, "They were unified in their belief that the FBI wasn't taking their accounts seriously."[15] In fact, many key witnesses would complain publicly about the superficial nature of their FBI interviews. After one brief FBI interview at his Florida home, Dwight Brumley, who watched the tragedy from US Air 217, observed:

> Here I am twenty-five years in the Navy, electronic warfare technician . . .
> I understand relative motion, relative bearing, and I thought I would have
> been a good witness, the only witness with that level of expertise to look
> down on what turned out to be TWA 800. I was very, very surprised and
> am still surprised that to this day no one has come to talk to me.[16]

That one FBI interview would prove to be his last interview with any government agency. Pilot Sven Faret and his passenger, Ken Wendell, observed the crash from a private plane. Says Faret, "We were interviewed by the FBI and NTSB. They took our report, but we felt they did not capture the detail we expressed, or the certainty of our facts."[17]

Although this lack of certainty would finally prove useful, it seems more the result of arrogance and inexperience than conspiracy. What does seem more purposeful is the information block on eyewitness testimony. Kallstrom argued that this was done to preserve the integrity of the evidence,[18] but it fits a larger pattern of evidence suppression, one that would often descend into dishonesty and occasionally even into cruelty.

THE treatment of Major Meyer and, to a lesser degree, Captain Baur, is a case in point. In the early stages of the investigation, it was enough to insinuate that the pair saw streaks coming in opposite directions and that Meyer at least had changed his story from seeing a missile to not seeing one. But as the investigation wore on, and Meyer publicly challenged official inaction, the stakes were raised.

Both Patricia Milton and Christine Negroni capture the official bias against the helicopter pilots and reflect that animus in their own summations. Milton tells us that the FBI was not impressed with the pilots from the beginning. The FBI saw the two men as "self-important" and that Meyer in particular was a "show-off" with a tendency to be "melodramatic."[19] Upon his second interview—his first lasted less than five minutes—"Meyer came off as an even less useful witness than he had appeared to be in the initial days after the crash."[20] Not surprisingly, as Milton tells it, the third crew member, flight engineer Dennis Richardson, "seemed the most credible."[21] Only one problem, a rather large one. As Milton relates earlier in her book, "Richardson was looking in another direction when the flash occurred."[22] Of the three, Richardson was the only one who could not and would not challenge the official explanation, whatever it might turn out to be.

Negroni hits even harder and lower than Milton does. First, she finds it curious that Meyer did not share his story with his colleagues until the next afternoon, the implication being that he concocted it.[23] Negroni follows Meyer's account immediately with a report from a Seattle psychologist who talks about how "rampant speculation" contaminates witness recollections. Even on casual examination, however, Negroni's insinuation makes no sense. Meyer claimed that the streak came from the west, not the east like Baur's, and that it was followed by two flashes of white light. Unknown to Meyer, scores of other eyewitnesses were confirming his version of events to the FBI, but Meyer was the first to voice it publicly. To this day, he also admits that the streak looked like a "shooting star," a phrase repeated by about a dozen other witnesses. He admits also that he was not initially certain that it was a missile. In his experience in Vietnam, he had come to know a missile in flight by its erratic flight path. The guidance system was continuously correcting.

It would be months before Meyer met another eyewitness, Richard Goss, who had seen the streak come from the north and west and helped Meyer put his own observations in perspective. Says Meyer, "When I saw Richard Goss's depiction of what he had seen, I knew why I hadn't seen an erratic flight path, why the arc was smooth, and I knew that what I had seen was a missile. I picked it up, you see, on the top here where it curves. I picked it up just about where it starts to turn."[24]

Scores of other witnesses verified this downward arc at the end of the object's flight. Witness 200 used a memorable metaphor to describe its path. "The dot traveled up a path shaped like a candy cane," reads his FBI witness statement, "straight up, then curving at the top from west to east."[25] This is the same direction as Meyer's streak.

Negroni is not content to attack Meyer's memory. She goes after his credibility and does so with a stunningly gratuitous low blow. "Meyer," she tells us, "began to lecture the others about his own distrust of government and what he believed were serious inaccuracies in the history of the holocaust." There you have it: How can one ever trust a Holocaust denier? To be sure, she gives no specifics as to what those inaccuracies might be or who made this insinuation.[26]

More to the point, Negroni quotes Meyer as saying, "I haven't trusted the FBI since Ruby Ridge."[27] She includes this quote to paint him as an antigovernment extremist so as to further diminish his credibility. But in selecting it, she reveals more about her own biases as a CNN reporter and those of her media colleagues.

A word of explanation is in order. As CNN itself would report on October 22, 1996, three months after the crash of TWA 800, "The FBI admits making serious mistakes at its 1992 siege of Randy Weaver's mountain cabin at Ruby Ridge, Idaho."[28] But "mistakes" doesn't do justice to what happened. As the Justice Department's own task force would later acknowledge, "The FBI's Hostage Rescue Team overreacted to the threat of violence and instituted a shoot-on-sight policy that violated bureau guidelines and Fourth Amendment restrictions on police power."[29]

More specifically, an FBI sharpshooter shot Randy Weaver's wife, Vickie, through the head while she stood in the doorway of her cabin holding her baby in her arms. At the time, the sharpshooter was not disciplined for this shooting.

When federal prosecutors in Idaho asked the FBI for materials pertaining to the incident, FBI manager E. Michael Kahoe and certain unnamed superiors at FBI headquarters resisted the request. According to the U.S. Attorney's office, the FBI ordered a subordinate to destroy all copies of an internal critique and make it appear as if the critique never existed. Under intense congressional pressure, the FBI eventually disciplined twelve agents and employees, including Larry Potts, whom Louis Freeh had just named deputy director.

This story took four years to surface for two reasons, neither of them reassuring. One was that the media had little interest in attributing victim status to the Christian right, regardless of the circumstances. The indifferent coverage of the Waco horror is an even more chilling case in point. The second, and more relevant, is that the major media had come to identify with the FBI, seeing the agency as the strong and straight right arm of the Clinton administration.

Yet, as the Waco and Ruby Ridge cases illustrate, these were not the best years for the FBI. With little restraint from the White House or major media, elements within the FBI could and did act lawlessly. Indeed, as both Filegate and Travelgate made clear, the White House would use the FBI to further its own political ends.[30]

To challenge the FBI during those years, as Meyer did, was to invite comparison with the darkest forces of the right. But Meyer is not the kook the FBI and its accomplices in the media want him to seem. His story has remained entirely consistent over the years. All new information only confirms its accuracy. Besides, on the night of July 17, when called to National Guard duty, he was on his way to the fund-raiser for Vincent Cannuscio, the town supervisor of Southampton. This is not the kind of behavior one expects from an antigovernment extremist.

Also of note, the most probing coverage of the TWA 800 case came not from the right, but from the left, specifically the *Village Voice*. If the *New York Times* and other media lapsed into willful blindness in their tacit support of the Clinton administration, the *Voice* refused to.

After its story on July 19, the *Times* paid remarkably little attention to eyewitness accounts. When "government officials" stopped talking about missile sightings, so did the *Times*. The paper's first article on the subject, and first serious reference in a month, occurred on August 17. The article featured one Michael Russell, an engineer who witnessed the explosion from a boat. According to the *Times*, "His sober, understated story was one of only a few that investigators have judged credible." The *Times* took its story straight from FBI sources and picked up its spin as well. These few "clear accounts" like Russell's, the reader is told, have "substantially weakened support for the idea that a missile downed the plane."[31]

That is correct—*weakened*. The *Times* continues to track with the FBI's spin, claiming that Russell's account of a quick flash well before the large fireball has "bolstered the idea that a bomb, and not an exploding fuel tank, triggered the disintegration of the airplane." At this stage in the article, the FBI account, as reported by the *Times*, devolves into fantasy:

> The winnowing of witnesses' accounts, investigators have said, involved teams of Federal agents and safety board officials. They watched for distinctive body language and listened for phrases that appeared to have been taken from newspaper headlines about the crash. Certain cues marked some witnesses as "pleasers," or people eager to say what they thought interviewers wanted to hear, said one crash investigator, who refused to be identified. Most of the accounts were embellished, with many approaching the outlandish, the investigator said.

The notion of "teams" of FBI officers and NTSB agents working together, methodically evaluating witness testimony, flies in the face of all known facts. The NTSB was roughly excluded from the process, and the FBI was notoriously unsystematic in its interviews.

The *Times* adds that there were "fewer than a dozen accounts" that the FBI considered "believable enough to hold clues to what happened." The NTSB's Bruce Magladry, however, had reviewed hundreds of these accounts and concluded that they were "generally similar to one another."[32] The article also fails to mention the intelligence analysts from MISIC, the ones who had reported to the FBI that "many of the descriptions given by eyewitnesses were very consistent with the characteristics of the flight of such missiles."[33] Sources within the investigation would later report that MISIC had identified at least thirty-four such witnesses.

Although she was in a position to know better, Patricia Milton would repeat the canard about the witnesses in her 1999 book. "Only about a dozen were standing in the right place at the right time," she writes, "looking in the general direction from which a missile would have had to come."[34]

The NTSB's own witness summary, issued in October of 1997, tells a different story. Although the NTSB's database contained information on only 458 of the FBI witness interviews, less than two-thirds of the total, it strongly suggests that many more than a dozen witnesses deserved serious attention. According to the NTSB's own calculations, 183 witnesses said they saw a streak of light. Of those, 146 provided a description of the path taken by the streak and 96 said that the streak originated from the surface. Sixty-four witnesses even reported a compass direction of travel or gave sufficient information so that a direction of travel could be resolved, and this without much help from the FBI.[35]

Importantly, according to the NTSB, "128 witnesses reported an immediate end of the streak, 85 described it ending in an explosion, 32 said it ended in a fireball, and 11 said it ended in a flash."[36]

It is quite likely that Michael Russell saw just the flash out of the corner of his eye, "the right side of his field of vision." He describes it as a "camera flash," much as Meyer did.[37] Russell then turned and saw the fireball some seconds later. Like the flight engineer on Major Meyer's helicopter, the less a witness had seen the more credible a witness he or she became.

Obviously, the FBI had access to more interview data than it let on when its agents told the *Times* that there were fewer than a dozen credible witnesses. This misdirection had to be purposeful. The *Times*, however, did not challenge the FBI data and did not bother to seek out witnesses on its own. The FBI surely recommended the one witness the *Times* interviewed. The major media followed the *Times* lead.

A review of the ten most significant TWA 800 stories on CNN during the month of August reveals not a single mention of the word *witness* or *eyewitness*. Yet by August 20, the FBI had interviewed more than seven hundred such eyewitnesses to the crash. Without their testimony, without the radar data and the satellite imagery and the video and the photographic evidence, government officials were free to channel the story as they chose. And this they did.

AT this point it might be helpful to ask whether an "unseen hand" was directing the investigation from the White House. The answer seems to be both yes and no.

Yes. By late in the day, July 18, this control had shown itself on the question of missiles. There was a single message emanating from a single source, and it went something like this: For reasons of highest national security, on a need-to-know basis, no information about missiles will be volunteered to the media and the public. Research can continue into the question. "Missile" can be kept on the table as a possible theory, but all other information will be tightly held.

There is no documentation to prove this contention. None likely exists, but all circumstantial evidence confirms it:

- The military's comprehensive deception about military assets.

- The P-3 crew's stonewalling of the FBI. Its "broken" transponder.

- The State Department's refusal to acknowledge a credible warning from the Islamic Change Movement.

- The inexplicable absence of satellite imagery.

- The suppression of video evidence.

- The intervention of the Justice Department on behalf of the FBI.

- The FBI's failure to acknowledge publicly the presence of the MISIC analysts.

- The changing rationales to devalue the telltale radar.

- The dismissal of the Kabot photo.

- The dismissal of the Krieger photo.

- The silencing and defamation of Major Meyer.

- The suppression of eyewitness information.

Were FBI officials as cautious about physical evidence as they were about eyewitness testimony, one could make the case that their withholding of missile information testified to their high level of discretion. But from the beginning, as shall be seen, the FBI systematically fed the media "evidence" of a bomb, at least until late August.

Thus, the *No*. Beyond the understanding that missiles were not to be discussed, that the military was not to cooperate in any meaningful way, and that the FBI was to control the investigation, the investigation was largely left to its own rhythms. These were discordant enough. This discord would, however, allow the Clinton administration extra room to maneuver. As

Christine Negroni correctly notes, "Flight 800 became the first accident where the issue of agency would be so hotly debated that the White House had to intervene."[38]

On July 25, the president did just that when he visited the victims' families on Long Island. There, he told the grieving relatives that "we do not yet know what caused Flight 800 to crash, whether it was mechanical failure or sabotage."[39] He did announce, however, that his administration would immediately tighten security at the nation's airports.

On that same day, feigning an open mind, President Clinton announced the formation of a commission to deal with the perceived attack on that doomed airplane. It would be called The White House Commission on Aviation Safety and Security and was officially established by Executive Order 13015 on August 22. Chairing the commission was to be Vice President Al Gore.

The new security measures did not mean that the White House knew the cause of the crash, or so administration officials were quick to point out. These officials included Transportation Secretary Federico F. Peña, who accompanied Clinton to Long Island, and adviser George Stephanopoulos. Said Stephanopoulos, "We felt it prudent to reassure people, even before a final judgment was made, about the safety of the airlines."[40] Remember that Stephanopoulos would not utter a word about his involvement in the TWA 800 affair in his memoirs.

Also on this same day, White House Chief of Staff Leon Panetta publicly formalized what had been quietly true from the beginning. "All coordinated information will be done through Bob Francis," said Panetta at a press conference held at JFK. That the White House would involve itself in so seemingly routine a matter is telling. Oddly, Panetta described Francis as "head of the National Transportation Safety Board."[41]

The president's visit to Long Island eight days after the crash would prove to be something of a milestone. On that same day, for the first time, unnamed "law enforcement officials"—most assuredly the FBI—told the *New York Times* that they "supported the theory that the plane was destroyed by a bomb."[42] At a separate briefing that day, Kallstrom reinforced the theory. "We know there was a catastrophic explosion," he admitted. "It was caused by some kind of bomb, obviously explosion." Catching himself, he added some corrective cover about the possibility of "a mechanical problem," but his intent was clear.[43] This admission represented a major shift in thinking without the benefit of any new evidence. Just a week earlier

Kallstrom had told the press, "We do have information that there was something in the sky. A number of people have seen it. A number of people have described it similarly. It was ascending."[44]

Something else happened on July 25 that deserves mention. Three days earlier, the NTSB's Bruce Magladry had begun to review the FBI witness statements by himself, with the "attendant prohibitions" mentioned earlier. Although the NTSB Witness Group Summary Report acknowledges that "this was the only way for the Safety Board to gain access to the information gathered by the FBI," Magladry inexplicably abandoned the task on July 25 and headed back to Washington, the job barely begun.[45]

From this day forward, there would be no more serious mention of eyewitnesses, radar, satellites—nothing. All talk of a missile had disappeared. The "bomb" theory had emerged almost out of whole cloth. With little evidence to support a bomb and none to support a mechanical failure, the administration had established an inherently false dialectic between bomb and mechanical failure only one week after the crash, and the media did not challenge it.

A DAY or two before this media spectacle, Jim Speer got a keen sense of the direction in which the investigation was heading. Speer was on the scene representing ALPA, the Air Line Pilots Association. Few people on the scene could match his credentials—Air Force veteran, twenty-five years of experience as a fighter pilot, a seasoned accident investigator, a TWA pilot, and a safety and environmental engineer as well. But in this investigation, Speer was hamstrung from the beginning.

For him and the others, the FBI agents were a constant intimidating presence. Indeed, investigators had to pass through three levels of security merely to come and go and were warned frequently and severely against disclosing any information. In one oddly amusing scene picked up by an ABC cameraman early in the investigation, a wisecracking NYPD cop from the joint task force on terrorism sorts through the damaged parts and says, "I wish Clinton would get off his ass and do something about this terrorism."[46] At this point, the FBI agent monitoring him realizes the camera is rolling and leans in to kill the terrorist talk. The cop, who doesn't see the camera, keeps right on talking. "Oh no, it's definitely an explosion," he tells the FBI agent. "When you see it for yourself, the little pieces are all over the place."[47]

Given these circumstances, Speer had to be inventive to get at the truth.

On this particular occasion, he came across a suspicious part that no one seemed willing to examine. So he took it himself to the FBI's field lab, explained that he had done some chemical testing in college, and asked to see how the FBI's chemical tester worked. And yes, he just happened to have a part parked outside that they might use in a demonstration. Speer explains what happened next:

> I asked them to swab it and test that in their demonstration, which they did, and the part tested positive for nitrates. Upon which they picked up the phone, called somebody, and in nanoseconds three FBI guys in suits come running in. They physically excluded me from conversation, turned to me and said, "The machine has frequent false positives; we will conduct the test again." And they did, four more times, maybe five. They would not let me watch the tests and also when the test was complete, they turned to me and said, "All the rest of the tests were negative; we will declare the overall test negative and the first one you saw, we'll call it a false positive."[48]

Both the FBI and the ATF used state-of-the-art EGIS equipment at the Calverton site on Long Island. Although Negroni and Milton try to dismiss this technology as "portable" or "makeshift," there was nothing crude about the testing process or the technology itself, valued at $200,000 a unit.

Assistant FBI Director Donald Kerr testified to the seriousness of the Bureau's effort before a Senate subcommittee. As he related, the FBI's Evidence Response Team arrived at the scene the evening of the crash to be followed the next morning by three examiners from the Materials and Devices Unit, and later that morning by three examiners from the Chemistry Unit. During the course of the investigation, Kerr boasted thoughtlessly that FBI Lab examiners lent nearly five thousand hours of on-site support and sent "116 pieces of debris" to the FBI lab in Washington for further testing.[49]

As to the on-site technology, President Clinton himself described EGIS as "highly sophisticated detection equipment" when he honored an Israeli request for the technology after a series of terrorist attacks earlier in 1996.[50] Israel already had a number of EGIS machines on-line and knew their value. At the time of the shipment to Israel, Washington sources referred to this equipment as "extremely sensitive." In fact, EGIS was then being used as the benchmark by which other detection systems were evaluated.

Manufactured by Thermedics Incorporated of Woburn, Massachusetts, the EGIS equipment weighs about three hundred pounds. Its "portability" is provided by a handheld sampling unit, which vacuums air from suspect articles and areas and transfers the resulting vapors to the analysis unit. A result described as "positive" for this machine not only shows the presence of an explosive, but it also specifically identifies that residue.

In fact, structural aluminum tests false positive less than one in ten thousand times. The particular part that Speer had identified, a leading-edge wing rib, caused problems for the FBI. It was an exterior part. It would not fit the newly minted bomb scenario, at least not in any conventional sense. Speer continues:

> We talked with ALPA and they talked to the NTSB on Monday, and they approached the FBI with some concern that maybe the part did need to have further investigation, and the FBI said, "All right, all right, we'll send it to our real lab in Washington."[51]

In one of those odd quirks of history, Maj. Fritz Meyer was assigned to fly this part from the Calverton hangar back to the Suffolk air base, from which it would be taken to Washington on a C-130. "They didn't know who I was," says Meyer. "I'm just a guy in a green bag flying the helicopter."[52]

Meyer adds confirming detail. He noticed that there were very large puncture holes along the leading edge. "Here you have an aluminum alloy, which is turned tightly into an eight- or nine-inch radius. It has great strength," says Meyer. "Something had driven through that with such force that it dimpled it inward. Not just once but regularly, about four or five holes which appeared to be almost in line."[53]

On July 23, *Newsday* also added confirming detail, reporting that "a chemical test showed traces of a rare explosive on a wing from TWA Flight 800." *Newsday* then quoted one senior federal official on the condition of anonymity: "The divers reported pitting in the external metal portion of the section."[54] Meyer wasn't quite sure where in Washington the wing edge was going, but as Jim Speer adds, "The part has not been seen since for five years now."[55]

To be fair, the FBI agents in question would not have thought they were involved in a cover-up. Their mission was to prevent the other investigators from gaining access to the information. As *Newsday* would report, the process for sending pieces of the aircraft to the FBI lab was "kept under close wraps," so close that even the ATF officials doing much of the preliminary testing were unaware of the process.

Milton reports an incident similar to Speer's in the first week of the investigation. In this case the ATF tested a thirty-foot piece of a wing's underbelly on its own EGIS scanning device. After the test, someone told the media that the part had tested positive for explosive residue. Again, the FBI promptly sent the part to its lab in Washington, and again it tested negative. But the FBI had failed in its mission to control this information, and Kallstrom was furious. His agents told him that they "suspected" that ATF agents were "tipping off journalists about possible hits on their portable machines."[56] After this, the FBI blocked the ATF even from running tests on its own equipment. All the ATF agents could do after this was prepare materials for the FBI to test.

CONSPIRACIES are far less vast than their critics like to think. At this point all but one or two people in the Long Island investigation were working to solve the puzzle, including the FBI agents who shut the ATF and others out of the investigation. It is likely that they sent the part to the FBI lab in Washington in good faith or something like it. What happened to the part in Washington, however, was out of their hands, out of Kallstrom's for that matter.

The FBI lab at this time was a veritable black hole. In January 1997, six months after the crash, the now notorious FBI lab scandal would break. In April of the same year, the Inspector General's office released a report documenting numerous cases of inaccurate and scientifically flawed testimony, evidence mishandling and contamination, and quite possibly worse. The report focused on misconduct in only three departments, all of them relevant—the Explosives Unit, the Materials Analysis Unit, and the Chemistry-Toxicology Unit.

As it happens, the first person Louis Freeh would suspend was Frederic Whitehurst, the one man with courage enough to blow the whistle on the morass at the lab. "The action taken by the FBI implies that he is being punished for 'committing truth,'" wrote Sen. Charles Grassley of Iowa to Freeh. "It appears to be a reprisal for his disclosures."[57] Such was the culture of the FBI circa 1996–1997.

Whitehurst, by the way, had first brought his concerns to the Justice Department in 1995. The White House was aware of the lab's problems all the while the FBI was shipping parts to it.

Christine Negroni admits that three of the FBI scientists working on the crash—Roger Martz, Rick Hahn, and James Thurman, an explosives expert—would be among those cited in the report. She makes this point to suggest that any explosive residue the lab identified was possibly in error. But she gets it exactly backwards. The lab scientists, either out of willful intent or incompetence, were apparently eliminating instance after instance of legitimate explosive findings, including all positive hits on the exterior, sure signs of an explosion outside the plane.[58]

For all its shortcomings, the FBI was only half the problem. Those investigators like Speer who were trying their best to decode the evidence found themselves caught between the Scylla of the FBI's brutish secrecy and the Charybdis of the NTSB's obstructionistic spite.

The FBI patronized the NTSB. The NTSB despised the FBI. The FBI distrusted the ATF. The ATF despised the FBI. NTSB irregulars distrusted the NTSB senior staff and vice versa. The FBI distrusted its lab and vice versa. And no one trusted the NTSB's Robert Francis except James Kallstrom, who probably shouldn't have.

Francis functioned the way a "political officer" might have in the Soviet Army. He served as the eyes and ears of the party in power. While NTSB Chairman Jim Hall complained of the FBI's intrusiveness and Francis's unauthorized complicity with the FBI, Francis sloughed it off. "This is a Washington hang-up," he said, "that one agency has to be in charge."[59] Francis had no real authority, but he exercised a good deal of power through the strength of his connections. Unlike Jim Hall or even James Kallstrom of the FBI, Francis seems to have been given a specific directive that went something like this: A mechanical problem caused the explosion. Insist on this explanation regardless.

There are multiple reasons why the NTSB would push so hard for a mechanical explanation. Robert Francis's advocacy preceded the evidence. His motives were altogether political. The motives of Dr. Bernard Loeb and Dr. Merrit Birky, the NTSB's two most influential managers on the scene, largely preceded the evidence as well, but in their cases, the motives were more institutional.

Birky prided himself that "he never believed it [terrorism] from day one."[60] Loeb did not take much longer to convince. "Crimes are corroborated very quickly," Loeb observed. "We weren't getting anything to suggest a criminal enterprise had taken place."[61] Early in the investigation, the two may not have known about the negation of all audio and visual evidence. But they knew that the FBI was culling off any physical evidence that suggested a criminal act.

Oddly, the removal of this evidence played into their own game plan. As Negroni attests, both Birky and Loeb were highly irritated by the FBI's claims of terrorism.[62] Unless one or the other had a back channel to the White House, it seems likely that they willed the investigation towards a mechanical explanation to justify their own presences and to spite the FBI, Loeb especially. Those who know him almost inevitably describe him in the negative—touchy, arrogant, thin-skinned, self-righteous. One investigator on the scene tells of him "having his own agenda," one that no one could quite understand.[63]

Regardless of their motives, NTSB management did even less to foster the truth than the FBI. Speer reveals the nature of the problem in this encounter with Dr. Birky during the first week of the investigation.

> We walked over and looked at the part, and I asked him [Birky] what he thought and he asked me what I thought and I said it looked to me like it has been next to a high explosion, and he says, "Well I have considered everything and I have decided that this has happened because of hydraulic action on impact with the water." And I looked at him right in the eye and said, "BS—you know as well as I that the terminal velocity of things falling through the atmosphere near sea level is 120 to 140 miles an hour. That kind of velocity does not do this kind of damage to structural aluminum." He looked back at the part and up at me and said, "Hydraulic action on impact with the water."[64]

That was not all. Speer continues:

> There was a piece of stringer attached to this and I said, "Since when have you seen hydraulic action on impact with the water cause sooting through the hole?" and with that he turned on his heel and stomped off.

THE White House could not have asked for more. In fact, on the morning of July 26, upon reading the *New York Times*, President Clinton had to be pleasantly surprised at the progress of the investigation and how well information from the night of July 17 had been contained. He had bought some much-needed time. Better still, his visit to Long Island had turned into a public relations coup, much like his visit to Oklahoma City a year earlier. No president had ever been more adept at hand-holding than he.

By July 26, all serious talk of a missile had disappeared, and the investigation had been channeled into a debate between "bomb" and "mechanical." Over the next four weeks, the drumbeat for a "bomb" would become so loud that the White House would have to intervene once again to silence it. As those in the know understood, TWA 800 was a puzzle that could not be solved, at least until after the election.

CHAPTER 4

DOG DAYS

For all the high-tech equipment put to work in the TWA 800 investigation, its most critical chapter would be both opened and closed by a keen-nosed dog.

The dog saga began on August 7, 1996, when a German shepherd screened out the rank odors of deep-sea immersion on the recovered wreckage and zeroed in on a stretch of flooring alongside the right wing at rows 25 and 26. The piece tested positive for both PETN and RDX at Calverton and again at the FBI lab in Washington. The FBI's James Kallstrom was all but ready to declare the crash site a crime scene. This seemed to be the confirmation he was waiting for. This is the story at least as Patricia Milton tells it.[1]

It seems to be at least half true, but perhaps no more than that.

The FBI had been tilting towards a bomb for the last two weeks, and its favored vehicle for the release of information was the *New York Times*. On July 28, 1996, the *Times* quoted Kallstrom as saying, "I think within the next 48 hours we'll get something that we think is going to give us the clues that we need."[2] The FBI delivered two days later.

"Jet's Landing Gear Is Said to Provide Evidence of Bomb," declared the headline of the *Times'* July 31 edition. "For the last several days, law enforcement officials investigating the crash of Trans World Airlines Flight 800 have been saying privately that they believed the plane was destroyed by a bomb," noted the *Times*, "but they have been waiting to find a piece of clear physical evidence to support their theory."[3]

The front landing gear seemed to be it. Although the landing gear had been retracted into its housing before the plane exploded, "serious concussive damage" disfigured its hydraulic mechanism. This was not easily done. With the exception of certain engine components, the landing gear is the strongest single part of an aircraft, made as it is of steel and titanium. "By the way it had been smashed," the *Times* quoted one investigator as saying, "the bomb experts thought it had been very close to the source of the explosion." The discovery, according to the *Times*, "caused a stir among the divers, Navy and Coast Guard technicians and Federal agents who recovered the landing gear on Saturday." There was no way to ignore it or conceal such a discovery.

The *Times* also implied that the part had been damaged by an explosion. With on-site results testing positive, "samples of apparent residue found on the landing gear have been sent to the F.B.I. lab in Washington to find if they hold chemical traces of an explosive."

As of July 31, however, the doors of the landing gear had yet to be found. The doors were critical. If they were found to have been blown outward, that would all but prove a bomb. If blown inward, that would all but prove a missile. But first they had to be "found." Without this particular piece of evidence—indeed with little suggestive evidence—the top FBI agents on the scene argued for a bomb. Still, at this juncture "a missile or rocket" had not been ruled out, and a mechanical failure remained "an outside possibility."[4]

Both bombs and missiles leave residue, and on August 1, CNN strongly implied that explosive residue had been found not only on the wreckage of the plane but also on the victims' bodies. When asked to respond to this allegation, Kallstrom answered, "I haven't said I haven't found it. I just haven't commented on it."[5] Kallstrom was not the first to suggest this possibility. A week earlier CNN had quoted White House Chief of Staff Leon Panetta as admitting that "chemical residues had been found on some of the bodies and plane parts."[6] Regardless of whether the cause was bomb or missile, interest in the crash remained high. In August of 1996, in fact, TWA 800 was the hottest story in America. And the *New York Times*, while at times "used" by investigators, was keeping the heat on the investigation.

"Luggage Spotted in Debris Trail Suggests an Explosion to Experts," announced the headline on August 6. Don Van Natta Jr., the paper's most aggressive reporter on the case, wrote that a trail of debris was found several miles closer to JFK than any wreckage found before. The debris included large suitcases and scattered clothing. According to the *Times*, the discovery strengthened the theory that an explosion occurred in or near the forward cargo hold and blew the suitcases out of the plane even before the nose separated.[7]

The *Times*, however, missed an even more important discovery. Located amid the luggage on the ocean floor was the number three engine from the right side of the 747. According to an intrepid reporter from a local New York TV station, investigators did not find the engine until August. The engine had fallen into the water so far to the west, so close to JFK, that the Navy had not initially videotaped the area.[8]

Robert Francis, of course, was not one to rush to judgment. "Obviously, we would have loved to have had the first big thing tell us the whole story," he was quoted as saying. "This is systematic and can be a long-term process."[9]

Among the other discoveries reported that day in the *Times* was the gnarled cockpit. A large metal beam from another section of the plane had rammed right through it, almost assuredly in those first few seconds before the cockpit blew away. Refusing to acknowledge an explosion, and teetering on the edge of self-parody, Francis listed the possible causes of this phenomenon:

> There's the hitting the water. There's the sinking to the bottom. There's the getting tangled with other things. There's the recovery. There's putting it on a deck. There's putting it into a tug. There's taking it off. There's putting it in a hangar.

"There's the getting tangled with other things"? As noted earlier, the NTSB wasn't quite the agency it used to be.

AFTER the August 7 discovery by the dogs of the PETN and RDX and confirmation in Washington, the pace accelerated at the investigation site. Patricia Milton provides the best behind-the-scenes accounts of what transpired, and she provides enough credible detail to suggest that James Kallstrom and the FBI were still keenly intent on solving this case.

As Milton tells it, Kallstrom maintained a high level of secrecy about the discovery of the explosive residue. He only grudgingly told NTSB Chairman Jim Hall of the findings and refused to say where the residue was found. He also shared the news with his own key staff and with Francis, whom he liked for his White House connections and his seeming pliability.[10]

On August 12, according to Milton, Kallstrom called Long Island from Washington to say he was delayed at a briefing on Capitol Hill. He asked Agent Joe Cantamessa, his technical guru, to stand in for him at that evening's briefing. After reading a statement prepared for him by Kallstrom, Cantamessa proceeded to take questions. In the process, he revealed that numerous tests for explosive residue had, in fact, proved positive on Long Island, but that they had all tested negative in Washington. Sure enough, Van Natta reported as much in the next day's *New York Times*. Van Natta focused in particular on the positive result for PETN from a test on the right wing, near where the wing and the fuselage are joined.

Taking his cue from the FBI, Van Natta referred to the sophisticated EGIS testing site as "a makeshift lab at Calverton" and acknowledged that tests at the FBI lab in Washington proved "inconclusive." Still, he took Cantamessa literally at his word, writing, "As many as 10 other parts of the airliner tested by the technicians in the hangar in Calverton registered positive for explosives."[11]

Kallstrom was, reportedly, furious. Even negative results were part of the evidence, Milton relates, and the evidence was never to be discussed.[12] Her explanation for this secrecy would ring truer had not the FBI been advancing a bomb thesis and feeding the *Times* evidence of the same for the past three weeks. It is, in fact, possible that Kallstrom used Cantamessa as a cutout to advance a sabotage scenario against resistance from the White House and the NTSB. Milton reports that Kallstrom's "deep freeze" of Cantamessa ended after a few days, and their mutual good feelings returned.[13]

Like the *Times*, CNN reported that attention had shifted "toward the center of the plane, where the right wing was attached to the fuselage, as a likely location for the explosion." CNN also mentioned that investigators were looking closely at a beam recovered from the center section. "The beam," claimed CNN, "was found in an area where the center fuel tank is located."[14]

One of the critical tools in any investigation is the debris field. Investigators can learn much by analyzing which parts left the plane and in what order. Had the initial explosion been the result of a mechanical malfunction, the keel beam would have been among the first parts found on the ocean floor. It is the spine of the plane and runs under the center wing tank. The bulk of the center wing tank, however, had been found in the eastern end of the debris field, far from JFK. As CNN notes, so was the keel beam. FBI documents also show that the keel beam was among the last parts to hit the water, not the first.

The morning of August 14 had to be a rough one at the White House. Van Natta's article in the *Times*—"Fuel Tank's Condition Makes Malfunction Seem Less Likely"—was the most provocative yet.

According to the *Times*, investigators "concluded that the center fuel tank caught fire as many as 24 seconds after the initial blast that split apart the plane, a finding that deals a serious blow to the already remote possibility that a mechanical accident caused the crash." For weeks investigators had been telling the *Times* that if a mechanical failure had triggered the explosion, the most likely source for the explosion would have been the center fuel tank, often called the center wing tank (CWT), situated, as it is, between the wings. But after discovering that pieces of this fuel tank were "virtually unscathed," investigators concluded that the initiating explosion must have occurred elsewhere, "slightly forward of the spot where the wings meet the fuselage."[15]

One official was quoted as saying that parts of the tank were in "pristine condition." Said another official who insisted on anonymity, "It is clear that whatever set off the tank did not severely damage the tank. Something else, most likely later, blew up the tank."

There was more. Investigators told the *Times* that the pattern of the debris "persuaded them that a mechanical malfunction is highly unlikely." A narrow strip of the fuselage ahead of the right wing, which had been recovered from the area closest to Kennedy airport, was the first to have been blown off the plane. From their analysis of the debris field, these investigators concluded the following, a summary that has all the appearance of unvarnished truth:

> The blast's force decapitated the plane, severing the cockpit and first-class cabin, which then fell into the Atlantic Ocean. The rest of the plane flew on, descending rapidly, and as it did thousands of gallons of jet fuel spilled out of the wings and the center fuel tank between them. At 8,000 feet, about 24 seconds after the initial blast, the fuel caught fire, engulfing the remainder of the jetliner into a giant fireball.

The *Times* threw in another kicker. The manufacturer of the EGIS technology told Van Natta that false positives occur in only a fraction of cases. Added Van Natta, "Some senior Federal investigators say the positive results over the last few weeks have some validity."

Van Natta's next line had to have sent shock waves through the White House: "Now that investigators say they think the center fuel tank did not explode, they say the only good explanations remaining are that a bomb or a missile brought down the plane." It should be noted that this conclusion was reached *before* the *Times* learned of the PETN and RDX confirmation at the FBI lab in Washington.

To be sure, Robert Francis was trying his best to keep the stalling game alive. "I don't think anything rules out anything at this point," he told the *Times*. But Francis was sounding increasingly shrill and out of touch, and the *Times* wasn't buying.

ON August 14, 1996, the very day this damning *New York Times* story broke, President Clinton called Victoria Cummock and personally invited her to sit on a newly formed airline safety and security commission to be chaired by Vice President Al Gore. Cummock was the widow of a Pan Am Flight 103 victim and an airline safety advocate. In inviting her, the president assured Cummock that he wanted to develop tough new counter-terrorism measures. With the timing of this invitation, he may also have hoped to offset that morning's bombshell announcement.

Given the perceived seriousness of the threat that August, Clinton also appointed to the commission former CIA Director John M. Deutch, Transportation Secretary Federico F. Peña, and others with experience in aviation safety and security matters. At this point in the investigation, one could forgive Clinton for thinking that he just might have to "dust off those contingency plans" after all. For obvious political reasons, however, the White House was reluctant to admit to a terrorist scenario.

Only one investigator had the wherewithal to thwart the White House's will—James Kallstrom. Patricia Milton portrays Kallstrom much the way Homer did Achilles: "a bear of a man bristling with fierce energy," "six feet tall and solidly built," "towering" over his foes, bearing the weight of the investigation "on his big broad shoulders," a "hero" to the victims' families.[16] The photos that show Kallstrom to be a squat, rumpled, middle-aged man of less than average height obviously conceal the force within, the force that blinded

Milton. Were she not so blind, Milton might have seen the true tragic heart of the epic tale she weaves, the transformation of this agent of justice into what one knowledgeable congressional aide would call "just another liar."[17]

Little is written about the week after the August 14 *Times* story, a day on which traces of nitroglycerin were also found on the plane.[18] President Clinton remained out west vacationing. FBI Director Louis Freeh remained out of sight. There would not be a single mention of him by the *New York Times* in regard to TWA 800 in the two months following the crash.

Besides, the FBI had its hands full in Atlanta with the deadly bombing of Centennial Olympic Park on July 27, which killed 2 and injured 112 more. There, a less-secretive FBI office had already identified the lethal device as a pipe bomb and had fingered its chief suspect—the hapless security guard Richard Jewell. While the network cameramen waited outside his apartment for the rare sighting, Jewell and his mom squirreled away within, virtual prisoners of the media. America was enjoying the Jewell spectacle that careless summer, relieved that there was no terrorist involvement in Atlanta either.

Neither Freeh nor his boss, Janet Reno, had much to do with TWA 800. As both were ineffectual, neither were they entirely reliable. The task of reining in James Kallstrom would fall to Jamie Gorelick, the deputy attorney general. If Robert Francis served as the "political officer" for the investigation on Long Island, Gorelick served a similar role in the Justice Department. She had assumed this role after Clinton crony Webster Hubbell resigned in disgrace, and she would hand it on to her successor, Eric Holder, who himself would be disgraced in the Marc Rich affair.[19]

Gorelick was much nimbler than either and kept a lower profile. An article in *Newsweek* of June 3, 1996, however, captured some sense of the trust placed in her by the Clinton administration. "Using the lexicon of the campaign, Deputy Attorney General Jamie Gorelick has told aides she wants a 'rapid response' to counter charges 'in the same news cycle,'" wrote the authors of Gorelick's PR plans to defend liberal jurists. "Gorelick is even setting up a campaign-like 'war room' in her office. In a campaign year, Justice can't afford to be totally blind."[20]

No, in a campaign year, with "survival" at stake, Justice could not afford to be blind at all. On August 22, Kallstrom was summoned to Washington to be served up a dose of survival reality. At this juncture in the investigation, even if Gorelick knew no more than what she read in the *New York Times*, she would have known that explosive residue had been found all over the plane and that the possibility of a mechanical failure was more "remote" than ever.

Kallstrom, however, knew more—much more. For one thing, he knew that the traces of PETN and RDX found in the fuselage along the right wing had been confirmed by the D.C. lab. For another, he knew what the witnesses saw. Tellingly, the FBI had performed its last interview two days before the meeting. The eyewitness accounts now numbered more than seven hundred. At least 244 of these were so specific, so consistent, and so credible that they could not be ignored. Defense Department analysts had debriefed some thirty-four of the witnesses. There were also scores of witness drawings, some so accurate and vivid they could chill the blood.

But there is something else Kallstrom must have known. Navy divers had found the crucial nose-gear doors in the debris field closest to JFK, well to the south of Flight 800's flight path, a mile closer to JFK than the bulk of the center wing tank. Equally damning, the debris from the 747 fuselage to the right of the doors was also found deep in this same zone.

In triaging the wreckage, FBI agents had identified and "logged in" the doors sometime during the month of August 1996.[21] It was clear that a fuel tank explosion could not have blown them so far off the flight path. But one other fact emerged even more clearly: The doors had been blown *inward*, almost undoubtedly by an external force. If linked to the other evidence, the doors provided a critical clue in breaking open the investigation. But although the doors were known to be at the hangar, and would even be discussed by NTSB staffers, no one in authority was drawing the necessary inferences. The doors would not be officially "discovered" until September 1997. The NTSB might not have discovered them at all had not "party members" like Boeing and TWA insisted that someone look.

Boeing spokeswoman Debbie Nomaguchi confirmed that a door and hatch identified by serial number in a confidential debris-field report were from the nose gear. As CNN reported on September 5, 1997, the structural damage to the doors "baffled" officials and called into question "a leading crash theory."[22] More than a year after the crash, with the bomb theory discounted, the "leading crash theory" just happened to be the spontaneous fuel-tank explosion. CNN's reporting on this discovery suggests the media's reluctance to grasp the obvious or pursue leads:

Examiners who have been looking at crash wreckage for the past 13 months are now said to be mystified about the significance of the damage on the doors, which are located below the flight deck and well forward of the plane's center fuel tank. The investigators are equally troubled by the fact that these nose gear doors were among the first things on the plane to have come off in flight.[23]

NTSB spokeswoman Shelly Hazle, however, downplayed the significance of the blown-in doors. "In every investigation," she noted blithely, "things come up all the time that we have to look at and are not readily explainable."[24] In time, independent investigator James Sanders would be able to explain a good deal, privy as he was to official documents turned over by a source within the investigation and granted in the discovery phase of his legal battle over evidence in the TWA 800 case.

As Sanders discovered, the nose-gear doors and the surrounding strips of fuselage had been blown off the plane and had landed in the same area well south of the flight path and deep in the Red Zone, the area closest to JFK. Their presences together suggested a powerful blast beneath and to the left of the plane. When initially recovered, Navy divers had tagged the debris surrounding the doors "Red Zone" and pinpointed each piece on a diving map by longitude and latitude. Someone consequently retagged the debris "Yellow Zone" without specifying coordinates. An unknown person then explained the retagging in a lengthy memo, alleging that this debris had originally been mistagged. Sanders uncovered two FBI documents establishing beyond any doubt the falseness of the explanation.[25]

The media, however, had long since lost interest in the doors. Unexplained in the news reports—or in the books by Negroni and Milton—was why these doors had been ignored for the missing year. By itself, the story of the nose-gear doors had little momentum in late 1997 and less thereafter. Like so much else in the investigation, it quietly disappeared.

GIVEN all the information at his disposal, Kallstrom must finally have realized what happened the night of July 17, if not in perfect detail, at least in its rough outlines. He must have known that there were two different ascending streaks of light—helicopter pilots Baur and Meyer were not just confused—and reports of two high-velocity explosions, one lower than the other.

He might have concluded that the first blast damaged the right wing where it meets the fuselage, and a second, much larger blast—the lower one—savaged the nose gear, ripped open the underbelly of the plane, spilled its cargo, and severed the plane's head. These possibilities, however, never even cross the mind of the James Kallstrom that Patricia Milton reveals in detail. The very absence of such rumination alerts the knowing reader.

This was surely a come-to-Jesus meeting on August 22. Kallstrom had been a good soldier the past five weeks. He had kept all talk of eyewitnesses and satellites and radar and missiles out of the news. But the evidence had led him far away from mechanical failure, and there was no easy way to turn back.

Although *Newsday* puts Janet Reno in the meeting with Kallstrom that day, Milton does not.[26] The only Justice Department official she mentions by name is Jamie Gorelick. To be sure, no account of the meeting provides any more than routine detail, but behaviors begin to change immediately afterwards, especially after the *New York Times* broke a headline story the next day, top right: "Prime Evidence Found That Device Exploded in Cabin of Flight 800." This article stole the thunder from Clinton's election-driven approval of welfare reform in that same day's paper and threatened to undermine the peace and prosperity message of the next week's Democratic National Convention.

The story that Milton tells of how this story came to be is not convincing. In her account, Kallstrom learned that the story was about to break on the way back from the Washington meeting and "was stunned." Milton has him wonder, "Could there be any doubt that someone in Reno's office had leaked the news?"[27]

Yes, there could be. No one in Reno's office had any interest in doing so. Just the opposite. Nor did anyone in that office know enough to satisfy the always careful *Times*. Janet Reno herself likely did not know enough. More concretely, the *Times* attributes the story to "three senior officials deeply involved in the investigation."[28] No one person in Reno's office fits that bill, let alone three.

A more likely explanation is that Kallstrom had orchestrated this story to force the White House's hand before he was effectively silenced. The last time a major story broke on explosive residue, Kallstrom was also in Washington. That one he blamed on agent Joe Cantamessa, this on Reno's office. Washington, it seems, was his alibi.

The one part of Milton's story that squares with the logic of that time and place is Kallstrom's efforts to kill the story. Whatever he had learned in the meeting on August 22 made him regret the article to come. And if the meeting didn't entirely break his will, it surely dimmed his enthusiasm for finding the truth.

"Investigators have finally found scientific evidence that an explosive device was detonated inside the passenger cabin of Trans World Airlines Flight 800," reported the *Times* authoritatively on the twenty-third. The paper referred specifically to the traces of PETN, or pentaerythritol tetranitrate, first identified by the dog more than two weeks previous. According to the *Times*, the positive test result came from "a part of a seat" from the area in "the epicenter of the blast," somewhere between rows 17 and 27, close to the area of the right wing and near the spot where the plane split in two.

These investigators told the *Times* that PETN is commonly found in bombs and surface-to-air missiles, "making it impossible, for now, to know for sure which type of explosive device destroyed the Boeing 747." Nowhere in the story, however, is there any mention of the RDX that Milton claims the FBI found with the PETN on the carpet strip in the same area, and Milton herself directly traces that specific find to this specific story.[29]

The *Times* reminded its readers that ten days prior the FBI had said that "one positive result" in the forensic tests would cause them to declare the explosion a crime. But the paper did give the FBI a little wiggle room, probably in response to Kallstrom's late pleadings, allowing that senior investigators "were not ready to declare that the crash was the result of a criminal act in part because they did not yet know whether the explosion was caused by a bomb or a missile."

On the face of it, this argument makes no sense. By the same logic, the FBI would not have declared Oklahoma City a crime scene until it was sure an ANFO-soaked truck bomb had caused the explosion and not, say, a SEMTEX-packed car bomb. The FBI's hesitation seems rather a desperate dodge triggered by the meeting the day before. On the eve of the Democratic National Convention, the last thing the White House would want is an admission that terrorists had killed 230 Americans in full view of Steven Spielberg's home in the Hamptons. The next to last thing, actually. The political consequences would be even worse had the Navy done it by accident.

THE news of the twenty-third took Robert Francis by surprise. It was not that he didn't know about the PETN confirmation. Rather, he didn't know that he was supposed to know. According to Milton, Kallstrom had called Francis immediately after the confirmation two weeks prior and stressed the need for secrecy. Francis was good at that. As Milton notes, "Kallstrom knew Francis could be trusted."[30] Kallstrom had grown to like Francis as well. Francis shadowed Kallstrom at every news briefing, ignoring the NTSB's own daily briefings back at Calverton. His cooperation with the FBI may have endeared him to Kallstrom, but it alienated his NTSB colleagues.

"I have participated in over 110 major transportation accident investigations while with the NTSB," investigator Henry Hughes would later tell a

Senate subcommittee, "and the TWA-800 investigation is the only one in which the NTSB Board Member in charge was never available to the investigative staff."[31]

Such charges didn't faze Francis. His job wasn't to advance the investigation. His job was to keep an eye on it. For him, the truth was never much of an issue. When asked about PETN in a television interview on the morning of August 23, Francis responded, "I don't know anything about the explosive."[32]

He further confused the issue at a briefing later in the day. "What I said this morning was accurate at that time," Francis told reporters. "When the FBI found out about this, it was shared with us in a timely manner."[33] The media were left to parse this bit of Clintonian doublespeak on their own.

An incident a week or so later shows just how indifferent to the truth Francis had become. At the time, Maj. Fritz Meyer's Air National Guard unit had been given the task of flying investigators from one site to another. One day Meyer flew to the Calverton site with Admiral Kristensen and a friend, a fellow Air Guardsman and FAA employee. At the hangar, the friend introduced Meyer to Francis, whom the friend knew from the FAA.

"This is Fritz Meyer. He is the pilot who was flying the night the plane went down," said the friend to Francis. They started talking. Meyer remembers there being four people in the group: him, his friend, Francis, and a young woman from the NTSB, Kristensen having gone off on his own.

As they walked, Francis turned to Meyer, then looked away collecting himself, and turned back and said, "You know, we're getting away from that missile theory."[34] Meyer just laughed at him in disbelief. The conversation took a turn to the serious when the group came upon the nosewheel that caused such a furor when found a month earlier. Observed Meyer, "It had striations across it, great, deep cuts through the alloy of the wheel casting." According to Meyer, Francis looked at him and said, "You know my people tell me that this is a sign of a high-velocity explosion."

"I made a mistake," admits Meyer. "I told this to a reporter about three months later, and he picked up the phone and called Bob Francis, and Bob Francis denied he had ever met me—had seen my face on television—but he had never met me in person." As was evident from the beginning, Robert Francis had an assignment, and he was sticking to it, truth be damned.

AUGUST 23 represented something of a turning point in the investigation. It was on this day, Christine Negroni notes, that the FAA began to inquire whether any dog-training exercises had ever taken place on the plane that would come to be designated TWA 800.[35] The FAA had never kept systematic records of such exercises. Further, from that day forward there would be no more eyewitness interviews done by the FBI, at least not for the next two months, and only a handful after that—and all of them for the wrong reasons. On the twenty-third itself, as CNN reported, Kallstrom was now saying that "it was possible that the PETN could have been brought on the plane by a passenger and was not part of a bomb." CNN adds an interesting detail: He was "reading a prepared statement."[36]

But there was a speed bump ahead. On the twenty-fifth, for the first time, the *New York Times* published a story with a "missile" lead. "The discovery of PETN," claimed the article, "has kept alive the fearsome though remote possibility that the airliner was brought down by a surface-to-air missile."[37] The article steers wide of any possible military involvement and relies only on information that had already been revealed, but it suggested just how far the reporting had spun out of control. On the next day, the twenty-sixth, the Democratic National Convention opened.

At that day's news briefing, Kallstrom consciously tried to spin the story away from terrorism. The aircraft, Kallstrom said, had been used as a military charter during the Gulf War five years earlier. Maybe a "passenger" did have some residue on his person. Yet, in checking with TWA and the U.S. Air Mobility command at Scott Air Force Base, Illinois, CNN learned that the plane had been completely refurbished after its last use by the troops, making this scenario much less likely.[38]

On the twenty-ninth, President Clinton dedicated only one paragraph to the question of terrorism or aviation safety, and this towards the very end of a long, self-congratulatory acceptance speech:

> [W]e will improve airport and air travel security. I have asked the vice president to establish a commission and report back to me on ways to do this. But now we will install the most sophisticated bomb detection equipment in all our major airports. We will search every airplane flying to or from America from another nation—every flight, every cargo hold, every cabin, every time.[39]

The implication was clear: If the FBI had not ruled out a missile, the White House had. The president, however, could live with a "bomb" and maybe even score a few political points off it. There was, after all, a momentum building at the *New York Times* for a terrorist scenario that even the White House did not seem able to halt.

The next day, August 30, the *Times* explained the details of such a scenario in a lengthy piece by Andrew Revkin. Revkin reported that investigators had prepared a second-by-second computer simulation of the disintegrating plane. The simulation was based on the physical evidence, the debris field, even the radar tracking, but not any eyewitness testimony.[40] Despite this deficiency, the simulation is still revealing. It shows that almost everything first blown out of the plane came from one area on the right side along the right wing. Two seats on the right side of row 23 had fist-sized holes in the back, and row 24 was missing altogether, as was much of the material from rows 20–27. Traces of PETN were also found in this general area.

On that same day, the FBI announced that it had discovered additional traces of explosive residue "on a piece of wreckage from inside the Boeing 747 near where the right wing meets the fuselage."[41] The location is critical. This is exactly where the first explosion seemed to be centered. At the briefing, the FBI did not identify the type of chemical, but "senior investigators" tipped off the *Times*' Van Natta that the substance was RDX. Formally known as cyclotrimethylenetrinitramine, RDX got its shorthand name from the British, who developed it during World War II. For secrecy's sake, they called it "Research Department Explosive," or RDX. More to the point, Van Natta learned that RDX was "a major ingredient of SEMTEX, a plastic explosive developed in Czechoslovakia that has become a favorite of terrorist bombers." In fact, one agent told Van Natta that finding the two ingredients together, RDX and PETN, was "virtually synonymous with SEMTEX."

Van Natta, who prided himself on his sources, was now being steered by them to exactly where they wanted this investigation to go—away from the "missile" and back towards the "bomb," even if it meant revealing more information. If PETN alone allowed for the possibility of a missile, PETN and RDX together argued much more strongly for a bomb.

Note, too, how voluble the once tight-lipped FBI had become. Milton's claim that in Kallstrom's FBI "evidence was never discussed, period" is revealed as no more than a PR strategy.[42] One FBI agent even shared with Van Natta the results right off the EGIS tests. So perfect is the set up that it causes one to doubt whether the PETN and RDX had, in fact, been found in the same area as Milton claims. On August 30, CNN reported that, according to its source, "the RDX was found on a curtain used in the cargo compartment of the jumbo jet."[43] Writing three years later, Milton reaffirms the RDX on the cargo-hold curtain.[44]

Also on August 30, in a joint statement by the FBI and the NTSB, the administration tipped its hand as to how the investigation was to be managed in the future. Regardless of the explosive residues found, the FBI would declare the act a crime only if it could identify supporting "physical evidence"—for example, "physical damage or patterns characteristic of a detonation."[45] Van Natta adds that this "very small piece of evidence" may be no larger than a football. What Van Natta did not realize at the time is that he had just been handed a blueprint for the cover-up that was to follow.

For the next three weeks there would be no new revelations. Consider, though, what had been learned or reaffirmed in just the last ten days.

- Traces of PETN had been confirmed in the cabin along the right wing.

- Two seats in the same area had fist-sized holes punched out in the back.

- One whole row was missing from that area.

- Computer simulations showed that this section along the right wing was blown out first.

- RDX was found on the plane.

- Even Kallstrom was spinning the news away from sabotage.

- Everyone was spinning it away from a missile.

Some interesting contradictions had also begun to develop, all of which would have future ramifications.

- The *New York Times* placed the confirmed PETN trace "on part of a seat." *Newsday* said it was on a "seat cushion."

- Writing later, Milton specifically places the same PETN discovery on "the two-sided tape that holds the carpet down, on row 25 or 26."

- Milton also quotes Kallstrom that RDX had also been found and confirmed on that same tape on August 7, the same day as the PETN.

- The *New York Times* is told about the RDX eight days after it learns of the PETN and only then after it publishes an article reopening the missile issue.

- Milton and CNN confirm an RDX find on a curtain in the cargo hold.

- The *Times* locates its RDX find on a piece of wreckage "near where the right wing meets the fuselage."

These details may seem trivial, but, as shall be seen, they would shape the entire course of the investigation. They were less the result of sloppy reporting—though there was plenty of that—than an imperfect and ever-shifting attempt to conceal what really happened on the night of July 17, 1996.

CHAPTER 5

RED HERRING

After the events of September 11, Al Gore must have hoped no one remembered.

But someone did.

On September 20, 2001, the *Boston Globe* broke the story of how the so-called Gore Commission had failed in its mission to address airline safety. The *Globe* claimed this failure "represents the clearest recent public example of the success that airlines have long had in defeating calls for more oversight."[1] The *Globe* traced that failure to a series of campaign donations from the airlines to the Democratic National Committee in 1996, in the wake of the crash of TWA Flight 800.

Although on the right track, the *Globe* had gotten only half the story. The complete story is much more chilling. Yes, the Clinton-Gore team did abandon security planning for the sake of campaign cash. But worse, the White House deliberately concealed the real cause of the crash, in no small part to justify that abandonment.

The full commission held its first executive session on September 5, 1996, and on September 9 submitted its tough preliminary report to the president. The report advanced twenty serious recommendations to strengthen aviation security. The proposals called for a sixty-day test for matching bags with passengers on domestic flights and a computer-based system of "profiling" passengers that, of course, immediately riled the ACLU. Also proposed were "vulnerability assessments" at every commercial airport in the country, increased numbers of bomb-sniffing dogs, better screening and training of the workers who examined bags, and more frequent tests of their work.[2] At a press conference on September 9, Vice President Gore declared his strong support of these proposals.[3]

But this support did not last for long. "Within ten days, the whole [airline] industry jumped all over Al Gore," commission member Victoria Cummock would claim. As the *Globe* correctly reported, this pressure took the form of an intense lobbying campaign aimed at the White House. On September 19, Gore backed off the proposal in a letter to Carol Hallett, president of the industry's trade group, the Air Transport Association. Wrote Gore, "I want to make it very clear that it is not the intent of this administration or of the commission to create a hardship for the air transportation industry or to cause inconvenience to the traveling public."[4]

To reassure Hallett, the *Globe* reported, Gore added that the FAA would develop "a draft test concept . . . in full partnership with representatives of the airline industry."

What the *Globe* did not report, however, is that on the same day the administration was sending this letter, it was signaling its cooperative spirit to the airline industry through calculated leaks to the *Washington Post* and the *New York Times*. The lead of the *Times* story reads as follows:

> Investigators from the National Transportation Safety Board, saying they are convinced that none of the physical evidence recovered from T.W.A. Flight 800 proves that a bomb brought down the plane, plan tests intended to show that the explosion could have been caused by a mechanical failure alone.[5]

Weeks before, the *Times* had reported that "the only good explanations remaining are that a bomb or a missile brought down the plane off Long Island."[6] In the interim, the evidence for a missile strike had grown only stronger as more explosive residue had been found on the plane and more eyewitnesses had been interviewed.

Now, however, officials were telling the public through the media that a mechanical failure brought down the airplane:

In fact, a senior N.T.S.B. official said, if there was a bomb, investigators probably would have seen "classic signs" of it by now, including metal that is pitted and bent by high-energy shock waves. Likewise, he said, the fact that they have not found any parts of a missile puts that theory in more doubt.[7]

This story came from briefings not at the New York crash site—Robert Francis was almost played out—but at NTSB headquarters in Washington. NTSB Chairman Jim Hall, who still maintained some credibility, had personally orchestrated them. An old political hand from Tennessee—described by an associate as "a personal retainer" to the Gore family—Hall was finally justifying his appointment.[8]

It followed, of course, that a mechanical failure did not require urgent security measures. This was the first time the NTSB had made such a declaration, and its timing was highly suspicious. The investigators took this new direction despite an admission to the *Times* that "they have no evidence pointing to a mechanical malfunction." They claimed instead that "the failure to find proof of a bombing" had led them to reexplore the possibility that an explosion of the center fuel tank destroyed the plane.[9]

ON the next day, September 20, almost surely to make some sense of its radical change in direction, the administration advanced a new story, one that proved to have extraordinary effect.

CNN fully snatched the bait. The headline of its on-line article, "Investigators: Test explosives set back TWA bomb theories," perfectly captures its slant.[10] The *New York Times* article on September 21 well summarizes the government's argument. "Federal officials," said the *Times*, claimed that "the jetliner was used during a test of a bomb-detecting dog five weeks before the crash, which they said could explain the traces of explosives found in the wreckage."[11]

The test took place at the St. Louis airport on June 10, five weeks before the crash. As the *Times* relates, packages containing explosives were placed in the plane's passenger cabin for the dog to find. These packages contained "the same explosives as those found by investigators after the crash." The explanation was not perfect. For one, as shall be seen, the explosives were not the same. For another, as the *Times* admitted the next day, "The packages were not placed in the same place where the traces were located."[12] Then, too, the records found in St. Louis failed to mention the tested plane by tail number. Instead, investigators used "records of what gates planes were parked at that day" to make their case.

Despite these limitations, investigators admitted that the dog exercise "deepened the mystery of whether the plane exploded because of sabotage or mechanical failure." The effect of this discovery was powerful. Don Van Natta summed up its impact: "For some investigators," he wrote in the September 22 *Times*, "the revelation of the bomb-sniffing dog amounted to a stunning setback." Van Natta quotes one investigator as saying that the news hit him like "a punch in the gut."[13] It should be recalled, however, that the search for the records had begun on August 23, the day after the pivotal Washington meeting. This was not to be a search for the truth. It was the search for a plausible cover story. Were a Robert Ludlum to have given this operation a name, "Red Herring" would be just about perfect.

The phrase derives from the practice by seventeenth-century English fox hunters of using actual smoked herring to test and improve a hound's sense of smell. The pungent odor of the fish was a powerful distraction, but a well-trained hound could identify it, filter it out, and continue the pursuit of the fox being trailed.

The phrase here works much too well. Van Natta, who pursued this case diligently, has admitted that the dog-training revelation sidetracked his pursuit of the sabotage angle. It may have even confused Van Natta's sources within this highly compartmentalized investigation, the ones who, weeks before, had thought it "highly unlikely" that a mechanical problem had caused Flight 800 to explode.[14] If the dog-training story could distract the *Times*, it could easily send the rest of the media pack yelping in the wrong direction. And it did. The interest of the major media in the TWA 800 story all but died on September 20, 1996. Worse, the pack would begin to turn on those who challenged the official version with a passion bordering on fury.

AS the official story goes, the FAA traced a likely source of the explosive residue to a training exercise at the St. Louis airport on June 10, 1996. Given the almost random state of documentation for these exercises nationwide, this had to have been a laborious task.

On September 21, 1996, the FBI found its way to Officer Herman Burnett, who oversaw the exercise. As it happens, this is the day *after* the stories about the dog-training exercise began to appear in the media.[15] In other words, the authorities were leaking this particular story even before anyone had talked to the officer in question. According to the FBI, airport management told Burnett that a "wide body" was available for training at Gate 50 that day. The officer then withdrew some exercise "aids" from departmental supplies and drove to Gate 50. Once there, he walked up the exterior jetway staircase and boarded the plane. This information is documented in a letter from the FBI's James Kallstrom to Rep. James A. Traficant, dated September 5, 1997.[16]

According to the FBI, Burnett "made no notations regarding the tail number of the aircraft, as it was not his policy to do so." As Officer Burnett told the authors, he made no notation of the gate either.[17] He did say, however, that he listed specific start and stop times on the training form, and the notation "wide body." No one claims he did more.

Burnett told the FBI that he saw no TWA crew, cleaners, caterers, or passengers when he "began the placement of the explosives at 10:45 AM," nor at any time when he was on board the 747. According to the FBI account, the officer concealed the training aids in specific places throughout the passenger cabin in a "zig-zag" pattern. Burnett let the explosives sit for a while, as FAA regulations dictate, and then returned to his car to retrieve the dog. "At 11:45 AM, the patrolman began the exercise by bringing the dog into the aircraft." Again, according to the FBI, "the exercise lasted 15 minutes, and the dog located all the explosives." Burnett then went back down the jetway with the dog, secured the dog in his car, and climbed back up to retrieve the training aids from various locations throughout this large aircraft. He placed each aid on the galley counter before carting them all back out. Burnett estimated that this activity took fifteen minutes.

Based on the scenario developed by the FBI, Burnett could not have left the plane earlier than 12:15 P.M. Given the time spent going up and down the jetway, a 12:20 or 12:25 P.M. exit is more likely. During this time, Burnett saw no one else on board the plane. He did not expect to. He carried out these daily exercises in as "sterile" an environment as possible—that is, without anyone present.

Existing records play serious havoc with the FBI scenario. They show that Capt. Vance Weir piloted TWA 17119—the plane that would become Flight 800—from St. Louis to Hawaii that day, and Thomas D. Sheary served as first officer. Weir's "Pilot Activity Sheet" from June 10, 1996, adds important detail. It indicates that on this day and on this plane he flew out of St. Louis for Honolulu at 12:35 P.M.[18] Please note the time of departure.

Federal officials were aware of this time as well. The letter from Kallstrom to Traficant (referenced previously) makes this clear:

> The FAA in St. Louis provided the FBI with a copy of a TWA document listing gate assignments for June 10, 1996. This document shows that a 747 bearing TWA # 17119, which is the number for the 747 that was to become Flight 800, was parked at Gate 50 from shortly before 700 hours (7 AM) until approximately 1230 hours (12:30 PM) on that date.

In other words, the plane that would become Flight 800 left the gate between 12:30 and 12:35 P.M. The police officer, however, did not leave the plane until 12:15 P.M. at the earliest and saw no one. To clean the plane, stock it, check out the mechanics and board several hundred passengers would take more than the fifteen-minute window of opportunity the FBI's own timetable presents.

Much more.

TWA regulations in effect in 1996 mandated that the crew of a wide-body report for briefing ninety minutes before scheduled takeoff. Crew members had thirty minutes to complete their briefing and board the 747 as the regulations also mandated that they board one hour before scheduled takeoff. This means that the crew was most likely on the plane by 10:50 A.M. Even if there had been a planned delay, the crew, the pilot, the first officer, the engineer, and a minimum of fourteen flight attendants would have been on board the 747 no later than 11:35 A.M. They would have been preparing the plane for a full load of passengers—stowing their belongings, performing safety equipment preflight, and checking food and beverage supplies. Besides a crew of at least seventeen, there would have been maintenance, food service, and gate agents coming and going during the exact period that the officer was alleged to be training his dog and seeing no one.[19]

David E. Hendrix, an investigative reporter for the Riverside, California, *Press-Enterprise* newspaper, interviewed Captain Weir personally and First Officer Sheary by telephone. They told him they saw no dog or officer on the plane that day. How could they be so certain? As they told Hendrix, they have each flown commercial aircraft for twenty-plus years, and neither has ever seen a dog-training exercise on his plane in all that time.[20]

So if not the 800 plane, which "wide body" could the officer possibly have used? Gates 50 and 51 at St. Louis Lambert International Airport (now gates C-36 and C-38, respectively) are at the end of Concourse C. According to TWA records provided by the FBI, the future Flight 800 aircraft was indeed parked at Gate 50. Parked at Gate 51 was another 747, number 17116, the sister aircraft, a veritable clone.[21] This second plane—bound for JFK International as TWA Flight 844—would not leave the gate until 2 P.M. This later departure would have allowed TWA staff ample time to load and board the plane after the officer finished the training exercise at about 12:15 or slightly later.

To be sure, this second plane was not parked at Gate 50 where the FBI conveniently alleges the exercise took place.

But how could either management or the officer remember the site of a routine exercise performed seventy days prior? According to the FBI, "The manager on duty, whose name the patrolman could not recall, told him that a wide body was available at gate 50." In other words, the officer could not remember the manager's name, but he could remember the gate. This very recollection is suspicious. No known documentation puts Burnett and his dog at this gate or on the Flight 800 plane. No one had anything but memory to call on.

Federal officials had searched the nation, and probably the world, to find an airport at which a dog exercise had taken place on a day when the Flight 800 plane was parked there. They placed the dog exercise on the Flight 800 plane fully indifferent to the truth. If the time of day did not square, so be it. Although Kallstrom would later boast of the more than seven thousand interviews his agents completed, his agents chose not to interview Weir or Sheary. They would not want to know any facts that might undermine the story they were pressured to create.

AFTER news of the dog exercise broke, the story began to spin back Robert Francis's way. Said Francis at a news conference, "If there was a bomb on the plane, there will be evidence that transcends the traces that have been found."[22] By now, he could feel confident that no such evidence would ever be brought to light.

A September 20 subhead from CNN—"Bomb not ruled out"—reveals just how matter-of-factly the media had begun to parrot the false dialectic between bomb and mechanical. It also suggests that "mechanical" was now the favored theory, at least by the NTSB and CNN.

Still, the NTSB needed more. The media may have been accepting the fiction that a dog-training exercise had taken place on the Flight 800 plane, but this was not enough. As CNN casually reported on September 20, the training aids were "well-wrapped packages of explosives."[23] If the explosives remained well wrapped throughout the exercise, the NTSB and the FBI could not make a convincing case that these training aids were the source of the residue. They had to go further. They would have to convince the media that there was not only an exercise on board, but that it was a sloppy, incompetent one. To pull this off, they needed a scapegoat and found one in an innocent African-American police officer with seventeen years on the force, two of those dedicated to daily dog-training exercises.

By now, the authorities could have cared less about Burnett's experience or his reputation. The NTSB summarized its findings on this case in February 1997 in a letter from Chairman Jim Hall to acting FAA Administrator Barry Valentine. "The dog handler," wrote Hall of the officer, "had spilled trace amounts of explosives while placing training aids on board the aircraft during a proficiency training exercise." This same officer, Hall added, "told investigators that he was aware that he had spilled trace amounts of explosives."[24]

"Based on interviews with the dog handler," the letter continued, "the Safety Board determined that he had conducted the training exercise without taking adequate time and precaution when handling the explosive training aids." The letter goes on to chastise Burnett, claiming that he had likely spilled residue from at least two different sources, all of which he had admitted to the authorities.

Patricia Milton's retelling is even more defamatory. "Yeah, I could have spilled more than a little," Burnett is alleged to have told the FBI. "The packages were old and cracked and we hadn't used them in a while, so more than usual might have come out."[25] After the interview Burnett and his dog, Carlo, became subjects of derision among the agents.

At a press conference later that day, Kallstrom hewed to the Robert Francis line. "He observed," says Milton, "that no amount of chemical traces would be enough now for the investigators to conclude a bomb had exploded on Flight 800."[26]

Officer Burnett tells a different story. Says the officer of his treatment at the hands of the federal government, "I am pissed off to this day." Although shaken by the experience, and understandably wary of the authorities, the officer tells a story dramatically different from the one served up by the NTSB or the FBI. "I never lost any," he says of the explosives. "I never spilled any." The officer related this to the authors with clarity and conviction. He adds, "There was never any powder lying loose." As to his alleged confession of the same, he answers, "I just hate that they twisted my words. I know what I did, and how I did it."[27]

To give further cover to this elaborate charade, Hall had to pretend that the St. Louis episode exposed some larger system-wide problem. In the letter referenced previously, he demanded that the FAA "develop and implement procedures" to assure "an effective K-9 explosives training program." In much the same way, the NTSB would later argue for changes in the wiring and in fuel tanks to avoid explosions that never happened.

In this same letter, however, Jim Hall makes a curious admission: "During the recovery of wreckage from TWA Flight 800, trace amounts of explosives were found on the interior surfaces of the cabin and cargo area." Unexplained by Hall is how explosives could possibly have been found in the cargo area, an area in which no one claims the officer ever planted training aids. Even more problematic, the residue found within the passenger cabin—in an area that runs roughly from rows 17 to 27 on the right side of the plane—in no way matches the "zig-zag" pattern in which the officer placed the aids.

It might seem academic at this point to match placements of the training aids with confirmed residue locations, given that the exercise did not take place on the plane in question. But on September 20, the investigation changed, and so thus does the inquiry into the investigation.

On that day, authorities began the full-time search for a mechanical explanation. The answer did not have to be honest—there was no honest answer; it only had to be plausible. The details of the dog-training episode show just how far they were willing to go to make a mechanical explanation stick. The difference between finessing the *New York Times* and lying to Congress is one not just of degree, but of kind. It is finally the difference between compromise and corruption and deserves to be documented.

September 20 also marked the first time federal authorities started hurting people to preserve illusions. Officer Burnett would be the first to suffer, but he would not be the last, or the most grievously injured. In this light, details become evidence, not against those who destroyed the plane but against those who concealed the true cause of its destruction. This is where the inconsistencies noted in the last chapter come in to play. A quick recall:

- The *New York Times* placed the confirmed PETN trace "on part of a seat." *Newsday* suggested it was on a "seat cushion."

- Milton specifically places the PETN on "the two-sided tape that holds the carpet down, on row 25 or 26."

- Milton also quotes Kallstrom that RDX had also been found and confirmed on that same tape on August 7, the same day as the PETN.

- The *New York Times* is told about the confirmed RDX eight days after it learns of the PETN and only then after it publishes an article reopening the missile issue.

- Milton and CNN state that one confirmed RDX find was on a curtain in the cargo hold.

- The *Times* locates its RDX find on a piece of wreckage "near where the right wing meets the fuselage."

As Burnett told the FBI, he made five separate placements of explosive devices within the plane in a zigzag pattern. These included smokeless powder, water gel, detonator cord, and ammonia dynamite. All of these were placed outside the area of damage on the right side of the plane, rows 17–27, in which the explosive residue had been found.

According to the FBI's letter to Traficant, so was the C-4, the most critical of the explosives. "A 1.4 pound block of C-4," reads the letter, "was placed in the pouch on the back of the backrest of row 10, seat 9." This was the only placement of C-4, and this, too, was outside the damage area.

Writing two years later, with the acknowledged help of the FBI, Patricia Milton launders the entire episode. In her account, Burnett places a second "container" of C-4 in "row 26, near floorboard 121"—within the damaged area where the right wing meets the fuselage.[28] This placement just so happens to correlate with her unique revelation that both the PETN and the RDX were found on the floor, under the carpet on the fastening tape "on row 25 or 26." Her source for this admission is Kallstrom. These chemicals were alleged to have been found on August 7 and were arguably the most important find to that point. By positioning the find on the floor, possibly in row 26, the FBI can claim that Officer Burnett's training aid was responsible for this find. By putting both RDX and PETN together, the FBI can argue through Milton that this residue was from the "SEMTEX, or C-4, comprised of PETN, RDX, nitroglycerine, and gunpowder" that Burnett allegedly placed there.

This scenario falls apart under the least scrutiny. For starters, SEMTEX and C-4 are entirely different explosives. Yes, SEMTEX is composed of a varying blend of PETN and RDX, but C-4 is not. Its composition is 91 percent RDX and 9 percent plastic stabilizer. It has no PETN in it.

It gets worse. All contemporary accounts of the confirmed PETN find put it on a seat. The *Times* puts the RDX on a piece of wreckage near the right wing. No account puts either the PETN or the RDX on the floor, not even the Van Natta article inspired by the August 7 discovery. No one puts the RDX and PETN together. And all accounts put RDX in the cargo hold, which Carlo the dog never visited.

Another word on red herrings—more literal this time. As Milton correctly observes, the smell of "brackish seawater and dead fish" made it difficult for the dogs to locate explosive residue.[29] Yet on at least twelve cited occasions, the dogs fought their way through the odors and identified parts of the wreckage that also passed the EGIS test. Much more explosive residue was likely lost to the long immersion. Stranger still, the FBI rinsed the wreckage on the pier as the parts were brought ashore, a decision "made by FBI laboratory personnel."[30] Other parts that registered explosive traces— the nose-gear doors come to mind—were simply lost or ignored. Under no circumstance could Officer Burnett have been responsible for all these traces, especially those on the exterior of the plane.[31]

Nor could Burnett have been responsible for the explosive residue reportedly found on the victims' bodies, reports attested to by no less than Leon Panetta and James Kallstrom. Not surprisingly, the FBI has classified the medical forensic reports on these bodies.[32]

The NTSB could have cleared up many of these issues when it sent one of its own people, Tom Lasseigne, to St. Louis to evaluate the dog-training story. According to the Chairman's Report of November 15, 1996, Lasseigne "anticipates the preparation of a factual report for the public docket by 12/20/96."[33] The report was never released. Freedom of Information Act requests for the report have not been honored.

As to the FBI, the administration seems to have worn down its resistance over time. In fact, one can trace Kallstrom's descent into bitter compromise through his own retelling of the dog story. Two months after the story broke, Kallstrom appeared on the PBS *News Hour with Jim Lehrer*. At this time, Kallstrom still hedged his bets on the dog exercise, admitting that he was not "absolutely" sure "that that's how the chemicals got there." The real proof, Kallstrom acknowledged, would be in the "evidence of the metal, the forensics to go with that."[34]

Kallstrom's tone had changed by the time of a congressional hearing in

July of 1997, a year after the crash. Here, Milton portrays Kallstrom heroically facing down his inquisitors, among them Congresswoman Patricia Danner. In Milton's retelling, all opposition to the official story line was motivated by greed, a desperate search for publicity, or some other "private agenda" like Danner's need to protect TWA, whose headquarters Milton placed in Danner's St. Louis district. "If the government was covering up the cause," Milton writes, "the airline could avoid the suits brought by the victims' families."[35] One problem here: Pat Danner represented the Kansas City area, about 250 miles and four congressional districts away from TWA headquarters.

Kallstrom's responses to Representative James Traficant of Ohio show how deeply he had been compromised. In speaking of the dog-training exercise, Traficant asked Kallstrom, "Do you know for sure that that dog was on the plane?"[36]

"We know for sure," Kallstrom answered. By the time of the congressional hearing, with no new evidence to contradict him, Kallstrom had grown more confident.

"Isn't it a fact," continues Traficant, "that where the dog was to have visited, that it is not the part of the plane where the precursors of SEMTEX were found?" (Traficant here refers to the PETN and RDX.)

"That's not true," Kallstrom answered. He then added the kind of detail that would make a defense attorney cringe: "It is very important where the packages were put, Congressman. And the test packages that we looked at, that were in very bad condition, that were unfortunately dripping those chemicals, were placed exactly above the location of the airplane where we found chemicals on the floor."[37]

As detailed earlier, none of the training aids were placed near where the chemicals had been found. And the Kallstrom letter is just one source of this admission. In September of 1996, when the FBI was less sure that the dog story would work, the *New York Times* reported as follows: "The packages were not placed in the same place where the traces were located." FAA bomb technician Calvin Walbert made a comparable claim. "Where the bureau got hits on the wreckage," said Walbert, "there was no explosive training aids anywhere near that."[38] Added Irish Flynn, FAA associate administrator, "It's a question of where those traces came from. The dog doesn't answer the questions."[39]

Kallstrom, however, had seemingly little need to answer any questions. September's "well-wrapped packages of explosives" became July's "dripping" chemicals. The residue traces once on the seat or on a piece of wreckage were now on the floor. All references to residue in the cargo hold had disappeared.

By 1999, however, Kallstrom was surely aware that citizen investigators had discovered one discrepancy after another. He has used Milton to tidy up the story for public consumption. She even has the dog exercise ending at 11:30, fifteen minutes before it actually started, but an hour before the plane departed.

The blame, however, is not Milton's alone. Not a single reporter in the major media bothered to check the airport documentation, and the media pack went yelping after the "mechanical" story as if it were valid. Negroni acknowledges that after the dog story broke, "the matter was pretty much closed."[40] By the time the FBI pulled out of the investigation in November 1997, Kallstrom could say the following without fear of being challenged:

> On June 10, 1996, the St. Louis Airport Police Department conducted canine explosives training aboard the victim aircraft. The residue collected after the explosion of Flight 800 was consistent with the explosives utilized during the exercise.[41]

What caused a presumably good man like Kallstrom to serve his staff and his nation so badly? On a case of this consequence, it is much less likely lust for money or power than it is fear, a fear that can paralyze when citizens lose confidence in the media.

Consider, for instance, the following e-mail the authors received from a New Jersey homicide detective who had served as our liaison to the St. Louis officer, Herman Burnett:

> It seemed apparent from what he said that the powers-to-be have come down on him and he's been told to stay away from anything to do with TWA-800, and he mentioned specifically that he's been told not to assist you [with your next videotape]. Unlike the first time I spoke with him, he hesitated frequently during his message, and I was left with the distinct impression that he was a little nervous, a bit uptight, maybe even a little scared. That was my cop-to-cop impression. Also, there was an implication during the message that should he violate the order against involving himself in anything TWA-800 related, then he might find his job in jeopardy.[42]

If one ever wonders why it is that "people just don't come forward," here is the answer in a nutshell.

FOR all its convincing detail, not everyone simply accepted the dog-training story at face value. At an FBI briefing, Victoria Cummock, citizen activist on the safety and security commission, asked to see the FAA log for the training exercise. "They said, 'It's not conclusive this particular plane was involved,'" she told the *Village Voice*. "They couldn't produce the log." FBI honcho James Kallstrom, however, tried to browbeat Cummock into submission. "It's absolutely confirmed that it was that plane," he reportedly told her.[43]

The authorities, alas, convinced just about everyone but Cummock. The public relaxed, and the pressure for increased airport security deflated quickly. The *Boston Globe* reports what happened next:

> By the time of the presidential election, other airlines had poured large donations into Democratic Party committees: $265,000 from American Airlines, $120,000 from Delta Air Lines, $115,000 from United Air Lines, $87,000 from Northwest Airlines, according to an analysis done for the Globe by the Center for Responsive Politics, which tracks donations. In all, the airlines gave the Democratic Party $585,000 in the election's closing weeks. Over the preceding 10-week period, the airlines gave the Democrats less than half that sum.[44]

Unaware of the specifics of the spin or the motivation behind it, Victoria Cummock nonetheless sensed that something was awry. "It was quite obvious," Cummock has told the authors, "that we were being railroaded."[45] Cummock grew alarmed in January 1997 when the vice president's staff circulated a draft final report that essentially eliminated all security measures from their findings. She was not alone in her concern. CIA Director and fellow commissioner John Deutch also protested.

As reported in the *Washington Times*, Gore withdrew the draft. On February 12, 1997, Gore issued a final report that has all the appearances of seriousness. Although released five months *after* the breaking of the dog-training story, the following excerpt seems to refer to the demise of TWA Flight 800, the event that triggered this report and the only possible such attack within the last eight years:

> When terrorists attack an American airliner, they are attacking the United States. They have so little respect for our values—so little regard for human life or the principles of justice that are the foundation of American society—that they would destroy innocent children and devoted mothers and

fathers completely at random. This cannot be tolerated, or allowed to intimidate free societies. There must be a concerted national will to fight terrorism.[46]

Following this paradoxical introduction was a series of recommendations that seem both forceful and reasonable, to wit, "3.13 Conduct airport vulnerability assessments and develop action plans." These recommendations did not trouble Cummock in general. What she criticized was their vagueness. She cited 3.13 above, like many others, for its absence of "specificity," "accountability," and "timetables/deadlines."[47]

"In summary," Cummock wrote, "the final report contains no specific call to action, no commitments to address safety and security system-wide by mandating the deployment of current technology and training, with actionable timetables and budgets."[48] Without tough and timely enforcement, she rightly believed that the recommendations would become just so many words on a page, pure Washington spin.

"After much thoughtful consideration and with a very heavy heart," Cummock filed a dissent against the Gore proposal. Gore stated publicly that he would include the dissent in the final report. But when he presented that report to the president, he not only failed to accommodate Cummock, but he also claimed that the report's findings were unanimous. "Both of those Gore lies are on video tape," reported the *Washington Times*. "NBC's Dateline has the tapes."[49]

With her dissent suppressed, Cummock sued the vice president, the secretary of Transportation, and the commission in District Court. In her view, as expressed in her ultimately successful appeal of a dismissed suit, "The Clinton Administration had formed the Commission simply to obtain rubber-stamp endorsement of a predetermined policy agenda, rather than to facilitate genuine deliberations."[50]

As her suit successfully but slowly made its way through the courts, the Clinton administration kept on spinning its apocryphal tale that "mechanical failure" destroyed TWA 800. This tale climaxed at the final NTSB hearing in August of 2000. Although the NTSB's Bernard Loeb was much more circumspect about the source of the explosive residue—"We don't know exactly how the explosive residues got there," he admitted—it no longer mattered. "We do know from the physical evidence I've just discussed," Loeb noted, "that the residues were not the result of the detonation of a bomb."[51]

As to the Gore Commission, despite Cummock's valiant efforts, it came to naught or something close to it. Al Gore, however, may yet pay a political price for his failure to act.

In the weeks following September 11, 2001, several political insiders referred to the destruction of Flight 800 as a terrorist incident. But only one did it twice. That person is Sen. John Kerry of Massachusetts. Appearing on *Larry King Live* on September 11 itself, Kerry suggested that TWA Flight 800 was brought down by a terrorist act. On September 24, on *Hardball* with Chris Matthews, the authors watched as Kerry casually recited a number of terrorist attacks against the United States, among them TWA "Flight 800." Like Larry King before him, Chris Matthews either did not catch the remark or chose to let it pass.

If the first admission seemed more or less innocent and accidental, the second one had to be purposeful. Indeed, Kerry's office took and responded to calls about his remarks on Flight 800 after the first incident. If a mistake, it seems highly unlikely that it could have happened again. But it did.

There is more evidence to consider. On September 20, one mainstream newspaper broke the story of how the so-called Gore Commission failed to address airline safety. That newspaper just happened to be John Kerry's hometown *Boston Globe*. As it happened, the paper released the story five years to the day after the dog-training story broke. This was a damning revelation, certainly to Al Gore. The *Boston Globe* was the only medium to the left of the *Washington Times* to have released this information, and the *Times* did so at least a year before the attack on the World Trade Center and the Pentagon.

Of course, it is possible that Senator Kerry merely misspoke about a terrorist attack against TWA 800 on two occasions, and it is possible, too, that the *Globe*'s entrance into the fray was merely coincidental, as was its timing. But given the brutal realities of presidential politics, it seems likely that these revelations were calculated and perhaps even coordinated.

As of this writing, John Kerry is the most visible and viable contender for the Democratic presidential nomination in 2004. When Kerry made his revelations, Al Gore loomed as Kerry's major opponent for the nomination. John Kerry knew that Gore plays internecine hardball. It was Gore, after all, who introduced the Willie Horton gambit against another Massachusetts candidate, Michael Dukakis, in the 1988 Democratic primaries.

But John Kerry seemed to have his sights on Al Gore's Achilles' heel. After the events of September 11, the story of how Al Gore helped subvert the investigation into TWA 800 and undermine airport security may yet prove to be a career-killer. Kerry's "slips" may put Gore out of the race even before he gets in.

CHAPTER 6

DECENT INTERVAL

*FBI agent James Kallstrom has been named head of antiterrorism for
New York. He was chief investigator of the explosion aboard TWA 800.
He's just weeks away from concluding that the World Trade Center col-
lapsed due to mechanical failure.*

—ARGUS HAMILTON, COMEDIAN

The corruption of the Flight 800 investigation was not James Kallstrom's
idea. It came from the top. But, reluctantly or otherwise, Kallstrom let it
happen. He allowed the investigation to become a farce, an unfunny running gag, an open sore in America's psyche, and the source of an unprecedented and deeply felt cynicism among its aviation community. To verify the
depths of that cynicism, one need only ask a TWA pilot or mechanic or
Boeing engineer what brought down that doomed airliner. "Mechanical failure" will not be among the answers.

A month after the destruction of the World Trade Center, Kallstrom abandoned a comfy sinecure as executive VP at credit-card giant MBNA, and
assumed the gritty top job at New York State's new Office of Public Security. The
new job may well be his own attempt at atonement. He has much to atone for.

Unlike the political agents at the NTSB—Chairman Jim Hall and Vice Chair Robert Francis—Kallstrom could find no easy refuge in willful ignorance or political opportunism. In 1996 at least, James Kallstrom was a serious man with an admirable record. He had established his reputation long before he ever knew the name Bill Clinton, a name that today he must regret ever hearing.

Kallstrom truly felt the pain—in his own words—"of walking into a Ramada Inn on day two or day three, and seeing a thousand-plus people that have just lost their daughter or their son, a mother or father in some cases, the entire family."[1] In reviewing the record, one finds an impulse towards truth-telling on his part that is unique in the investigation.

His instinct to tell the truth, however, warred with the pressure to remain silent. A few months after the attack, for instance, TWA attendant Marge Gross, whose brother was killed in the crash, heard a reporter yell to him, "You can't tell me it was anything but a missile that took that plane down." According to Gross, Kallstrom shot back, "You're right, but if you quote me I'll deny it."[2] After the dog-training exercise was revealed two months into the investigation, denial would become Kallstrom's MO.

THE "problem," NTSB investigator Hank Hughes told a Senate subcommittee, "was recognized about two months into the investigation." The problem that Hughes documented before Sen. Charles Grassley's judiciary subcommittee was a serious one, "the disappearance of parts from the hangar."[3] And Hughes was a serious man.

The NTSB investigator had been examining accident scenes most of his adult life, first on the highways of Fairfax County, Virginia, and then with the NTSB, the last decade on aviation accidents. Patricia Milton interviewed Hughes and writes favorably about him, describing him as a sensitive man who took his work seriously. How he came to appear before Grassley's committee in 1999—"a kangaroo court of malcontents" according to the by-then embittered Kallstrom—she chose not to explain.[4]

As Hughes told the Grassley committee, he and his team had grown increasingly suspicious about airplane parts disappearing from the hangar. To test their suspicions, they took a complete inventory of the hangar on one particular day to see if anything would come up missing the following day. "Not to our surprise," he told the senator, "we found that seats were missing and other evidence had been disturbed." Soon after, in something of a sting that Hughes encouraged, some accommodating FBI agents caught two or three other FBI agents in the hangar without authorization at 3 A.M. on a Saturday morning. "I supervised that project," said Hughes of the work under way in the hangar, "and these people had no connection to it."[5]

The agents who broke in did not do so of their own accord. Given Hughes's testimony, they or their colleagues had been there before, at least a few times. What were they looking for? In all likelihood, "physical evidence." After September 20, after Kallstrom had admitted, "No amount of chemical traces would be enough now," the so-called "physical evidence" became hugely important.[6] For all practical purposes, the phrase would become the investigation's mantra.

The International Association of Machinists and Aerospace Workers (IAMAW) confirmed Hughes's testimony in an unflinching public report quietly buried by the NTSB. "During the investigation of TWA Flight 800 cabin wreckage began to disappear from the cabin wreckage hangar," reads the IAMAW report. "Indications were that the disappearance was due to the removal of wreckage by the FBI."[7]

At the final NTSB hearing, Chairman Jim Hall claimed that his investigators had "examined every piece of wreckage for any physical evidence that the crash of Flight 800 had been caused by a bomb or missile." Had they found such evidence, he added, they would have referred the matter back to the appropriate law enforcement agencies. "Let me state unequivocably [sic]," said Hall in his inimitably clumsy way, "the Safety Board has found no evidence."[8]

NTSB officials would "find" no evidence because they didn't look. Those at the top could indulge their myopia and speak at least somewhat truthfully only of what they had let themselves see. Those who worked below them worked on in the dark, conscious that something was wrong but not quite sure what. The triage system that the FBI had set up on day one, presumably to protect evidence, was now being used to conceal it. As is evident from Hughes's testimony, the FBI stepped up its operation after mid-September, most likely to redeem wreckage that had been allowed through the process when the agency was still acting in good faith.

In the months ahead, Kallstrom would still play the role of truth seeker—he could hardly do otherwise—but the role-playing would represent at best a stall for time. Patricia Milton, for instance, has the NTSB brass wondering, "Why wasn't Kallstrom willing to concede the cause was mechanical?"[9] This question surfaced with Kallstrom's demand in late

October that the NTSB construct a mock-up of the plane, a demand that Bernard Loeb and others at the NTSB resisted.

"Frankly," Loeb was reported to have said, "I'm more convinced than ever that a reconstruction of Flight 800 is ridiculous."[10] In a technical sense, Loeb was correct. The mock-up they eventually built would lack the wings, the nose, the engines, and certain key parts. It would also have gaping holes in the fuselage, reshaped metal, and rearranged seats.

Kallstrom argued that the press would demand a reconstruction, and Jim Hall eventually sided with Kallstrom. "Reconstruction, [Hall] felt, would not be the proper course of action, but it could be viewed as politically correct."[11] In Christine Negroni's account, it was White House Chief of Staff Leon Panetta who finally ordered the $500,000 reconstruction to begin.[12]

What Kallstrom seems to have understood more instinctively than his peers at the NTSB was the need for a "decent interval." This phrase is sometimes applied—in bitter irony—to the final two years of the Vietnam experience, two years when the U.S. had withdrawn its support in all but name. After the horrific FBI assault on the Mount Carmel community in Waco, Texas, just three years prior, there was no such interval. The FBI destroyed the remains of the building in unseemly haste and was justifiably criticized for so doing. Kallstrom would not repeat that mistake. He would construct a Potemkin plane and stage a Potemkin investigation. If some irrepressible bit of evidence emerged, or if someone came forward with the truth, he could still accommodate it. Fact is, he probably would have welcomed it. He could not have liked the limitations under which he worked.

Adding to Kallstrom's frustration was the increasingly odd behavior of the Bureau of Alcohol Tobacco and Firearms. Despite the agency's limited role in the investigation and its lack of access to any evidence of consequence, the ATF started publicly siding with the NTSB. In January 1997, the ATF released its own report, citing "evidence of possible design flaws" in Boeing aircraft as the likely culprit, an analysis so far beyond its mission and its competence that it made even the NTSB uneasy.[13]

Embarrassed earlier by the FBI, the ATF was getting its own revenge. Besides, the agency knew which way the winds were blowing out of Washington. This time, it would catch them. A politically sensitive agency if there ever were one, the ATF had staged the initial disastrous raid at Waco, "Operation Showtime," largely to impress its new bosses in Washington. The agency did not quite succeed. This time it would do better.

To be sure, one does the individual agents of the ATF, the NTSB, and the FBI an injustice to speak collectively of their respective agencies. As Hughes's testimony suggests, and as the FBI agents' cooperation confirms, the great majority of investigators did their best to solve the mystery of TWA 800. Even those FBI agents caught breaking into the hangar may not have understood the use to which their efforts would be put. Still, too many people chose not to see. And those who did see, and who did come forward, almost inevitably paid a price.

Hank Hughes was not alone in his protest. Despite their nondisclosure agreements and an intimidating environment—at least one investigator had his phone tapped by the FBI for six months *after* he left Long Island[14]— many investigators tried to break the truth out. ALPA investigator Jim Speer is one of them.

Before September 11, 2001, Speer had kept his protests within the investigation and was suspended for his troubles. Since then he has gone public. "Now we have a national terrorism war on our hands," Speer explains. "Had the truth been allowed to be brought out at that time, they could have begun improvements in security five years ago, and this event would not have happened."[15]

Among the illegal acts Speer witnessed was the retagging of the keel beam. As explained in chapter 4, a spontaneous explosion in the center wing tank would have blown the keel beam out almost immediately. It is the spine of the plane and runs under the tank. As FBI documents show, and as the *New York Times* reported, the keel beam was among the last parts to hit the water, not the first. It was found deep in the C, or "Green," Zone, the one farthest from JFK. For no known reason, investigators crossed out C 061 and changed it to B 061—and then changed the designation once again from B to A, the zone closest to JFK.[16] "The validity of the Tag database," reports the IAMAW in a bit of ironic understatement, "has been in question from the beginning of the TWA Flight 800 investigation."[17]

Says Speer, "The NTSB/FBI has changed the recovery location tag of the keel beam, so that can mean only one thing to me—that they are trying to make the recovery location of the keel beam fit a scenario that they already have decided has happened." Adds Speer wryly, "That's not how you do accident investigations."[18] Speer's comments suggest that the FBI and the NTSB, at least at a certain level, now had the same mission—create a plausible mechanical scenario. The fine points of this work would be left to the NTSB.

TWA employee Linda Kunz served on one of the NTSB investigation teams. In the course of her work, she caught certain NTSB officials changing tags on seat parts.[19] By retagging these seats, investigators could redefine the breakup sequence of the airplane to fit a mechanical scenario.

To document this chicanery, Kunz had two New York state troopers take photographs, a common investigative practice. But this was no ordinary investigation. The only discipline leveled was leveled against Kunz. Over TWA's protests, she was removed from the investigation and threatened with prosecution for exposing the falsified evidence. "She snapped photographs in violation of the rules at the hangar," scolds CNN reporter Christine Negroni, "and very nearly got TWA kicked off the investigation."[20]

NEGRONI'S comments point to a problem arguably even more profound than the failure of the FBI—the abdication of the media. When the FBI changed sides, the media did too. Part of the problem, the obvious part, is that the major media had come to rely much too heavily on their sources within the investigation. A secondary problem, the unspoken one, was that of political sympathies. Six weeks before the election, the last thing that any two key people in any major newsroom wanted was a scandal that would give Newt Gingrich a Republican president.

The *New York Times* was most conspicuous in its conversion. On November 17, just four months after the crash and two months after the dog story, the *Times* was running an article on the investigation with headlines like "How a Quack Becomes a Canard." This piece detailed how "conspiracy theories" mutate in an age of easy global communication.[21]

Virtually all dissent from the accepted wisdom now invited only scorn or derision from the major media. Milton and Negroni are relentless in their depiction of dissidents as "conspiracy theorists" or the even more patronizing "conspiracy buffs," unthinking souls who have fallen victim—in the ever so arch words of the *Times*—to "the pitfalls of conspiracy mongering."[22]

The major media would casually equate Flight 800 "conspiracies" with Roswell, Bigfoot, Elvis sightings, even Holocaust denials. They were all of a kind. Never mind that 230 innocent civilians had been killed in potentially the single greatest crime ever on American territory in full sight of thousands of people, without any official word on how it really happened. The major media, circa 1994–2000, had chosen sides.

The media's most conspicuous target was an unlikely one. Pierre Salinger had first come to prominence as President John F. Kennedy's press secretary and had maintained a high profile ever since, as a U.S. senator from

California, an internationally well-connected PR consultant, and as a Pulitzer Prize–winning journalist. Indeed, he won his third Pulitzer for his reporting on the Pan Am 103 crash at Lockerbie, Scotland. A faithful Democrat, he waited until November 7—three days after the election—to tell an audience of aviation officials in Cannes, France, that intelligence sources had revealed to him that the U.S. Navy had accidentally shot down TWA 800.

At a press conference in New York immediately after this story broke, a furious James Kallstrom denounced Salinger's report as "pure, utter nonsense."[23] Flanked by Admiral Kristensen, Kallstrom went on to assure everyone, especially the victims' families, how thoroughly the FBI and the NTSB had investigated any possibility of U.S. Navy involvement. Kallstrom then asked for questions. CBS producer Kristina Borjesson describes what happened next:

> A man raised his hands and asked what I thought was a pertinent—and impertinent—question. He wanted to know why the Navy was involved in the recovery and investigation while a possible suspect. Kallstrom's response was immediate: "Remove him!" he yelled. Two men leapt over to the questioner and grabbed him by the arms. There was a momentary chill in the air after the guy had been dragged out of the room. Kallstrom, Kristensen, Hall and their entourage acted as if nothing had happened. There was something very disquieting about the goonish tactics. A dispassionately dismissive response from Kallstrom would have been a more convincing way to tell us that the Navy had nothing to do with the disaster. In any case, right then and there, the rest of us had been put on notice to be on our best behavior.[24]

Patricia Milton described the questioner as "an unkempt figure among the reporters," suggesting that an unkempt reporter is somehow unusual and that he thus deserved what he got.[25] Milton does not tell us what happened next. Borjesson does:

> The conference continued. Admiral Kristensen explained that the Navy had only two assets in the area that night: a P-3 Orion submarine-hunting plane 80 miles south of the crash and the battleship *Normandy* about 185 miles southwest.[26]

The reporter had every right to be suspicious. Had he not been removed, and had he done his homework, he might have asked—among other questions—what the P-3 was doing on a sub-hunting exercise after the likely shoot-down of an American airliner, what official Washington thought to be an "act of war," or why the admiral placed the P-3 eighty miles south of its actual location at the time of the crash.

Given this context, Salinger is hardly the fool he has been made out to be. He did not, however, have the kind of documentation necessary to make the public claims he did, at least not in the climate he made them in. Worse, from his perspective, is that at least some of his documentation had already been posted on the Internet, a medium that the traditional print and electronic media held in a fear-based contempt. According to Salinger, he received the documentation "directly from a French intelligence agent." He acknowledged that it had been on the Internet as well, but he added that "part of the information" that he obtained had not been on the Internet and had come from a second source.[27]

The Internet message itself deserves attention. It came from Dick Russell, a retired United Airlines pilot and ALPA crash investigator. In August 1996, Russell had e-mailed a select group of colleagues that a "TWA Flight 800 was shot down by a U.S. Navy Aegis missile fired from a guided missile ship which was in area W-105 about 30 miles from where TWA Flight 800 exploded." He had received the information from a friend in the FAA who had been told this at a "high-level briefing." Russell asked his colleagues to keep the information to themselves, but one of them obviously did not.

To talk to Russell is to believe him. Having spent twenty-six years in aviation safety work, he had no reason to risk his reputation on spurious accusations. He asked his source for a copy of the radar tape as confirmation and received it. He took his information to ALPA first and then to the media, and as Russell says, "They kissed me off."[28] As shall be seen later, Russell did not get the full story, but there was a large element of truth to what he forwarded and what Salinger received and voiced.

The day after the press conference in Cannes, Kallstrom called Salinger in Paris and invited him to New York to share his information, assuring him that the FBI stood ready to act on any new evidence. Salinger accepted the invitation, saying, "I'm just trying to do the right thing for the United States."[29]

On November 13, six days after his announcement in France, three FBI agents and a Secret Service agent went to Salinger's New York hotel to interview him. Kallstrom was not among them. When Salinger asked where Kallstrom was, the agents told him that Kallstrom had been "tied up." This was not the case. Milton explains his reasoning: "Kallstrom believed Salinger's charges were so preposterous that he didn't want to lend them the credibility that a one-to-one meeting with the head of the FBI's New York office would confer."[30]

Despite the petty gamesmanship, Salinger persisted. He had more information at hand than an Internet message and raised some interesting questions. One was why the P-3's transponder was off. The FBI assured him that "it had been broken for months."[31] Given the P-3's electronic sophistication, this answer could not have been very satisfying. Salinger also had a print of the Linda Kabot photo. Unable to identify the airborne object in the photo, the agents explained that it was "on the wrong side of the sky."

Finally, Salinger asked about the USS *Normandy*. Milton supplies the answer, "The agents told him that the ship had been 181 miles south of the crash site when Flight 800 exploded, and not in the position to hit the plane with any of its armaments." At the time the agents may not have known the *Normandy*'s position. At the press conference a few days earlier, Admiral Kristensen had placed it "about 185 miles" south of the crash site. But in 1999, when Milton's book was published, the FBI and Milton both had to know the ship was much closer indeed.

This point needs to be stressed. At the FBI's final press conference just one year later, Kallstrom would admit that the FBI interviewed the crew of the *Normandy* and *three* submarines "due to their immediate vicinity to the crash site."[32] How immediate? When asked about the three vessels within six miles of the crash site by Reed Irvine of Accuracy in Media, Kallstrom replied, "We all know what those were. In fact, I spoke about those publicly. They were Navy vessels that were on classified maneuvers."[33]

In November 1996, Salinger was closer to the truth than the FBI. No matter. The media declared open season on him. The *Times* headline from November 17—"Salinger the Crash Theorist Raises More Eyebrows Than New Questions"—captures the criticism in one of its more temperate expressions.[34]

A MAN of some clout, Salinger refused to retreat at the media's first salvo. In March 1997 he surfaced once more. With his assistance, *Paris Match* prepared a fifty-seven-page article advancing the theory that the plane was shot down by a Navy missile.[35] The administration struck back hard, smearing Salinger and subpoenaing Dick Russell to give up the radar tape in his possession.

Kenneth Bacon, the chief spokesman for the Pentagon, now got into the act. "We have absolutely no evidence that there was any incident like this," he told the press. "All missiles owned by the Navy, by any ships, submarines or planes in the area, have been inventoried, personnel have been interviewed, records have been checked."[36] Bacon would gain his own notoriety a few years later for illegally leaking Linda Tripp's personnel records to the *New Yorker*.

Officials did admit to the *New York Times* that "a Navy P-3 plane and a submarine were near the flight path on a practice mission" but added, "Neither was armed with missiles."[37]

This is a curious admission. Had the *Times* reporter checked the paper's own files from the last Salinger flare-up four months earlier, he would have read about Admiral Kristensen declaring the P-3 and sub to be eighty miles away, which is decidedly not "near the flight path." Twelve days after this article appeared, the P-3 crew would tell the NTSB in the presence of the FBI that its practice mission with the submarine *Trepang* took place "a minimum of 200 miles south" of the crash site.[38] Someone obviously wasn't on message.

Salinger may not have gotten the story completely right, but at least he was trying to expose the truth. And even at this point in the investigation, as the *Times* noted, "The missile theory is one of three that investigators say might explain the crash."[39] The administration's attack on Salinger, however, served its purpose. "I have reasoned that if Mr. Salinger, who is a former prestigious government official, could be treated so poorly," commented witness Paul Angelides, "what is in store for me if I speak out?"[40] Angelides was not alone in thinking this.

If the Salinger case unnerved potential critics, the Jeremy Crocker case chilled them to the bone. On December 5, 1996, this soft-spoken engineer appeared on Peter Ford's popular California radio show to discuss his theories about TWA 800. On December 9, he visited the downtown Los Angeles library to do some additional research on the crash.[41] He was never seen again.

A longtime Palm Springs resident, Crocker created mathematical models of the flight and studied its aerodynamics. By all accounts, he was a meticulous researcher who was careful not to jump to conclusions. Although he believed a missile downed the plane, he did not speculate as to who had fired it. Other TWA 800 dissidents credit Crocker with being well ahead of any other private researcher on the information curve. Says one: "No one's theories/speculation were more serious than Crocker's, or would have made the government more nervous."[42]

The authors' own investigation did not confirm any evidence of foul play. If there had been, Crocker had made a share of enemies in his citizen's crusade to shut down crack houses and block rapacious development. Still, his disappearance remains one more unsolved mystery in a case that has lots of them, one that spooked other citizen investigators.

One investigator who refused to be intimidated was retired Naval Cmdr. William Donaldson. An all-state football player in high school, Donaldson joined the Navy after college, flew more than seventy strike missions over North Vietnam and Laos in an A-4 Skyhawk, served as the Air Traffic Control Officer on the carrier *Forrestal*, and was posted with NATO in Naples, Italy, as a Nuclear Weapons Targeting Officer. In the course of his career, he had worked on numerous accident investigations as a safety officer, including one on an aircraft that was accidentally downed by a missile. He did not like what he saw of the TWA 800 investigation.

In April 1997 he sent a letter to the editor of The *Wall Street Journal* challenging a previous letter by Jim Hall.[43] This letter would mark the beginning of a four-year crusade as head of the Association of Retired Aviation Professionals, one that would end only with his death from a brain tumor in August 2001.

A man of commanding presence and a no-nonsense presenter of fact, Donaldson rattled official Washington. Fortunately for the White House, the media did everything they could to avoid him or diminish him. "On the second anniversary of the crash," writes Patricia Milton, "conspiracy buffs found a new face in William Donaldson."[44] Milton dismisses Donaldson's main theory that the plane was struck by two terrorist missiles with the mantralike repetition that "there was simply no physical evidence." She states that the NTSB "stopped returning his calls" when Donaldson began to claim that "a Canadian frigate had shot the plane down," an inference of insanity here that flirts with slander.

The Navy, in fact, provided the four most compelling advocates of a missile attack in veterans Maj. Fritz Meyer, Master Chief Dwight Brumley, Commander Donaldson, and former Chairman of the Joint Chiefs Admiral Thomas Moorer, who backed Donaldson.

Many other citizen investigators would devote their every free hour to the mystery of TWA 800, some of whom would do some excellent original research, including Tom Shoemaker, Ian Goddard, Michael Hull, Marilyn Brady, Graeme Sephton, Michael Rivero, and physicist Dr. Thomas Stalcup. Veteran Reed Irvine of the watchdog group Accuracy in Media played a key role as well, particularly in his support of Donaldson. There was a good deal of spirited dissent in this community on the particulars, but none on the most fundamental question of bomb, missile, or mechanical. All agreed on missile or, at least, some force outside the plane.

As to the major media, one would be hard-pressed to find a single article built on original research. In that area, Pierre Salinger served up the most newsworthy story during the lull of the decent interval from September 1996 to November 1997.

ONE story that merited more attention than it got was that of the tightly guarded trawling operation. The operation seemed very routine—even if it did begin on November 4, Election Day. The trawling followed months of diving operations by the Navy and other agencies, in excess of four thousand dives in all. "By November 2," writes Milton, "more than 85 percent of the plane had been recovered."[45] Please note this number.

The debate over trawling mirrored the debate over the reconstruction of the plane. Kallstrom, allegedly looking for the "Eureka piece" that would solve the puzzle of the plane's demise, advocated strongly for it. Loeb and Hall were against. Trawling, however, would cost $5 million, ten times as much as the reconstruction. Despite the higher cost, Milton states that "the standoff over trawling was settled much more quickly." The reason she gives is not particularly persuasive, namely that "more wreckage would be found."[46]

And so the operation began. Four fishing boats, contracted by the Navy, dragged wide rakes along the ocean bottom and collected everything in the path into large nets. This procedure was not unlike dragging for scallops and clams, with one notable exception—an armed FBI agent manned each boat. This was a new wrinkle. Consider the following exchange from the final NTSB hearing in August 2000 between Jim Hall and Al Dickinson, the head of the NTSB investigation. Hall first asks about the diving operation.

> *Jim Hall:* Did we have someone on each ship at all times? Or did the FBI?
> *Al Dickinson:* Yes, it was either us or the FBI. When we got into the trawling, it was a six-month period over the winter months, we did not have NTSB people there, but the FBI had agents on each one of the ships.[47]

The operation lasted for six brutal winter months before ending abruptly and inexplicably on April 30, 1997. Commander Donaldson argued that the reason it ended as it did was because the FBI found what it was looking for. In his own research, he retrieved an FBI Trawler Operations Manual that had been left behind on one of the boats.

The manual gives all appearances of being authentic. It cites the mission of the operation concisely as follows: "Objective: To extract *every piece of man-made* debris from the trawling area with the expectation that some piece may hold a clue which will help us make a determination as to the cause of the crash."[48] Of more seeming interest, the manual provided images of three particular parts for which the agents on board were to have been looking. One was the "fuel scavenge pump." This was the one pump allegedly not found and the source, some thought—particularly the trial lawyers—of the spark that ignited the fuel tank.

The other two parts definitely raise eyebrows: a "Stinger missile eject motor" and a "Stinger missile battery coolant unit." Reports that a fisherman had retrieved the ejector motor and thrown it back in the ocean, Donaldson believed, stirred the government to action. The operations manual also listed a secure phone line for the agent to call should the parts be retrieved.

To chart the course of this investigation, however, is to understand that the president and others knew almost exactly what happened within hours, if not minutes, of the event. They knew that neither a Stinger missile nor a scavenge pump had brought down TWA 800. Given all the evidence they had already concealed or ignored, they were not about to invest $5 million in a search for parts that did not matter even if they existed. These parts, however, made useful cover. The FBI's two-man "missile team" might have even thought that the agency was taking its limited mission seriously. But, in fact, what the trawlers were seeking was spelled out in the objective, namely "*every piece of man-made* debris" that radiated out from the point of the first explosions, even if considerably north, south, or west of the debris field.

Maj. Fritz Meyer, like many other witnesses, had seen two bright, initiating explosions. The first he identified as a "high-velocity explosion of military ordnance." Radar expert Michael O'Rourke, contracted by the FBI, confirms that something dramatic happened at that very moment, reporting that "some portion or component of the aircraft kicked out to the right nearly immediately after the loss of transponder signal."[49]

O'Rourke's contention does not at all square with the NTSB's fuel-tank theory. The component "kicked out" of the plane at very nearly Mach 2, a force and speed much too powerful to have been caused by a low-velocity explosion. "Some of this wreckage evidently landed in a debris field that was officially never located," argues physicist Dr. Thomas Stalcup in his assessment of the radar data, a debris field that may well have contained what even the NTSB admitted was "significant missing structure."[50]

Of the second explosion Major Meyer saw, the lower one, he could say only that it was a "high-velocity explosion of some brilliant white light—I don't know what it was." But it was brilliant enough and powerful enough to shake a bridge in Westhampton ten miles away and blow the nose off a 747. This was no ordinary missile. In all likelihood it was not a missile at all.

The government had a good idea of what the source of each explosion was. From the beginning, however, the FBI made sure no one else did—even the investigators on Long Island. Jim Speer had a front-row seat on this particular abridgement of the truth:

> So we're watching videotapes of the bottom of the ocean, and I notice that the time clock stops in the given run. If you're running a path down here, there should be a continuous run and there are gaps in the time clock. So I look up at our FBI agent/chaperone and say, "Well, you know that tape has been edited." "No, it hasn't." I said, "Look at the gaps in the time clock here. There is no reason for gaps to occur unless the tape has been edited. I want to see the unedited version." "No" was the response.[51]

The government spent the additional $5 million either to confirm *who* caused the explosions and/or to prevent anyone else from discovering *what* caused them. These are the only explanations that make sense. At this stage, no other problems were worth that much to solve.

Patricia Milton makes another unwitting revelation on the trawling operation, one that raises more questions than it answers. According to Milton, the investigation team had recovered "more than 85 percent" of the plane when the trawling began. After dredging more than forty square miles of ocean bottom, the trawlers recovered "more than two tons of wreckage: two percent of the plane."[52]

"To recover 2 percent of a jumbo jet was still a considerable amount," Milton writes in the same paragraph, "but recovering 98 percent was a remarkable and heroic achievement."

In no known system of math do 2 percent and 85 percent equal 98 percent, especially without additional inputs. The 87 percent figure is probably closer to the truth. The FBI may well have inflated it to 98 percent for propaganda purposes. After all, how could the Bureau abandon its search for the

"Eureka piece" with 13 percent of the plane still missing? In any case, by the time of the final NTSB hearing, the recovery percentage had settled back down to 95 percent.[53]

WITH political cronies running Justice and the NTSB, the administration could do whatever kind of math it pleased. On May 1, 1997, the White House introduced its unique political calculus to the FAA. "Clinton to Go Outside Aviation Circles for New F.A.A. Chief" read the headline of an otherwise unexceptional article in the *New York Times*.[54] The White House announced that Jane Garvey, acting administrator of the Federal Highway Administration, had been chosen to head the Federal Aviation Administration.

Like Hall and Goelz at the NTSB, Garvey had risen rapidly in the world of aviation. A high-school English teacher, she had parlayed volunteer work with the Dukakis for Governor campaign in Massachusetts into an appointment as a deputy commissioner in the Massachusetts Department of Public Works. A decade later, she rode her connections to a posting as deputy administrator of the Federal Highway Administration under Clinton.

If the media were unfazed by Garvey's appointment, the Aircraft Owners and Pilots Association was not. Its leaders openly criticized her lack of a pilot's license or technical experience. In 1997, however, the White House was more interested in political reliability than in piloting skills, especially at the FAA. This was the least cooperative of all the agencies involved, the one that started the radar imbroglio and refused to back off. It surely needed a new, trustworthy hand at the helm, and it got one.

On July 10, 1997, a week before the first anniversary of the crash, the House Aviation Subcommittee inquired into the progress of the investigation. The following exchange between NTSB Chairman Jim Hall and Representative James Traficant, D-Ohio, reveals just how little real progress had been made:

> *Traficant:* To this point, has any physical evidence [been located], conclusive forensic evidence, to prove it was a mechanical failure that caused the explosion of the center fuel tank? Yes or no.
> *Hall:* We're looking at that.
> *Traficant:* I want a one [word] answer.
> *Hall:* No.[55]

This is a stunning admission. The NTSB was admittedly no closer to proving a mechanical explanation for the crash than it was in September of 1996 when it first went public with this conclusion.

Throughout this long period of uncertainty, the media had uncovered not one fresh angle or observation. The *Times* headline from November 14, 1997, well captured the mood of the investigation during this interval: "A Bold Start Stretched to 16 Fruitless Months."[56]

"They screwed this investigation up so bad it probably never will be straightened out," argues Jim Speer from a perspective that seems very nearly the consensus of the pilots, engineers, and mechanics working at Calverton. "We have felt ever since we were there that the thing has been covered up— that the truth was not allowed to be sought out and discovered."[57]

In the absence of truth, in the absence of light, corruption flourished. For the first ten months of 1997, unknown to the other investigators, agents from the FBI and CIA were at work creating arguably the most spectacular lie ever to be visited on the American people, one that dispelled any notion of Kallstrom's sincerity. Within a few days they would present it. Within a few weeks they would arrest the three whistle-blowers that stood in their way.

The decent interval was coming to an end with an indecent vengeance. Although few knew it at the time, American justice was about to experience one of its darkest moments.

CHAPTER 7

HANGAR MAN

Capt. Terrell Stacey knew the aircraft as well as or better than anyone in the investigation. A senior manager at TWA, he had flown the 747 into JFK from Paris the night before it became Flight 800. Indeed, he was in charge of all TWA 747 pilot activity within the airline. So it was logical that he would be among the first TWA employees assigned to the NTSB investigation.

Upon arriving at Calverton Hangar, Stacey was assigned to the NTSB eyewitness team. The team's mission was to interview those who had seen an object climb from the area of the ocean and intercept Flight 800. But as described earlier, the Justice Department and FBI stepped in and ordered the witness team to disband. Still, Stacey was a good team player. It would take more than one insult from the Justice Department to make him lose faith in the system. But the more he saw of the investigation, the less faith he had.

Elizabeth Sanders had gotten to know Stacey through her years as a flight attendant for TWA. She, like others who knew Stacey, thought of him as "a straight arrow, go-by-the-rules kind of guy" and respected him for it.[1] Flight 800 would bind their fates in ways that she never could have anticipated.

When the plane went down Sanders, now a trainer for TWA, was emotionally wrought. She had trained several of the attendants on board, one of whom had called her mother just before take off in high excitement about this, her first international flight. "TWA is such a family," Sanders remembered thinking, "that for a family to lose fifty-three members is devastating. How could this happen? Fifty-three of us are gone." Sanders, Stacey, and the other TWA employees found themselves at one memorial service after another. The feeling among the TWA family then—as now—was that a missile had brought down the plane. As the official investigation sputtered, the frustration among them grew.

Elizabeth's husband, James Sanders, could not help but pick up the vibes. A medically retired police officer from the L.A. area, Sanders had spent the last eleven years as an investigative reporter with a primary interest in the POW issue. He knew his way around government, and he knew the way government could work. Aware of the dissatisfaction within the TWA community, Sanders sought out a few good sources within the investigation on Long Island. The best of them proved to be Terrell Stacey. For discretion's sake, Sanders would refer to him only as "hangar man."

AFTER a phone introduction arranged by Elizabeth, James Sanders and Terrell Stacey agreed to meet. In October 1996, after the official investigation had lost all momentum, Sanders flew from Richmond to Newark and watched the familiar site of the Twin Towers come into view as his plane touched down. Stacey pulled up to the curb outside the terminal, recognized Sanders from social functions at which their paths had crossed, and beckoned him into the vehicle. From there, they drove to a large restaurant near the airport.

It was midafternoon, and the place was almost empty. Still, they decided to sit as far away from any ears as possible. After ordering appetizers and coffee, Sanders placed a legal pad on the table and began taking notes in Stacey's presence. "What he told me over those first hours," relates Sanders, "was one thing—'I know there's a cover-up in progress.'"

Stacey talked and drew illustrations of what he had seen and how the investigation had gone awry. He would later state under oath that he believed Sanders's cop-shop experience might help him find a truthful answer. As the meeting progressed the pair became comfortable with one another. Over the course of the meeting Stacey revealed a good deal, including the following:

- There was no analysis of how each part contributed to the overall picture; the NTSB could seize upon any individual part to make whatever point it wanted.

- Within a day or two this conjecture would be presented to the national media as the latest theory when, in reality, it was nothing more than guesswork, a stall for time.

- The FBI did not communicate or share information with the NTSB.

- The FBI, at will, could come into the hangar and remove any piece of the aircraft; these were not signed out or otherwise tracked by the NTSB investigation.

- Prior to a part arriving at the hangar, then being tagged and placed into the NTSB computer, there was no control or tracking of evidence, as required in criminal cases.

- The FBI conducted tests without ever sharing the results with the NTSB.

- It was unknown how the center wing tank (CWT) low-level explosion could produce enough energy to simultaneously put the Cockpit Voice Recorder (CVR) and Flight Data Recorder (FDR) out of action. This had proved an unsolvable problem during the informal discussions at the hangar.

This was plenty to start with. At the time, most of this information came as news to Sanders. After more than two hours of meeting, Stacey drove Sanders back to Newark, and Sanders flew home to Virginia. The meeting would forever change both their lives.

On September 22, 1996, the always-contrary *New York Post* reported that the FBI had interviewed 154 witnesses of a missilelike object rising into the sky. "'Some of these people were judged extremely credible' a top federal official told the *Post*."[2] The paper had also reported that the FBI had sat down many of these witnesses with U.S. military experts, who debriefed them and independently confirmed that their descriptions matched surface-to-air missile attacks, a fact later confirmed by the FBI in a Senate hearing.[3] Shortly after Stacey and Sanders began their source-to-journalist relationship, Stacey confirmed this story, adding that the thirty-four most credible witnesses had been taken to the sites from which they observed the object's flight. There the Missile and Space Intelligence Center (MISIC) analysts set up survey equipment and plotted the exact position of the observed streak and of the subsequent explosion. According to Stacey, all thirty-four witnesses saw an object rise from the surface and intercept the flight path of Flight 800. As noted earlier, the FBI kept this line of inquiry tightly under wraps.

Stacey was a cautious individual. He carefully measured each thought and did not confuse fact with speculation. More than three months into the investigation, he insisted on no particular hypothesis. He was certain of only one thing: The government was not conducting an honest investigation.

A few weeks after this first meeting, Sanders and Stacey met a second time. On this occasion, Stacey turned over an NTSB computer printout of the Red and Yellow Zones of the debris field. The Red Zone is the field closest to JFK airport and contains debris that first fell from the stricken 747. The Yellow Zone is a much smaller area to the east of the Red Zone, containing much of the front portion of Flight 800. The printout was dated November 13 (1996). All debris that had made it past the FBI was tagged and entered into the NTSB computer the day it arrived at Calverton and came under NTSB control. This database has never been released to the public.

Sanders computerized what appeared to be key pieces of debris in the NTSB Red Zone database printout and soon noticed a pattern. The very first damage to the plane centered on rows 17 through 19 with a general right-to-left bias. This pattern then extended forward along the right side of the fuselage. The apex of this "L"-shaped pattern was to the rear of the second door from the front where the leading edge of the right wing joined with the fuselage. Sanders believed that the narrow pattern suggested that this first event might not have been catastrophic. Another, more powerful blast had to have blown the nose off the 747.

Sanders also learned that more than 98 percent of the center wing tank remained with the stricken 747 until its final descent into the Atlantic. If an internal CWT explosion had been the initiating event, the CWT would have been among the first pieces to fall from Flight 800. In mid-August this is what federal officials had been telling the *New York Times* before the story changed.

With this evidence in hand it was time for another meeting with Stacey. On November 24, 1996, Sanders flew to Newark airport, rented a car and drove to Stacey's home in rural New Jersey. In Stacey's den, Sanders unfolded his debris-field map and, using 747 schematics as flip charts, showed Stacey the narrow trail of damage Sanders had found crossing the plane from the initial blast. At that point, Stacey revealed for the first time the existence of a reddish-orange trail across the cabin interior of the plane in the same area of the passenger cabin, rows 17 through 19. He noted, too, that the NTSB had just produced a duplicate of Sanders's initiating-event diagram.

"They are perplexed," Stacey said of the NTSB management. He also told Sanders that the coroner was supposed to be releasing a report saying, "It was *not* the center fuel tank that caused the plane to crash—per analysis of body damage."

The conversation frequently returned to the reddish-orange residue, of which Stacey provided more detail. The residue was on the foam-rubber seat-cushion backing attached to the metal frame, and the foam rubber was rapidly deteriorating. Stacey claimed that the FBI had taken several samples in late August but refused to share the test results and ignored requests by his NTSB team for the same. In September 1996, the red residue had become a hot topic at Calverton.

Had the residue proved inconsequential, the FBI would likely have told Stacey and the other investigators, "Forget it. The red residue is glue. It's found at crash scenes all the time." But no one did. Nor did anyone tell Stacey that the FBI chemists had chosen not to test the residue because it was obviously an adhesive. No, the FBI and NTSB brass would offer these rationales only after the residue trail was publicly revealed in March 1997. The story that the FBI would quietly tell inquisitive NTSB staffers in December 1996 was that the test results could not be shared because they were evidence of a crime. In this instance, the FBI was likely telling the truth. Five years later, and only then through the coercive powers of the Freedom of Information Act, Sanders would learn that these results had indeed been classified under national security.

At their face-to-face meeting in November 1996, Sanders and Stacey agreed that without forensic testing there was no way to know the source of the residue. As Stacey observed, however, the residue appeared to have flakes on the surface. These could probably be coaxed into a plastic bag with very little help.

In the second week of December 1996, Sanders received the NTSB computer printout of the Green Zone, the site of the last debris to fall into the ocean. This still-classified document confirmed the Red-Yellow Zone printout. More than 98 percent of the center wing tank had fallen with the last wreckage into the ocean.

A FEW days later Sanders received an NTSB document in the mail from Stacey, a document that began to explain the political manipulation guiding senior NTSB and FBI investigation managers. Entitled "NTSB Chairman's Briefing/Status Report November 15, 1996," the document summarized NTSB Chairman Jim Hall's briefing by senior NTSB managers at the Calverton hangar. Although the language is often disingenuous, the report reveals more than it intended. Consider, for instance, the Radar Data section of the report, which says in part:

> Ron Schleede will write a letter for Bernie Loeb's signature to Ron Morgan for a full explanation of the FAA handling of ATC and radar tapes concerning TWA Flight 800. The letter will reference the technician who did the analysis resulting in conflicting radar tracks *that indicated a missile*. It will inquire why that information was reported to the *White House* and sent to the FAA Technical Center before the Safety Board was given access to the data [emphasis added].[4]

Were the letter from another investigation, one might assume that the NTSB wanted more details from the FAA to augment its knowledge base. But in this investigation, that was not the case. Here, the NTSB was clearly pressuring the FAA to make its technicians recant their missile testimony.

This pressure is evident in this letter to the FAA, sent under Loeb's signature:

> As you know, during the first few hours after the accident, some FAA personnel made a preliminary assessment that recorded ATC radar data showed primary radar hits that indicated the track of a high-speed target that approached and merged with TWA 800. One of your staff called our office about 0930 on July 18, 1996, to advise us of the preliminary assessment of the radar data by FAA personnel, suggesting that a missile may have hit TWA 800 . . . After the Safety Board received the ATC radar data and reviewed it, it was determined that the preliminary assessment by FAA staff was incorrect. We understand that FAA official[s] now agree with the Safety Board's determination. I would appreciate it if you

could verify that all specialists and/or managers involved in the prelimi-
nary radar analyses fully agree that there is no evidence within the FAA
ATC radar track that would suggest a high-speed target merged with
TWA 800.[5]

Six years later the NTSB continues to classify the radar data and the
analysis referenced in the above letter, refusing to release it even under the
Freedom of Information Act. These evasive tactics suggest that Loeb's letter
to the FAA was an attempt to shape the outcome of the TWA Flight 800
investigation. To its credit, the FAA shied away from signing on to Loeb's
designs:

Dear Mr. Loeb,

The review of the printout from the program indicated that there
were radar tracks, which could not be accounted for by the FAA staff. This
information was immediately relayed to the appropriate law enforcement
organizations with the understanding that it was preliminary and did contain some unexplained data . . . Although we understand and share your
desire to allay public concern over this issue, we cannot comply with your
request . . . By alerting law enforcement agencies, air traffic control personnel simply did what was prudent at the time and reported what
appeared to them to be a suspicious event. To do less would have been
irresponsible.[6]

Loeb's letter makes two salient admissions: One was that the FAA did
report "conflicting radar tracks that indicated a missile"; the second was that
this track "approached and merged with TWA 800."

Not surprisingly, this radar track was expunged from the database prior
to the NTSB's releasing it to the public.[7] But the existence of a high-speed
object "merging" with Flight 800 had been well documented. The absence
of any such evidence in the released database—even the appearance of such
evidence—is deeply troubling. After all, why bother to conceal an "anomaly," if that's all it was? In fact, FAA radar tracked at least one unknown
object. Each FAA radar makes a 360-degree sweep every 4.6 seconds. A multiple radar overlay sequence was required to see a high-speed track "merging"
with Flight 800. Whoever tampered with this data runs the risk of criminal
prosecution under USC 18, Section 1001. To this day, the NTSB refuses to
release a certified copy of the database.

The NTSB Chairman's Report contains additional evidence of willful misdirection. The document, for instance, notes that "there was a forty-second gap between the last recorded radar hit and the time the explosion was mentioned on any ATC [air traffic control] tapes."[8]

In fact, an Eastwind Airlines pilot, David McClaine, observed TWA Flight 800 as it exploded and "immediately called BOS ATC"—Boston Air Traffic Control. It can be heard on audiotapes and read on transcripts released by the FAA.[9] There is no actual forty-second gap. McClaine cites the time specifically as "less than 15 seconds, but say, 10 seconds, around there." The gap owes its alleged existence either to an NTSB alteration or an analysis problem somewhere within the cockpit voice recorder (CVR), flight data recorder (FDR), radar tapes, or FAA ATC tapes; as shall be seen in more detail later, there is strong evidence of tampering with the FDR and the CVR. Somewhere within all this altered evidence lies the answer to the forty-second problem identified in the NTSB Chairman's Report.

This report makes some other interesting observations. For example: "Fragment evidence found in the CWT was indicative of an explosive event, not necessarily a missile or bomb but rather associated with the CWT explosion."[10] To be sure, this account is self-serving, but its value proved short-lived. If investigator-in-charge Alfred Dickinson was still claiming that "an explosion had occurred in the center wing tank"[11] at the December 1997 hearing, by the time of the August 2000 hearings, Bernard Loeb had quietly changed scenarios. He now argued that "the earliest event in the break-up sequence was an overpressure inside the center wing tank that caused structural failure of its forward section."[12] The concept of a fuel-tank "explosion" may have swayed the media, but it could not convince the scientists and technicians investigating the crash. They came to realize that no credible mechanical problem could have caused an "explosive event" inside the center wing tank.

For the record, an overpressure is a low-order event that does not cause an instant, powerful "explosion." The difference between the two is more than semantic. To accommodate the shift from one explanation to another, it would become necessary to alter the right side of the CWT and the right side of the passenger cabin between the critical rows 17 through 27, an act almost too brazen to believe were it not so well documented.[13]

When Sanders received the ten-page NTSB Chairman's Report from Stacey in December 1996, he was working with *Inside Edition* reporter Mark Sauter, who immediately recognized the significance of the information contained within. Sauter was not an ordinary establishment reporter, if indeed

Inside Edition can be considered establishment media. He combined a Harvard degree and master's from the Columbia School of Journalism with a background as a Special Forces officer. The combination resulted in a focused energy that could cut through even the thickest bureaucratic morass.

Sauter called the NTSB, asking for an official response to several of the more serious issues raised by the November 15, 1996, memo. Not surprisingly, real answers proved elusive. NTSB's public affairs officer, Peter Goelz, claimed "there were errors" in the document, but he would not say where.[14] Now that the NTSB was in a damage-limiting mode, Goelz tried to cast doubt on the credibility of the board's own document by diminishing unspecified parts. After a day of maneuvering, the NTSB claimed that one such "error" involved the FBI's failure to return photos to the NTSB. This seemed to be a minor point. But the NTSB left the issue of errors hanging by suggesting this was only one out of many.

Intrigued, Sauter flew to Washington to follow up. He found Jim Hall at a hearing on air bags at the Capitol and walked over to the public affairs staff hovering around the chairman. He wanted Hall to comment on his staff's inability to answer simple questions about the accuracy of the chairman's own memo. While Sauter and his film crew waited, an NTSB official approached.

"Are you waiting for the chairman?" he asked.

"Yes," Sauter responded.

"He's not going to answer any questions," the man said.

"We'll see," was Sauter's response.

"But maybe you'll talk to me. I'm Peter Goelz, the head of government and media relations for the NTSB. Maybe I'll answer some."

Sauter was surprised. He expected Goelz to be taller, trimmer, less rumpled. "What is this report we're talking about?" Sauter asked.

Goelz replied that it was a draft of "working minutes from a regularly scheduled review of our investigation." This was a major admission. He had just disproved the ambiguous suggestion that Sauter possessed a false document. Goelz told Sauter that this was just a "first draft" and "certainly not" the final one. He admitted, too, that there were "a few inaccuracies in that first draft."

When Sauter asked Goelz to identify them, Goelz could only cite the issue of the photos. "And the truth on that," said Goelz, "was shortly before that meeting we did get some photos back. They had been given to somebody in Calverton. It was not a big deal."

Goelz was dissembling. A political crony of Chairman Hall, he was prepared to say what the situation demanded. He and Hall had gotten to know
each other in the Clinton-Gore Tennessee campaign of 1992. Neither had
any experience related to the work with which the NTSB is tasked, but
Goelz had the ability to stay on message, a useful talent in Clinton's
Washington. He would soon enough be promoted to managing director.

The truth, revealed three years later through sworn testimony by two
NTSB investigators before a Senate committee, was that the FBI refused to
allow any non-FBI person to take any photograph for investigative purposes.[15] Typically, the NTSB used photos to build visual evidence that its
investigative teams could use at their nightly analysis meetings. This was not
a typical investigation. The NTSB took no photos. Linda Kunz was thrown
out of the investigation for daring to try. The FBI shared its photos with the
NTSB weeks after a given request, if at all.

Sauter continued to search for one factually correct statement from Peter
Goelz. "What about the missile the FAA technician said was on a collision
course with Flight 800?" Sauter inquired.

"We saw those radar tapes shortly after we got on the scene. Our staff
has reviewed those tapes and they show absolutely no sign of a missile,"
Goelz responded.

In Clinton's Washington, truth had become highly subjective. The FAA
had not just observed "suspicious events" on the radar. They had, in fact,
observed a high-speed object approach and merge with Flight 800.

Two years after this interview, another reporter would learn firsthand
that Goelz's first instinct was to deny, regardless of the truth. Robert Davey,
a reporter who frequently writes for the *Village Voice*, faxed Goelz a question
about nitrate residue being found on center wing tank debris-piece CW-504.
Goelz faxed Davey back, saying no nitrate was found on CW-504. Again, his
response was factually false. A NASA chemist had found nitrate on CW-504
and asked the NTSB for permission to continue testing to determine if the
nitrate came from an explosive. The NTSB's Dr. Merrit Birky told the
NASA chemist to cease and desist.[16] When Davey faxed this NASA report to
Goelz, Goelz responded that there had been a misunderstanding. He had
thought that Davey was using "nitrate" as a code word for "explosive." If
Goelz is to be believed, he simply misunderstood the question. The alternative is to accept that Peter Goelz was just another spinmeister caught in the
act of lying by a very good reporter.

Instructive in the ways of this investigation is the case of Kelly O'Meara.

O'Meara had served as Long Island Congressman Michael Forbes's chief of staff before becoming a reporter. In fact, it was her aggressive pursuit of the truth about TWA 800 that led to her controversial departure from Forbes's office.

Early in 1998, someone inside the NTSB had quietly released new radar data showing a large number of radar blips moving in unison between twenty-two and thirty-five miles south of the crash site. This piqued O'Meara's interest. Reporting for *Insight* magazine, which is published by the *Washington Times*, O'Meara interviewed Goelz, now the NTSB managing director, and asked him what the data meant and why it had not surfaced before. O'Meara had no sooner left his office, however, than Goelz called Howard Kurtz of the rival *Washington Post* to plant a story defaming her. Kurtz would quote Goelz as saying, "She really believes that the United States Navy shot this thing down and there was a fleet of warships."[17]

As O'Meara's audiotape revealed, however, it was the mocking and evasive Goelz who raised the issue of a missile, not O'Meara. Wrote *Insight* editor Paul Roderiquez, "In my experience as a veteran newsman, journalists would never roll over and allow government bureaucrats to use them to slime their colleagues. Yet that precisely is what recently happened."[18]

On December 20, 1996, *Inside Edition* ran a segment based on the chairman's report and Sauter's interview with Goelz. The segment focused exclusively on the internal conflict between the NTSB and FBI. Sanders was assured that the "red meat" in the chairman's report would be broadcast in the future if additional confirmation were developed. It wasn't to be. This was the last segment *Inside Edition* aired on the subject. By the time Sauter had gathered sufficient evidence of serious malfeasance within the investigation, *Inside Edition* had lost the nerve to take on the administration's hired guns at the FBI and Justice.

As Sauter was wrapping up his D.C. interview with Goelz, Terrell Stacey picked up the phone at his rural New Jersey home and called Sanders. It was December 8, almost five months after the crash.

Sanders's normal practice was to tape-record all business-related calls, then take notes from the audiotape and record over the interview. Most of the early conversation centered on identifying the role of each NTSB official named in the chairman's report. As the conversation began to wind down, a critical dialogue between Stacey and Sanders occurred:

Sanders: In any case, I won't keep you anymore here. I wanted to check in with you. So I'll just anxiously await the residue and whatever . . .

Stacey: Whatever else I can scrounge . . . I'll make that [scraping possible missile residue into a plastic bag] my top priority because that group, like I say, Les and them were talking about finishing up, so that place ought to be fairly secluded in a few days—there won't be a lot of people.

Sanders: Oh, outstanding, good.

Stacey: OK. Very good.

Sanders: OK. Talk to you later.

Stacey was firmly committed to obtaining a sample of the residue and having it tested. A positive test would prove not only evidence of a missile but also of an intentional compromise of the investigation. For reasons that will become clear in the next chapter, it is important to note that Stacey was comfortable with the decision he had made to provide the residue for testing. He was not asked to take it. He had volunteered. He had also volunteered to gather "whatever else I can scrounge."

At the moment this phone conversation took place, Elizabeth Sanders was driving to her commuter apartment near JFK airport. Stacey drove within a mile of the apartment coming to and from Calverton Hangar. If Liz had been involved in any way in the investigation, she would have been the person to whom Terry Stacey gave the residue. She was not.

Stacey called Sanders two days later. He had been about to scrape off the residue when a VIP tour came through the hangar, and he thought better of it. Stacey said the hangar was going to shut down for the holidays, and that he would probably not get back inside until some time in January 1997. Sanders and Stacey were playing with fire. Their debris-field analysis was easy to ignore. But the forensic evidence of the residue combined with the documentary evidence of the debris field would force the major media to pay heed. This was journalism with consequences.

As December 1996 wound to a close Stacey gave Sanders a year-end briefing. Sanders noted the following.

- The coroner said there was no pattern of lower-leg damage on the victims, suggesting that the explosion in the CWT was not the initiating event.

- New York Air National Guard Capt. Chris Bauer's tape-recorded statement had been heard. Bauer claimed that a "burning object" going east to west hit another object and caused it to explode. Stacey believes Bauer's superiors ordered him not to say "missile."

- Alcoa metallurgists were working with the FBI.

- The NTSB had asked many times for residue test results. "No response."

- The two-man FBI missile team "fe[lt] strongly it was a missile." This team gave a presentation to NTSB investigators in November 1996. They said that shoulder-fired missiles were capable of hitting Flight 800. They argued that it probably wasn't a radar-guided missile because it wasn't picked up on radar. Infrared guidance was their best guess. Third-generation infrared goes for "center of the heat."

- The only missile the FBI was allowed to investigate was shoulder-fired. At this point in the investigation a missile could, in an emergency, still be admitted to, as long as it could be blamed on terrorists.

Sanders and Stacey next communicated on January 9, 1997, at 8:45 P.M., when Stacey called and said two residue samples were en route by FedEx. The next day, about 3:20 in the afternoon, Sanders received the package. He soon learned the testing process would be more difficult than anticipated. After talking to chemists at the University of Virginia and UCLA, it became apparent that no one outside government could test the residue *and* provide an analysis of what the residue elements represented.

Sanders made arrangements with West Coast Analytical Services, a commercial laboratory in the Los Angeles area, to determine what elements were found in the reddish-orange residue. Step two was to give one copy of the elements to David Hendrix, a reporter at the *Press-Enterprise* newspaper in Riverside, California. Hendrix and Sanders had worked on various investigative projects for more than ten years. Hendrix had excellent sources within the federal government who fed him documents and information related to the Flight 800 investigation. The two reporters went their separate ways to interview people within the missile industry. They needed to know whether these elements were consistent with those found in the exhaust residue of a solid-fuel missile. They both received the same answer: The elements were consistent. No other explanation for the residue was apparent.

Months later, a retired missile-industry scientist added a confirming detail: These elements would also indicate an incendiary warhead explosion. The high amounts of magnesium, calcium, aluminum, iron, and antimony were all key ingredients of incendiary devices and would not be legally allowed in any "glue" associated with airplane cabin interior. Calcium, which is used when extreme heat is desired, made up 12 percent of the reddish-orange residue. All told, 99 percent of the elements by volume in the residue samples were consistent with elements expected to be found in an incendiary warhead.[19] Additional research revealed that "energized explosives" used in warheads create much more heat when magnesium, boron, aluminum, and zinc are added to RDX and/or PETN. These elements comprised a significant percentage of the residue Sanders received from Stacey. As noted earlier, PETN samples—and reportedly RDX samples—had been found and confirmed on Flight 800 debris from this same area of penetration, the right-side passenger cabin between rows 17 and 27.

Sanders learned that polymer-bonded explosives (PBX) combine PETN, RDX, and other explosives in a "rubber-like polymeric matrix" during the manufacturing process to promote stability. PETN is sometimes inserted into silicone rubber during that process; silicone made up a significant percentage of the residue Stacey removed from Calverton Hangar. Other explosive binders include polyester, polyamide, vinylidine chloride, and polyurethane. These binders do, in fact, resemble adhesives such as the 3M 1357 HP, the one that the FBI and NTSB would soon enough allege to be the source of residue. To diminish its significance further, they would simply refer to it as "glue."

On February 3, 1997, Stacey called Sanders with the numbers of the seats from which the FBI had lifted reddish-orange residue samples in early September. These included row 18, seats 6, 7, and 8; row 19, seat 7; and row 27, seat 2. Stacey had seen residue on rows 17 and 18 so these selections did not surprise him or Sanders. They believed that the FBI pulled a sample from row 27 because explosive traces had been found in the vicinity, perhaps on those very seats.

Nine days later, on February 12, Stacey and Sanders had their final face-to-face meeting, this time on Long Island. Sanders briefed Stacey on the residue elements, and Stacey briefed Sanders on what had transpired at an NTSB meeting he had attended only moments before.

At that meeting senior members of the NTSB had said that the Flight 800 cockpit voice recorder revealed a vibration traveling through the frame of the plane at over two thousand feet per second. The NTSB had access to data establishing that a vibration from a fuel-air explosion travels through an airplane frame at about 340 feet per second.[20] This gave the NTSB yet another powerful piece of evidence that a missile had struck TWA Flight 800. But the NTSB decided against retaining one of only two firms in the world with the expertise to analyze the vibration and pinpoint its origin. This information still remains classified.

By early March 1997 a decision was made to publish a series of newspaper articles describing Sanders's investigation of the government's apparent cover-up. At the time, Sanders and senior *Press-Enterprise* staff, along with a First Amendment lawyer, believed that the rule of law would prevent the FBI and Justice Department from violating the Constitution, federal criminal laws, and Justice Department regulations. They were being naive.

On March 5, Sanders interviewed Stacey for the last time, this time by phone. Notes from this conversation read as follows:

Hangar Man conversation (1) Brookhaven residue test [this was a sample from hold area of the plane that had reddish-orange residue. The first sample did not produce results to the government's liking, so a second sample was lifted and sent to Brookhaven], (2) entry/exit holes.

Stacey went into fairly extensive detail. Reconstruction of the right side was not yet complete toward the front. Stacey noted considerable speculation about the damage in the area of the R-3 door (on the right side of the plane, third door from the front). Unknown to Stacey, the right-side area he described had been dramatically altered. Sanders would learn this years later and then only the hard way.

THE next day Stacey had two, hour-long telephone conversations with David Hendrix to help Hendrix prepare the articles on the reddish-orange residue. Hendrix typed questions into his office computer prior to the interview, which was his normal practice. During the interview, Hendrix wore a headset in order to type in contemporaneous notes. Stacey proved to be both straightforward and cooperative.

It is important to get a feel for the nature of this interview. Three months later, although the interview was still relatively fresh in his mind, Stacey would present a dramatically different story to two FBI agents as he struggled to shape a scenario that would please them. As it happened, Hendrix alone interviewed Stacey; travel and phone records show that James Sanders was en route from Virginia when this interview occurred. Hendrix asked about the red residue, which Stacey first noticed in August on a "fairly uniform area."

> *Hendrix:* Is it anywhere else in the plane, other than on the rows [17, 18, 19]?
>
> *Stacey:* None on any other area (other than seats) [in rows 17, 18, 19].
>
> *Hendrix:* Has anybody else seen or commented about the red residue?
>
> *Stacey:* Everybody in [the] investigation team has seen and commented about it. [I] don't expect to see FBI info. [The] FBI [is] conducting [a] criminal investigation. Could be that the FBI exchanges info with [the] NTSB at [a] higher level. That's the frustrating thing, those samples were taken in August and no results have been shared (at this level). Everybody has seen the residue. I don't know (why anybody hasn't talked); it was a hot issue for a while, and they moved on to something else, and we heard nothing else from it. It was an anomaly being looked into[,] is how it was described.
>
> *Hendrix:* Anybody we can call who will tell us about the red residue, with or without their name being used?
>
> *Stacey:* Don't know of anybody I would want to [have interviewed].
>
> *Hendrix:* Have FBI investigators commented about it, even in passing?
>
> *Stacey:* Recorded as samples being taken, but no results. That's just something that never made the news.
>
> *Hendrix:* Some other anomalies?
>
> *Stacey:* The way [there] is fractur[ing] and curling, and the fact that there's some titanium in [the] center wing tank that heated [and affixed itself] to [the] center wing tank—something drastically happened. There's nothing on the plane that says missile in large letters, but it may all be there in small pieces. There may be large letters there but nobody knows about it except the FBI. A lot of tests and interviews but no idea about the results. There are things on the record—holes, damage, that are unexplained strictly by mechanical failure and [the] plane going through [the] windstream and hitting the water. Each scenario (mechanical, bomb, and explosion) eventually does not fit.

Hendrix: Why doesn't [the] metallurgy report talk about [the] nose falling off and what might have caused it to?

Stacey: They don't know. All they can say is what happened from a certain time. Those red zone pieces that came off the plane (front spars, doors, rows 17, 18 and 19). FBI says [the investigators inside the Hangar] can't let that be known (red stuff) because of the criminal aspect of the investigation.

Hendrix: What would happen if [a] large group got together and said, this is what we think's happening, somebody do something about it?

Stacey: That's been done (in meetings of investigators), in a large group (wanting information) they (FBI) say they can't do it because of the investigation.

Hendrix: Any bodies have red residue on it?

Stacey: No info of that happening.

Hendrix: Where are the residue seats in relationship to the dog-sniffing bomb tests?

Stacey: Don't know where; will try to find out.

Hendrix: How long were the seats on the ocean bottom?

Stacey: Don't know; will be on the log.

Hendrix: Any other clues to missile?

Stacey: (Puzzling about how residue bonded to [the foam rubber]) [The foam rubber may have] held or absorbed the residue from [the missile]. China Lake [Naval Weapons testing area in California]. Lots of experts from missiles [section] been here, but nobody's said anything.

Hendrix: How about the exit hole in the schematic? Where do I locate it?

Stacey: There are entry and exit holes all over this plane. [There is a] hole on [the] other side of C galley, that [is] a hole. Have to understand in reconstruction, that you're putting [the] plane back together. Hard to tell when [a] certain hole [aligns with another hole]. There is that large hole there, just forward of the wing area. [We are] Looking in reconstruction for line of site [sic] areas. If there was a hole that said missile on it we would be home; you certainly can say in that area where the residue was found, there certainly are plenty of holes both in and out. Other places like [the] L-3 door [left side of plane, third door back], is [a] very heavy structure [that is] bent in and [pieces are] missing . . .

Hendrix: Do you believe it was a missile?

Stacey: Yeah, I'd have to say I do; eyewitness accounts, interviews I've conducted, the ANG [New York Air National Guard] pilot. He said [an] object traveled and hit [Flight 800] and exploded. His superiors have told him to quit using the word missile. The immediate nature of what happened; voice recording stopped; there has been a lot of interest by the FBI in the missile theory. Lots of people have studied missiles.

Hendrix: I understand the FBI missile team believes it is a missile.

Stacey: Yes. I know at least two on [the missile team]. They're trying to prove their theory. [They have] given briefings and explored all the area. [They] are actively pursuing it.

Hendrix: Any other FBI think it [is] a missile?

Stacey: Can't speak to that. They don't say anything outside what they publicly believe. [I] can't say they've said they are convinced. Others on the investigation team believe it was a missile.

Hendrix: They (FBI)[missile team] ever said that in a meeting or is it only chat?

Stacey: Both—some official briefings; in briefing they talk about missile capabilities—hand held, shoulder fired; [a missile shot is] certainly within [the] capabilities [of shoulder fired]; Kallstrom has vociferously denied friendly fire. [The FBI missile] team in briefing says missiles [are] capable of hitting [planes] at that altitude. [There is] talk [within the Hangar] about work[ing] with eyewitnesses and triangulation, where [the missile] might have come from. Primarily [w]hat they talked about were stinger type and Russian [missiles] and others.

Hendrix: [Do] people on investigation team think friendly fire possible?

Stacey: Oh yes.

Hendrix: Suspicious or belief?

Stacey: Belief among some and suspicion among others.[21]

Terrell Stacey was a cautious, methodical person, not prone to speculate or to shape answers to fit a scenario. The residue had been a "hot" topic within the investigation. "It was an anomaly being looked into," is all the senior crash investigators had declared.[22] Were it only glue, they would not have allowed this mystery to linger. What is more, the FBI told the NTSB investigators not to reveal the existence of the residue trail to the media because it was part of their criminal investigation.

Inside the hangar, among serious people, the residue issue was treated with caution and concern bordering on paranoia. Once it became known that some of the residue had escaped the hangar, however, the residue issue would be treated as something of a joke by federal bureaucrats trying to re-direct the media spotlight. It was decidedly not a joke.

ONE day after interviewing Stacey, David Hendrix placed a call to the New York City FBI headquarters. He identified himself and gave the FBI press person a general description of the questions he wanted the FBI to answer prior to his publishing an article on the subject of the residue trail.

Hendrix placed the call shortly after 6 A.M. West Coast time. Sanders had arrived from Virginia on a TWA flight about five hours earlier. Now Sanders sat in Hendrix's office prepared to listen to the FBI response. It would be a long wait. Twelve hours later, Kallstrom personally returned Hendrix's call. After the opening pleasantries, Hendrix asked the first question:

> *Hendrix:* I'm doing a story saying there is apparent residue trail through TWA Flight 800 that tests out as missile propellant. I have confirmation that you had residue in your possession no later than August third and that the trail across the fuselage was completed at Calverton no later than the end of August.
>
> *Kallstrom:* It's not true. I don't plan to talk about the evidence. There is a red residue trail. It has no connection to a missile. I'm not going to get into it. There's a logical explanation but I'm not going to get into it. That is a non-starter. I wish we had something that was definitive of any theory. The notion that you would run an article saying this is proof of a missile. There's no basis in fact. To my knowledge that is not factual.
>
> *Hendrix:* The FBI took [samples] from seats in Rows 17, 18 and 19 (sic). What were the results of those tests?
>
> *Kallstrom:* We're not in the habit of discussing lab tests.

More than four years later, Sanders would obtain FBI documents estab-lishing that one of the tests Kallstrom refused to talk about revealed some-thing so sensitive that it was classified under national security.[23]

After his initial questions, Hendrix began to read some of the elements and the percentages of each. At this point Kallstrom turned on an office speaker so unknown persons in his office could hear. Hendrix's questions had serious implications: Either residue had escaped from the hangar, or someone at the FBI lab had leaked highly confidential information from tests conducted in August. At the moment, Kallstrom could not know precisely what story to tell, as he did not know how much of the truth had escaped FBI control. So he stalled for time as he assessed the damage.

Glue seems to have been the explanation that had been prepared in the summer of 1996 when the FBI noticed the reddish-orange trail. As Patricia Milton tells the story, the FBI had tested the "reddish-orange chemical" at the FBI lab in Washington in August 1996. The agent "worked all night" before concluding that the chemical was "upholstery glue." The manufacturer allegedly confirmed this urgent finding, and Kallstrom was well aware of it.[24] This all begs the question of why Kallstrom did not say to Hendrix, "Are you nuts? It's glue. Check it out. It's 3M 1357 HP glue," or why Kallstrom had not shared this seemingly innocuous information with Stacey and other NTSB personnel despite their requests.

Only one answer presents itself: The residue was not glue. Glue made for a good cover story *only* as long as the residue remained within the investigation.

Glue is, in fact, used on airplane seats, although in much smaller amounts than the government alleges. As long as one carefully selects the test to be performed, an FBI lab technician could look at the residue and say it was a "chlorinated polymeric material consistent with glue." The binding agents in explosives and solid fuel are made of material similar to many glues and paints.

Forensic evidence in an independent investigator's hands was a possibility the FBI did not contemplate. Its agents had grown soft dealing with the major media whose reporters had little knowledge of or interest in forensics. Sanders, however, was a retired police officer. During a career in law enforcement, he personally observed how scientific evidence carried the day in court time after time against the most carefully constructed alibis.

As his work evolved, Sanders realized that he was not only investigating the cause of the crash, but he was also investigating those who were concealing that cause, a possible criminal offense. His activity threatened the politically motivated outcome that the government had been improvising.

Within minutes of the interview's end, Kallstrom appears to have alerted the decision makers to the major threat that had just surfaced. The Justice Department sprang into action. Using the power of the grand jury, Justice began the process of recovering the potentially incriminating evidence.

The government had from Friday evening, March 7, 1997, until Monday morning, March 10, to make a final decision about how best to explain the residue to the establishment media. Its response was contrived over the weekend. The Justice Department took the lead. It would be necessary to violate federal criminal statutes, case law, and the Justice Department's own internal rules and regulations in order to regain control of the investigation. But the Clinton faithful within the Justice Department were old hands at damage control.

Once again, they would not disappoint.

CHAPTER 8

DAMAGE CONTROL

"New Data Show Missile May Have Nailed TWA 800," screamed the one-inch, front-page headline across the top of the *Riverside Press-Enterprise* on March 10, 1997.

For almost three days concerned parties within the government had been preparing for this moment. Until the article appeared, however, they could not respond. They did not know the extent of the damage they would have to control. Evidence suggests, however, that they had a plan of action prepared in case the information about the residue trail escaped from the hangar. The response would simply be this: The residue was "glue."

There was indeed glue in the area. It was used to fasten the plastic tray tables to the metal seat backs. This was not the residue in question, but it was a brownish color, close enough to deceive a credulous media.

Written by Loren Fleckenstein, the thirty-inch-column *Press-Enterprise* story identified James Sanders as an "investigative reporter," provided information on his previous nonfiction books, and described his inquiry into the FBI and NTSB Flight 800 investigation over the preceding five months.

"The pattern of the first wreckage to hit the water," wrote Fleckenstein, "combined with evidence of missile-propellant residue in the Boeing 747, clearly indicates that a missile carrying an inert warhead smashed through the airliner, author and investigative reporter James Sanders has concluded."[1]

The article quoted the NTSB's Peter Goelz in dissent. "We will be testifying before Congress on Tuesday that as of today there is no physical evidence of a bomb or a missile in any of the records that we have recovered." The article also quoted the FBI's James Kallstrom. "I wish we had something that was definitive of any theory, but the FBI does not," he told the paper.

The *Press-Enterprise* cited an anonymous FAA crash analyst who reviewed the NTSB documentation. "They made him believe some outside object pierced the jumbo jet right to left and started the catastrophic sequence that eventually dismembered the plane."

This story would create a significant problem for the Justice Department. Sanders was clearly identified as an "investigative reporter." The article's text confirmed that he was on the trail of potential criminal activity within the Flight 800 investigation. As to those charged with containing the investigation, their worst nightmare had been realized. Forensic evidence had been removed from the hangar and tested. The elements found in the reddish-orange residue proved to be consistent with exhaust from a solid fuel missile.

THOSE orchestrating the government response had another worry. They suspected that Sanders had additional residue. As soon as they fixed on an alternate explanation, he could produce a second or third sample for testing, possibly publicly.

Almost immediately, Justice Department officials zeroed in on what they sensed was Sanders's Achilles' heel, his wife, Elizabeth. A senior trainer for TWA, she loved her job and her colleagues. It was something of a second career for her. Of Filipino descent, Elizabeth had worked as an instructor of Polynesian dancing before becoming a flight attendant. TWA opened the world to her, and it became her family. Her distress on the night of the crash of Flight 800 was profound.

The Justice Department found its rationale on page A-12 of the *Press-Enterprise* story where Elizabeth Sanders was mentioned by name. In fact, James Sanders had had no real choice but to mention her. Elizabeth was a TWA employee and the wife of the journalist. TWA figured prominently in the articles. Disclosure was mandatory.

The Justice Department exploited this disclosure to devise its strategy.

To mention Elizabeth Sanders in the article created an "inference of guilt." Where such an inference existed, it was technically permissible to pursue her without the investigation constituting harassment, intimidation, or the violation of her civil rights. The courts refer to this process by the tautology "normalcy"—that is, the normal way in which federal prosecutors operate. If it is normal, so say the courts, it is proper. If it is proper, it is legal.

Despite being advised that Elizabeth Sanders did not wish to speak to or meet with the FBI, Special Agent James Kinsley went first to her residence in Virginia and then to the Norfolk airport in an apparent attempt to haul her off a TWA flight. Had she been involved in the very shoot-down of the plane, the FBI could not have been more severe in its interrogation of her friends and coworkers at TWA and of her neighbors in Williamsburg.

On the same morning as the article appeared, March 10, 1997, James Sanders arrived in New York City. There he made the rounds of the city's major publishers. After each visit to a publisher, Sanders stopped by the Associated Press to visit with reporter Richard Pyle. Pyle told Sanders that the government was going to issue a statement on the residue by noon. It did not happen. The time of the release was gradually set back, then canceled as of 3 P.M. The government resorted instead to the great art of the Clinton administration: *spin*. Its operatives started gradually and anonymously leaking word that the residue was nothing more than glue. They offered no backup, but the major media had long since ceased to ask for any. The media began to report that the missile theory had once again been shot down.

One network, however, held promise for Sanders. It was CBS. Sanders had granted an exclusive interview to Emmy Award–winning producer Kristina Borjesson. After the interview had been videotaped, however, Borjesson grew alarmed when she realized no one on the *Evening News* was editing the piece. Frustrated, she walked into a morning meeting of news executives and asked why the network wasn't doing the story on Sanders and his documents.[2]

"You think it's a missile, don't you?" queried an executive she didn't recognize.

"I don't know what the hell it is," Borjesson shot back, "but don't you think we should be doing a story that asks a few questions about this guy and his documents?" The silence that followed was, as Borjesson admits, "deafening." When she had walked into the room, she honestly believed she was about to correct an oversight at a level where it could be corrected quickly. "I walked out of there," said Borjesson, "feeling like I'd cooked my own goose."

When CBS finally aired the story, it used what Borjesson calls "a classic avoidance tactic" to keep Sanders off the air while reporting his side of the story. Borjesson describes the way it worked in this instance:

On the *Evening News*, Dan Rather, reading off of a TelePrompTer, told America about Sanders's allegations. Rather's narration continued while the camera cut to a photo of the residue that Sanders had provided. Then it was time for the FBI's response to the allegations. The FBI's TWA 800 task-force chief, James Kallstrom, appeared *live*. Looming large in a multi-monitor image, Kallstrom told Dan that the red residue was glue . . . Without one follow-up question, not even one asking how it could be that Sanders was able to get a piece of evidence from the hangar where security was supposed to be so tight, Rather thanked Kallstrom and moved on to the next story.

The day after the Sanders story broke, March 11, NTSB staff members testified before the House Aviation Subcommittee. When asked about a residue trail across rows 17 through 19, the NTSB's Bernard Loeb responded, "One thing I can say categorically is there is no such thing as a red residue trail in that airplane."[3]

"There is a reddish-orange substance that is on virtually all of the seats in the forward part of the airplane," Loeb continued. "For that matter, I am sure it is on all of the seats in the airplane because we believe that that red residue material is an adhesive."

Recall that on March 7, four days earlier, James Kallstrom had told Dave Hendrix of the *Press-Enterprise*, "There *is* a red residue trail." Four days later, Loeb would tell Congress that there was "no such thing as a red residue trail in that airplane."

Was either man lying? Once again, the answer hinged on the word *is*.

MULTIPLE sources inside Calverton Hangar did indeed verify Terrell Stacey's claim that a red residue trail ran across the passenger cabin in rows 17, 18, and 19, as would, ultimately, the FBI's arrest warrant for Sanders.[4] What is more, the samples Stacey removed from the hangar prove that the reddish-orange trail was imbedded in the foam rubber.

When Loeb made his statement, however, he was quite likely telling the truth, at least technically. All evidence indicates that the foam rubber had been stripped from the relevant seat backs some time after Kallstrom's interview on Friday afternoon, March 7, 1997, and before Loeb's testimony on Tuesday morning, March 11, 1997. The NTSB's Hank Hughes would, in fact, later testify that he discovered missing seats and seat cushions in a nearby Dumpster.[5] After the act of removal was complete, no reddish-orange foam rubber could be found at the hangar. All that remained were rust-colored bare metal and some hard plastic panels glued to the backs of some of the seats.

Disingenuous though it was, Loeb's testimony before Congress on March 11 changed the public debate. If he and his colleagues could produce glue from the plane, of virtually any sort, they could plant the impression that the red residue trail was fiction, as was the missile that left it.

To sustain the NTSB's story, the senior NTSB scientist at Calverton Hangar, Dr. Merrit Birky, chairman of the Flight 800 Fire and Explosion Group, sent some "brown to reddish-brown colored material" to NASA for testing. He would claim that the substance, upon testing, was revealed to be "consistent with a polychloroprene 3M Scotch-Grip 1357 High Performance contact adhesive."[6] The NTSB then circulated this report among the establishment media, as though it were independent proof that Sanders's residue was glue.

Aware of the intrigue, Sanders picked up the phone and called Charles Bassett, the NASA chemist who had tested some of the samples for the NTSB. To clarify matters, Bassett provided Sanders with an affidavit. In it Bassett admitted that the tests he conducted "did not identify specific elements, by quantity, within the reddish-orange residue of the sample submitted to them by Mr. Sanders."[7] As Bassett acknowledged, this made it impossible to compare Sanders's sample with the one sent by Birky.

To complicate matters, someone tampered with at least one of the rectangular samples the NTSB sent to NASA for testing. The sample in question is uniformly pinkish-red in color. It looks nothing like the darker, streaked red-orange of Sanders's sample nor the "reddish-brown colored material" the NTSB claims it sent. Worse, none of the adjacent area on the relevant seat, 19-2, is red at all.[8] Sanders discovered this when photographing the reconstructed plane as part of his limited discovery in December 1998. Someone had apparently smeared the NTSB sample with red dye to lend the illusion of redness and sent it on to NASA.

Despite the pressure, Dr. Bassett at NASA made a tough and honest declaration. He had no idea whether the residue he had tested was the same residue Sanders had tested. In the absence of any official effort to compare the composition of 3M adhesive Scotch Grip 1357 to the residue found on Sanders's sample, physicist Dr. Thomas Stalcup had the adhesive tested at a Florida State University lab.

As Stalcup discovered, Scotch Grip 1357 contained no silicon and barely perceptible trace amounts of calcium and aluminum. Silicon is a common solid-rocket-fuel ingredient. Calcium is the pyrotechnic that provides the burn when mixed with oxygen-providing perchlorate. Aluminum powder fuels the rocket. Sanders's sample, by contrast, contained 15 percent silicon, 12 percent calcium, and 2.8 percent aluminum. In total, these three key components comprise nearly 30 percent of Sanders's sample, but less than three one-hundredths of 1 percent of the adhesive. "The results," notes Borjesson in something of an understatement, "are completely different."[9]

After learning the results, Stalcup called the NTSB's Birky to inform him of the discrepancy. In the tape-recorded telephone conversation, Dr. Birky unwittingly gives away the game:

> *Birky:* 3M had already changed their formula. They had represented that to us when we tried to get some reference samples. Well that's old material. We haven't the foggiest notion what that formula is, nor do we have any of the old formulation, we don't know what was used at that time on those seats. So, in trying to prove that we have the same samples as Sanders, I'm not sure it gets us very far. Supposing you come out differently?
>
> *Stalcup:* Right, right.
>
> *Birky:* Then what are you going to say? Well, you're not going to put the thing to bed.[10]

Birky had exposed the fatal flaw in the government position. Its agents had tested another substance altogether, and they knew it. They could have easily tested a sample comparable to Sanders's—indeed, they could have tested one of Sanders's own samples—but they feared the results. "Supposing you come out differently?" said Dr. Birky. "Then what are you going to say?"[11]

Among the samples the FBI had in its possession was one it had seized from CBS's Borjesson. Sanders had sent her one of the samples so CBS could do its own independent testing. Although CBS News had no interest in the sample, *60 Minutes* did. Borjesson warned Senior Producer Josh Howard that a federal grand jury had been convened to deal with legal issues around the TWA 800 investigation, but Howard wasn't put off. "We've dealt with grand juries before," he told her.[12] Borjesson was elated. In the world of news, she told him, *60 Minutes* was the "last broadcast with balls." Borjesson put the sample in Howard's desk for safekeeping until she could locate a lab.

A few days later Borjesson got a call from her executive producer. The FBI wanted to talk to her "about some stolen evidence." As she learned, management had meekly handed over the untested sample to the FBI, "where it disappeared forever."[13]

On April 14, 1997, James Sanders, accompanied by his attorney at that time, Jeff Schlanger, met with the Justice Department, represented by Valerie Caproni, Chief of the New York Justice Department Criminal Division; Ben Campbell, her assistant; FBI agent Jim Kinsley; and two other government officials. Caproni was the same attorney who muscled the NTSB out of the witness interviews in its first few days. Arguably, she was a participant in the subversion of the investigation. Now she was prosecuting those who would expose that subversion.

Two years later, Schlanger recalled this meeting, under oath, at the Sanderses' trial, where the couple were charged with conspiring with a source inside the federal TWA Flight 800 investigation to obtain forensic evidence and have it tested. He did so under direct examination by James Sanders's trial attorney, Bruce Maffeo:

> *Maffeo:* What did the government then proceed to say?
>
> *Schlanger:* Essentially there was some back and forth. At least talk from the government about why Mr. Sanders should cooperate. And ultimately it ended up with the statement that if he didn't cooperate, they would not subpoena him before the grand jury, but would rather seek an indictment against him. And the next time that we saw them he would be on the wrong side of an indictment.
>
> *Maffeo:* Did the government indicate at that meeting what, if any, actions they were prepared to take with respect to Liz Sanders?
>
> *Schlanger:* At the very end of that meeting there was a change in the status of Mrs. Sanders from being just a subject in the investigation, to a possible target in the investigation. And that was communicated directly to myself and Mr. Sanders.
>
> *Maffeo:* And when you say [it] was communicated directly to you, what was your understanding that if she did not cooperate?

Schlanger: That the government would at least attempt to seek an indictment against her as well.

Maffeo: Now . . .

Schlanger: It wasn't if she didn't cooperate. It was if Mr. Sanders did not
cooperate.[14]

The selection of Elizabeth Sanders as a target alarmed her husband, but
did not surprise him. Justice had been playing hardball with Elizabeth since
the *Press-Enterprise* articles appeared a month earlier. The sole source of
information allegedly linking Mrs. Sanders to the acquisition of the residue
samples would prove to be Terrell Stacey. But at this point, the government
had not even talked to Stacey. Its agents made the threat against Mrs.
Sanders despite a total absence of evidence against her.

This intimidation took a particularly memorable turn in late April 1997,
when Kensington Publishing released James Sanders's book, *The Downing of
TWA Flight 800*. The book detailed the information Sanders had gathered
and concluded that the plane had been struck by a Navy missile. Just as crit-
ically, the book alleged that the government had concealed this information
from the American public. In the book's acknowledgments section, Sanders
had written, "Thanks to Liz's [Sanders] support system, Lee Taylor, Lucille
Collins and TWA Norfolk agents." Shortly after publication of the book, FBI
agents in New York demanded that Mrs. Collins, who was Mrs. Sanders's
immediate supervisor at TWA, and Mrs. Taylor, a close friend and colleague,
be brought to New York for questioning. Both individuals were subjected to
FBI questioning and both reported that many of the questions were of a
highly personal nature concerning the Sanderses' marriage and private lives.

The agents were not even coy about using Elizabeth to get at James
Sanders. When her attorney asked the FBI to communicate through him
and stop the harassment, he was ignored.

The Justice Department underestimated Elizabeth Sanders. Although
confused and disheartened by the FBI's pursuit of her, she advised the government through counsel that she declined to cooperate in its investigation
of her husband's journalistic pursuits.

Elizabeth believed in her country as only the child of immigrants can.
The idea that the wife of a journalist could be made to reveal information
about his investigations struck her as contrary to everything she had learned.
Regardless of the cost, she could not even conceive of betraying his source
and her friend Terrell Stacey, Hangar Man.

To escape her pursuers, Elizabeth Sanders had to take leave from TWA and avoid her home or anyplace else the agents might find her. For eight unnerving months in 1997, she found refuge with a friend in a lonely house trailer in the Northwest semi-wilderness. She was cut off from her career, her coworkers, her mother and sisters, her husband, and her adolescent son. The experience threw her into a profound depression from which she has never fully recovered.

The Justice Department would allege at trial that when Elizabeth removed herself from FBI harassment, it constituted "consciousness of guilt." In truth, she had been made a target in the absence of any evidence, real or imagined. This was the classic definition of vindictive prosecution, retaliation for its own sake.

Among the documents the FBI wanted from the Sanderses were their phone records. This took some doing. According to the Code of Federal Regulations, the relevant subpoenas for a journalist could be issued only with the approval of the attorney general and after alternative investigative steps have been attempted and failed. Absent "exigent circumstances," such subpoenas were to be limited to verification of published information. What is more, federal regulations prohibited the government from seizing a journalist's phone records without first giving him notice of intent. In theory, the journalist then had the opportunity to go to court and block the seizure.

The Justice Department sidestepped all such requirements. Its solution was stunningly audacious. It simply chose to deny that James Sanders was a journalist. The cynical observer has to marvel at Justice's *chutzpah*. The *Press-Enterprise* articles prominently identified Sanders as an "investigative reporter." He had no other occupation for the past decade. The legal concept of "normalcy," however, once again exempted the Justice Department from playing by the rules by which the public thinks it plays. Sanders was denied the opportunity to block the subpoena. He would be pursued as a common criminal instead of a journalist.

Working under the theory of normalcy, the FBI seized Sanders's phone records to track down Terrell Stacey. Despite the Sanderses' silence, two steely FBI agents found their way to Stacey's rural home in June 1997. Their job was to intimidate, to create a feeling of terror and helplessness, to get Stacey to roll over before he regained his composure, before he developed the presence of mind to request an attorney. The agents did their job well. Stacey succumbed to the pressure and spent seven hours talking to the FBI without an attorney present.

Stacey knew that if he, too, chose not to cooperate, it would cost him significant legal fees and quite likely his job. He instantly faced a weighty decision. How long could he keep his daughter in college? How long could he make the monthly payments on his beautiful home? How long could he continue the lease payments on his three cars? How long could he pay for a defense team capable of opposing the awesome power of the Justice Department? The only alternative was to cooperate, ingratiate himself with those who held the power to ruin him. Telling the truth, telling the agents that he was involved in a serious and potentially criminal investigation of their own superiors, would not sit well with anyone.

Stacey would learn—from the FBI and Justice Department agents who confronted him over the following months—what they wanted to hear. He began to deliver a portion of that message—enough to avoid a felony indictment, and the essence of normalcy in action.

FBI agent Kinsley's handwritten notes, taken during the interview, reveal Stacey to have been reasonably forthcoming.[15] He told Kinsley of the content of his meetings with James Sanders and listed the documents turned over to Sanders. Kinsley's notes read in part: "FedEx piece of plane to Sanders because Sanders said he could test it." Putting aside the self-serving "piece of the plane" to describe the residue, this statement did not, under any circumstance, rise to the level of conspiracy.

When he typed the report three days later, Kinsley made the necessary correction: "STACEY had discussions with [James] SANDERS regarding the residue. At that time SANDERS had requested a sample of the orange residue."

There is no hint that Sanders "requested a sample" in Kinsley's field notes (also recall from the last chapter's phone transcripts that no request was made by James Sanders). The reason is simple. Stacey made no such statement. Unfortunately, this may explain why the FBI does not tape-record its field interviews.

Kinsley's field notes did, however, contain incriminating information about contact between Stacey and Elizabeth Sanders: "[Stacey] at Xmas party week before Xmas, Liz chit chat. Subsequent phone call Liz called Stacey pressing issue for Stacey to get residue." Stacey would not testify to such a phone call in court. Phone records proved beyond any doubt that such a phone call did not take place in the period between the Christmas party and January 9, 1997, when Stacey walked out of Calverton Hangar with the residue.

On June 26, 1997, Stacey and his attorney, John McDonald, met Justice Department lawyers Valerie Caproni and Ben Campbell. Kinsley also attended the meeting, taking several pages of field notes. Kinsley's notes state, "Liz call, [after] > holidays, normal pleasantries, then asked me to get samples. This call convinced me to get the samples." This statement from Stacey further implicated Elizabeth Sanders in a conspiracy to remove the residue. But it would hold only if the massive documentation already in Justice's possession—phone records, hangar sign-out logs, credit card statements, and TWA travel logs—did not directly contradict the implicating statement. In fact, it did.

Records show that Elizabeth Sanders and Stacey did speak on the phone at 8:30 P.M. on January 9, 1997. But this was four hours *after* Stacey had signed out of Calverton Hangar with the residue. The normalcy doctrine, however, does not require the Justice Department to present conflicting evidence to a cooperating witness. Stacey would remember only what the prosecutors wanted him to.

According to Elizabeth Sanders, Stacey began the conversation saying he was about to call her husband because he had sent the residue to him at their Williamsburg address earlier that evening. Per Kinsley's notes: "On way back to Hol[iday] Inn that day [Stacey] went to FedEx—pd cash—to Arena Dr."[16] The Sanderses lived on Arena Street, Williamsburg, Virginia, in 1997.

One does not have to take Elizabeth Sanders's word for what Stacey said during their twenty-minute conversation. Documents in the possession of the Justice Department proved beyond a reasonable doubt that Stacey had removed the residue on January 9 prior to 4:30 P.M., four hours before the conversation took place.[17] The phone records prove there was only one phone call between Elizabeth Sanders and Stacey at the Ronkonkoma Holiday Inn, or any other phone on Long Island, during a forty-five-day period surrounding January 9, 1997. Stacey himself acknowledged that there had been one and only one phone call to or from Elizabeth Sanders during this period. Stacey would repeat this admission under oath during the criminal trial. Valerie Caproni, Ben Campbell, and Jim Kinsley knew the evidence exonerated Elizabeth Sanders. But true justice was, at this stage, beside the point. They had personally promised to indict Elizabeth Sanders if her husband did not give up his sources. Now, they were fulfilling that promise.

Kinsley's notes also reveal that Stacey called James Sanders after dropping off the samples at FedEx: "He didn't know I got it so I told him [it was] in [the] mail. He [Sanders] was excited." Nor did Sanders know that Stacey was going to obtain two samples: "He [Sanders] wanted him [Stacey] to scrap [sic] off [residue], but [the residue] wouldn't scrap [sic] off so S[tacey] took two strips. Then FedEx that day [to Sanders in Williamsburg]."

Residue from a missile is not part of an aircraft. The tortured case the government was trying to make would seem to have fallen apart with Kinsley's notation. This statement should also have resulted in exhaustive court-ordered testing of the residue prior to trial. By its very nature, however, such testing would have questioned the ethics, even the legality, of the Justice Department's strategy. This was not to be. It would be beyond the normal. Instead, the judge mandated that the residue be considered part of the aircraft.

At the second meeting with Caproni, June 26, 1997, Stacey admitted the following: "He was concerned that himself or TWA might get thrown off the investigation if he was caught handing over documentation to Sanders. He stated that he didn't think he was breaking the law but he was concerned about his image."[18]

This statement, and the documentary evidence held by the Justice Department, constituted a prohibition from the further "targeting" and harassment of the Sanderses, but only if the rule of law actually applied in the case. Again, the normalcy doctrine gave Justice cover to circumvent the rule of law, a useful maneuver when the lawfulness of one's own department is under attack.

FBI field notes at the June 26 meeting, which bear repetition, say Terrell Stacey removed the two strips of foam rubber of his own volition:

> He [James Sanders] wanted me to scrap (sic) off [flakes of residue] but [the flakes] wouldn't scrap [sic] off so I took 2 strips, then FedEx that day.

The Justice Department and FBI had a serious problem with that statement. Stacey had admitted that the removal of the foam rubber from the plane was his decision, and his alone. Yes, Sanders wanted missile "residue." But no, Sanders had never asked for any part of the airplane and had no idea that Stacey would take the "strips" of his own accord.

The government's line of attack would falter if Stacey's statement were not altered. The only criminal section the Justice Department had to work with was Title 49, section 1155(b): "A person that knowingly and without authority removes, conceals, or withholds a part of a civil aircraft involved in an accident, or property on the aircraft at the time of the accident, shall be fined under Title 18, imprisoned for not more than 10 years, or both." If the flakes of residue "he wanted me to scrap[e] off" were from a missile's exhaust or the by-product of a warhead detonation, the flakes did not come under the definition of Title 49, section 1155(b). They were not "part of a civil aircraft," nor were they "property on the aircraft" (that is, luggage or cargo). This may seem like a small distinction, but Justice knew otherwise.

The government would have to prove that the residue Sanders had tested was glue from the seats. Putting aside the pettiness of such an effort, the FBI already knew the residue was not 3M 1357 HP adhesive.

Moreover, Stacey had clearly said that he, on his own, had made the decision to remove two pieces of foam rubber. This admission refuted any possible conspiracy. Stacey's motive was clear. He had provided a journalist with forensic evidence in the hope that it would reveal the true cause of Flight 800's demise and unravel the cover-up that prevented the truth from surfacing.

Allowing the prosecution of the Sanderses to descend into such territory was simply too dangerous. The normalcy doctrine would save the day each step of the way. Although, for instance, the government officials had acknowledged that its earlier subpoena for Mr. Sanders's telephone records was illegal, it issued a second subpoena for Mr. Sanders's telephone records in August 1997.[19] Again, they did this without notifying him or complying fully with the provisions of the regulations adopted in 1980.

Sanders was undeterred. Continuing his probe into the investigation of the crash of Flight 800, he filed a number of Freedom of Information Act (FOIA) requests from August through October 1997. On November 18, 1997, Sanders told a *New York Post* reporter, Al Guart, that he had used FOIA to investigate possible wrongdoing by government officials, including James Kallstrom, James Kinsley, Valerie Caproni, and Benton Campbell. Guart claimed that he knew Caproni and would get a response from her.

The next morning, Guart's exclusive story appeared on page two of the *New York Post:* "Evidence-Swipers May Face Fed Charges."[20] This being the day after the FBI closed its criminal case on TWA 800, Justice could now focus on those who threatened the government's fiction as to why the case had been closed.

In the *Post* article Caproni went public for the first time with the government's chillingly effective strategy to silence James Sanders. As she described it, the Justice Department had no obligation to follow the subpoena rules for reporters because it found no basis for concluding that Sanders was acting as a reporter. The article also stated that, according to "law-enforcement sources," the Sanderses would probably be charged in the next two weeks. On this point at least, the officials were accurate.

FBI agent Jim Kinsley wrote and signed the affidavit in support of application for an arrest warrant that would be used to bring the Sanderses into custody.

Although the residue could not be a focal point of the judicial proceedings, it had to be included in the warrant. Remember that Bernard Loeb had told a congressional committee that "there is no such thing as a red residue trail" and that the reddish-orange substance was on "virtually all of the seats in the forward part of the airplane." The arrest warrant suggested otherwise:

> From Row 17 to Row 28 of the seating area there is a reddish residue on the metallic frame and backs of the passenger seats. The residue is manifested most strongly on seats from Rows 17 through 19. According to TWA maintenance records, the seats on which the residue can be seen had been refurbished, and glue was used to affix fabric and plastic to the metallic frames of the seats. Other rows of the airplane were not similarly refurbished, or were made by different manufacturers, and a similar residue cannot be seen on them.[21]

"Rows 17 to 28" had a history. When the investigation was still serious, this was the area of keenest interest, the area recognized to have first blown off the plane, the area in which the PETN and RDX had been found. "Rows 17 through 19" were exactly the rows Stacey had identified as the path of the residue trail. Loeb's blithe generalization did not square with the FBI's evidence. The government was having a hard time keeping its story straight. The arrest warrant continued:

> On March 10, 1997, the *Press-Enterprise*, a newspaper in Riverside, California, published a series of articles asserting that a U.S. Navy missile was responsible for the crash of TWA 800. In those articles, the newspaper extensively quoted the defendant JAMES SANDERS. SANDERS was identified in the articles as a former police officer, accident investigator, and Virginia-based writer.

As it happens, the U.S. Navy is not mentioned in the article published by the *Press-Enterprise* on March 10, 1997. More important, Kinsley misrepresented Sanders' profession. On page one of the article, above the fold, Sanders was identified as an "investigative reporter." This page-one identification posited First Amendment protection and precluded the Justice Department and FBI from legally harassing the Sanderses, but they did so anyway. Kinsley placed this information in the warrant presumably to mislead the grand jury. Keep in mind that the grand jury is a captive audience of the prosecution—in this case, Justice Department lawyers Valerie Caproni and Ben Campbell.

The arrest warrant continued in its summary of the *Press-Enterprise* article:

> The defendant JAMES SANDERS stated that the seat parts from TWA 800 were covered with a "red residue" and that chemical analysis of the residue was consistent with solid rocket fuel. The defendant JAMES SANDERS concluded that the test results, coupled with a "residue trail" which his source allegedly told him traveled from one side of the cabin to the other along the seats inside the aircraft, confirmed that a missile had punched through TWA 800 and caused it to explode.

In fact, Sanders did not tell reporters from the *Press-Enterprise* that the elements detected in the chemical test were "consistent with" solid rocket fuel. Sanders gave the *Press-Enterprise* a copy of the elemental test from West Coast Analytical Services. The paper found its own sources that said the residue was consistent with exhaust from a solid-fuel rocket. Sanders found additional sources, independent of the *Press-Enterprise*, who gave the same analysis. The *Press-Enterprise* also sent Sanders's written analysis and documents to a former government crash expert who concurred with Sanders's conclusions. All of this was, in detail, presented in the March 10 article.

Perhaps the warrant's most flagrant misrepresentation was its claim that Sanders relied exclusively on the "test results" and "residue trail" to conclude that "a missile had punched through TWA 800 and caused it to explode." The very subtitle of the article, "Debris Pattern Provides Key to Mystery," conspicuously documents a separate, more prominent thesis. The article elaborates: "The pattern of the first wreckage to hit the water, combined with evidence of missile-propellant residue in the Boeing 747, clearly indicates that a missile carrying an inert warhead smashed through the airliner, author and investigative reporter James Sanders has concluded."[22]

The residue elements and residue trail across the first three rows of seats to exit the aircraft were part of a much broader picture painted by the NTSB debris-field document that Terrell Stacey removed from the hangar and gave Sanders to analyze. That 140-page document so seriously undermined the NTSB "mechanical" hypothesis that the government has never released it.[23]

In Patricia Milton's account, James Kallstrom asked the Justice Department whether theorists like Sanders might have "violated the law by fabricating information and obstructing justice."[24] This request was presumably too blatant an assault on the First Amendment even for the Clinton Justice Department. Still, Kallstrom's thinking guided the arrest warrant. Its essential claim was that Sanders "misrepresented" the residue elements, saying that the elements, and the elements alone, provided "conclusive" proof that Flight 800 was brought down by a missile. Sanders, of course, had said no such thing.

The warrant also asserted that the head of West Coast Analytical Services, Jack Northington, "indicated that he told JAMES SANDERS that the tests were not conclusive that solid rocket propellant was present." But here is what Northington actually told a Los Angeles–based FBI agent, who wrote an honest account of the interview: "Northington then prepared and sent a final report to SANDERS which contained the scientific results of their analysis. The reports made no specific conclusion about the significance of any of the substances found."[25]

Kinsley had translated the neutral "no specific conclusion" into the negative "not conclusive." Kallstrom continued the disinformation campaign in a press release that accompanied the arrest warrants. "Despite the laboratory test results," read the release, "James Sanders misrepresented those results in media reports for which he was a source."[26]

The *Press-Enterprise* articles clearly stated that the elemental analysis was "consistent with" a solid-fuel missile—not "conclusive" proof. Likewise, Sanders's book, *The Downing of TWA Flight 800,* presents the reader with a list of the elements detected in the West Coast Analytical Services test and provides the percentage of each element. "All these elements," wrote Sanders, "are consistent with a list of the residue from a solid fuel missile."[27]

Terrell Stacey's file containing grand jury testimony and field agent notes from Stacey interviews, obtained under discovery, has multiple references to his expressed irritation with Sanders and *Press-Enterprise* reporter David Hendrix because they insisted on using "consistent with" when talking about the residue test results. He repeated that frustration when testifying before the grand jury:

Stacey: At some point [Sanders] indicated that he had the results from the lab and that someone had indicated that it was "consistent with" rocket propellant.

Q: What was your reaction to that?

Stacey: I was somewhat skeptical and wanted more definitive information. It didn't have a lab report, and I was skeptical of the term "consistent with."

Q: Was there any discussion again about the results of the laboratory analysis?

Stacey: At that time? I believe again we talked about the term "consistent with" rather than fact, you know.

Q: And what did you tell him about that?

Stacey: Well, that again I didn't like that term "consistent with." A lot of things could be consistent with other things.

This paradoxical questioning would be mildly amusing were the stakes not so high. The prosecution attacked Sanders inside the grand jury room for not overstating the strength of his evidence and attacked him outside for overstating it.

Despite Kallstrom's buildup, neither Northington nor his organization ever claimed any expertise in the area of missile exhaust. "We could probably detect residues from rocket propellant," Northington would write to Sanders, "if we knew what the rocket propellant contained." The FBI had obtained this e-mail on March 11, 1997, from West Coast Analytical Services. Its agent knew Northington was not an expert on the subject of missile exhaust, not remotely so. Sanders knew this, too, which is why he never asked for a conclusion in the first place.

As of December 5, 1997, the FBI was still playing games with the evidence. Kinsley's arrest narrative notes that Northington "provided the FBI agent with two bottles containing segments of the material he received from the defendant JAMES SANDERS." What Kinsley failed to note was that in addition to the two tested pieces, the FBI had also recovered an unused piece of residue. This, Sanders would only learn at his trial sixteen months later. But the implications are undeniable. The government had the ability to test the residue Sanders had received from Stacey. There was no need for the charade Dr. Birky of the NTSB went through with NASA. This was not, however, a convenient fact. It would stay concealed.

In a world of carrots and sticks, the oleaginous Peter Goelz got the carrot. On December 4, 1997, he was named managing director of the NTSB. In the early morning hours of the next day, December 5, the Sanderses got the stick. The FBI released the arrest warrant for James and Elizabeth Sanderses to the press. The FBI's New York office Internet site proudly, and almost comically, headlined the story, "Conspiracy theorist and wife charged with theft of parts from airplane." So proud was the FBI of this arrest that it animated the headline and had it scroll across the top of the page.[28]

THE Sanderses were not charged with theft of parts from an airplane. They were charged with conspiracy, aiding and abetting a source to obtain parts of an airplane, namely "residue." Their motive was transparently not to steal these parts but to test evidence, evidence of potential federal lawlessness.

The major media, however, found it comfortable to report the Sanderses' transgression as theft. The *New York Times* would later note without a hint of irony or outrage that "the Sanderses were charged under a Federal law enacted in 1996 after a truck driver in Florida was accused of taking a piece of the wreckage of the May 1996 ValuJet crash as a souvenir."[29] In fact, the law had been enacted in the 1960s to discourage souvenir hunters from carting away wreckage at a crash scene before authorities arrived. But the motive behind the act was, as described, to discourage scavengers. The *Times* also noted that the Sanderses' attorney "tried yesterday to portray the matter as a free press issue," but the very word *tried* suggests the *Times*' lack of sympathy.

Newsday's on-line headline cut right to the chase: "Missile theorist, wife and pilot accused of stealing." The copy reinforced the point, again without a hint of sympathy or understanding for what Sanders and Stacey were hoping to accomplish:

> Authorities said Stacey stole the swatch at the behest of Sanders' wife, Elizabeth, who is on leave as a senior trainer of flight attendants for TWA. With Stacey's cooperation, the author and his wife also were charged Friday with stealing "parts of a civil aircraft involved in an accident," a felony, according to a criminal complaint filed in U.S. District Court in Brooklyn.[30]

The *Newsday* article summarizes the government case. The official spin: Not only was Elizabeth Sanders deeply involved, but Terrell Stacey was also a reluctant participant.

Stacey said he balked at first when Sanders asked him for samples of "a red-dish residue that appeared on seats in the cabin of TWA 800," the FBI documents said. Stacey, however, eventually agreed to provide the residue along with seat fabric it was on after getting a telephone call from Elizabeth Sanders.

Through this selective misinformation, the FBI was turning the potential Long Island jury pool against the Sanderses. The protagonist of the *Newsday* article was none other than James Kallstrom. "This criminal investigation is far from over," *Newsday* quotes Kallstrom as saying. "These defendants are charged with not only committing a serious crime, they have also increased the pain already inflicted on the victims' families." The irony, of course, is that Kallstrom had called off the criminal investigation into the destruction of Flight 800 just a few weeks before. The Sanders affair was the kind of "serious" case he could actually solve.

The timing of this charge could not have been accidental. Three days later, the NTSB would hold its first public hearing on TWA Flight 800. The message from Kallstrom was clear: Challenging this administration had consequences. To make sure the hearings did not embarrass the FBI, Kallstrom sent the NTSB's Jim Hall an extraordinary four-page letter that same week.

"Until the NTSB has definitively determined an accidental cause for the crash," he wrote, "I believe it is prudent to withhold from public disclosure or discussion the identities of witnesses and the raw investigative details of the criminal investigation." These "details" included all eyewitness testimony, the showing of the CIA animation of the crash, and all talk of explosive residue, including the residue streak that Sanders had investigated. Discussion of these topics, Kallstrom continued disingenuously, "could complicate our efforts if the criminal investigation were to be reactivated."[31]

Jim Hall acquiesced immediately. He canceled the testimony that was, in fact, designed to discredit the eyewitnesses, pulled the showing of the CIA animation, and, as *Newsday* related, "also agreed to cut discussions of explosive residue found on the plane's seats."[32] It did not much matter. Months before, *Newsday* and the other media had casually swallowed the government's line that any residue found on the seats was glue.[33]

The Sanderses surrendered at the FBI field office in Uniondale, Long Island, on December 9, 1997. FBI agent Jim Kinsley was in charge of the arrest detail. He personally handled James Sanders's booking procedure while two young FBI agents booked Elizabeth Sanders. In response to

Elizabeth Sanders's question, the one female agent noted that all transport decisions—including decisions on handcuffs—were left to the senior agent, Kinsley. Kinsley's subsequent performance suggests that there was more at stake here than the exercise of justice.

When the younger male agent suggested that the Sanderses remain at the more comfortable FBI office until it was time to go to court, Kinsley rejected the suggestion. The same agent then asked that handcuffs not be used. Again Kinsley said "no." The young agent argued for handcuffing the Sanderses in the front. Kinsley said no again. Finally, the young agent asked that the transport cars be moved to the ramp, away from the media. Kinsley denied him once more.[34]

The agents bound the Sanderses' hands behind their backs and paraded them through the throng of reporters and photographers to FBI vehicles in the parking lot. Upon arrival at the Federal Eastern District Court at Uniondale, Kinsley ordered the cars to stop in front of the courthouse, hard by a cluster of cameramen and reporters. When the driver proposed to use a ramp in the rear, as was customary, Kinsley said no again. It was time for a second "perp walk," a technique long since declared unconstitutional.

This time, however, a bailiff who insisted on proper procedure would thwart Kinsley. In fact, the bailiff would have to request three times that the cars go to the ramp in the rear before Kinsley yielded.

Three hours later the agents took the Sanderses from their cells and again bound their hands behind their backs. They led them up a flight of stairs to the main courthouse foyer. Kinsley then paraded the Sanderses on still another "perp walk" through the courthouse.

"The day I was arrested was surreal," recalls Elizabeth Sanders. "It was something I would never thought could happen to an innocent, normal person in the United States."

JUST before Kinsely could continue the parade into the crowded courtroom, James Sanders heard a male voice say, "I've had enough of this BS." This unknown FBI agent then took control away from Kinsley and removed the handcuffs before the grateful Sanderses entered the courtroom.

A not-guilty plea was entered for both Sanderses, and the magistrate announced a $50,000 bail. Shortly thereafter the legal proceeding ended, and the reporters filed out the front door to await the Sanderses.

It stunned the Sanderses that none among the media managed to frame even one First Amendment question. When Jeff Schlanger, the Sanderses' lawyer at that time, attempted to bring this issue into focus, *Newsday*'s Bob Kessler began to argue the government line. He insisted that the Justice Department had not found sufficient evidence to declare James Sanders a journalist entitled to First Amendment protection. Another reporter asked Schlanger why his client did not immediately return the residue and turn Stacey in to the FBI. James Sanders shook his head in disbelief. Was it only a generation ago that the *New York Times* made Daniel Ellsberg a hero by publishing the purloined and fully classified *Pentagon Papers*?

For Elizabeth Sanders, the worst had yet to come. Shortly after her arrest in December 1997, the government demanded that TWA fire her. On December 17, 1997, Chris Rhoads, general manager for the TWA In-flight Services, Eastern Region, initiated the following letter to Elizabeth Sanders:

> This letter will serve as a directive to meet with me at 11:00 on Monday December 22, 1997, room 215, Hangar 12, JFK, to discuss your suspected theft and unauthorized possession of company and/or government property. Due to the status of this matter, you have been suspended from flight and pay status.

Terrell Stacey had been removed from flight status but remained on the payroll. He had pleaded guilty to theft. The government did not demand that he be fired. Elizabeth Sanders had pleaded not guilty and was removed from the payroll. Later she was denied medical benefits as well.

This letter gave Elizabeth only five days from the day it was written to fly to New York. TWA mailed it to the Sanderses' home address, knowing Liz was not at that location. The letter was not certified. The "copy to" portion of the letter said it was also forwarded to Jeff Schlanger, the Sanderses' attorney in New York. He never received it. Elizabeth found out about the letter only because she called the TWA flight attendants union about another matter and was immediately put in touch with the union attorney. She advised the attorney that she was not involved in the investigation of TWA Flight 800, that she had been framed and was going to fight the injustice in court.

After the call, Elizabeth Sanders headed directly to the airport and flew to New York. Escorted by her attorney, she appeared in person to face down those within TWA who had tried to summarily fire her at the government's request. The meeting lasted all of two minutes. TWA's Chris Rhoads, obviously shocked to see Elizabeth, handed her a written statement from the TWA Legal Department. It had fear written all over it.

The letter recapped "the theft of fabric swatches" and the "unauthorized testing" of that fabric by "your husband." The letter repeated the FBI canard that the test results were erroneous and that the results "caused the victims' families additional anguish and grief."

As a result of Elizabeth's actions, continued the letter, "TWA's status as a party to the NTSB investigation into F800 was and remains under the threat of expulsion." If this were not hurtful enough, TWA added one last, gratuitous blow:

> We also suspect that your actions were motivated not out of a desire to seek the truth, but were instead motivated by the financial gain and notoriety you and your husband stood to gain by publication of the book.

Although the outcome seemed preordained, TWA would hold a hearing "to determine what role you played in these events."

The TWA statement amazed the Sanderses. James Sanders had met with a TWA executive shortly before the March 10, 1997, newspaper article revealed the gist of his investigation. In a meeting of several hours, Sanders laid out his case and described all the documents in detail. He explained the reddish-orange residue, its removal from the hangar, elemental testing, and what the test meant. He told the TWA executive that an additional sample was available to counter any government disinformation. Within days Sanders had received a message that the head of the TWA Legal Department at St. Louis Corporate Headquarters had been briefed and was preparing a civil suit against the federal government, to be filed if Sanders's allegations placed the government on the defensive.

Nine months later, the world had changed. Struggling to survive, TWA had buckled under obvious government pressure. Elizabeth Sanders had to go.

CHAPTER 9

THE BIG LIE

November 18, 1997, marked the official end of the criminal investigation of TWA 800. On that fateful day, at a climactic press conference, the FBI announced for the first time that "no evidence has been found that would indicate that a criminal act was the cause of the tragedy of Flight 800."[1] It was on this day, too, that any serious media interest in the case died. Not that anyone noticed. Reporting had been lifeless since the spurious dog-training story more than a year earlier.

What made November 18 so memorable—and so controversial—was less the FBI press conference than the fifteen-minute, CIA-produced video that concluded the day, one of the most spectacular and successful deceptions ever visited on the American people.

As with all perceived successes, everyone wanted credit. A *New Yorker* profile post–September 11 gave the honors to the late FBI antiterrorist expert John O'Neill.[2] The *New Yorker*'s source was counterterrorism security chair Richard Clarke. According to Clarke, O'Neill insisted that TWA 800 was out of range of the most-likely shoulder-fired missile, the Stinger. O'Neill believed that the "ascending flare" must have been something else, like "the ignition of leaking fuel from the aircraft." Clarke also credits

O'Neill with persuading the CIA to create a visual re-creation of the same.

Not unexpectedly, Patricia Milton gives credit largely to Kallstrom. It was he who requested the CIA to examine "the 270 eyewitness accounts of a missile-like streak in the sky." Kallstrom, in fact, appears in the video, quite sympathetically at that.[3]

The CIA takes credit for the video's most memorable revelation, namely that the witnesses saw not just fuel, but the plane itself after the explosion—*ascending!* This insight came to the CIA like an epiphany. The one analyst traced the moment of awareness to the precise hour of 10 P.M. on December 30, 1996. Said he, "There was a realization, having all the data laid out in front of me, that you can explain what the eyewitnesses are seeing with only the burning aircraft."[4] For all the talk of cooperation, Kallstrom lent witness statements to the CIA in small, frustrating batches, starting with "30 or 40" out of more than seven hundred. The analyst, in fact, came to his startling conclusion after reviewing only about 12 percent of the interview statements, many of these hasty and slapdash in the first place. The CIA did no interviews of its own.[5]

"Within 24 hours" of its realization, a CIA analyst called the FBI to share the news. Over the next ten months the CIA remained in continuous contact with the FBI as the analysts "documented and refined" their work. This included a formal FBI briefing on February 6, 1997, and a letter to James Kallstrom six weeks later on March 24. At a later briefing, on October 22, 1997, Kallstrom "expressed his desire to use the video" at the upcoming press conference that would effectively announce the FBI's withdrawal from the case.

To help "refine" the CIA's work in progress, the FBI reinterviewed certain witnesses at the CIA's request. A travel industry employee from North Carolina, referred to in the FBI 302s—the official witness statements—as "witness number 73," was one of them.

In her first interview, on July 30, 1996, she had told an FBI agent that she was standing on the beach when she noticed a 747 "level off."[6] The flight pattern caught this experienced observer's attention because she thought the altitude too low for the plane to be doing this. With her eye still on the plane, she watched in awe as a "red streak" with a "light gray smoke trail" moved up towards the airline at a forty-five-degree angle. Then, the "red streak went past the right side and above the aircraft before arcking [sic] back down toward the aircrafts [sic] right wing." She saw "the front of the aircraft separate from the back" and watched in mounting horror as the burning pieces of the debris fell from the aircraft. She provided a drawing that showed the scenario in some detail, including the "upside-down Nike swoosh" that ended at the plane's right wing.

Nine months later, in April of 1997, the FBI interviewed Witness 73 once more. The new account added a few details useful to the CIA's rewrite. This time, the witness admitted she had had two cocktails sometime earlier in the evening. This time the FBI quoted her as saying that the plane "appeared to ascend for approximately ten seconds" just before the explosion.[7] The FBI also alleged that she could not remember which wing the object struck.

"Multiple witnesses tell me agents on rare second or third visits to persons who saw ascending objects tried to get the witnesses to change their original stories," wrote Cmdr. William Donaldson to FBI Director Louis Freeh. "Many of these people are now afraid of and disgusted with their own government."[8] Honest investigators within the NTSB's witness group were as alarmed by these refinements as Donaldson was. They requested "a fuller explanation" from the CIA to help them understand the agency's evaluation of witness statements, the evaluation captured in the video.

One highly useful document sheds light on the video and the motivations behind it. It is the word-for-word transcript of the NTSB's conversation with the CIA.[9] That this April 1999 meeting took a year and a half to arrange suggests that no one at the top was eager to make it happen. At the table for the NTSB were managers Bernard Loeb and David Mayer as well as five industry members of the witness group. Representing the CIA were the deputy director of the Office of Transnational Issues, the two analysts who did the work on the video, and the agency's general counsel. "We don't go anywhere without our lawyer," joked the deputy director to an assembled crowd that included other officials from the CIA and the NTSB, including its managing director, Peter Goelz.

The video under discussion that day has all the grace of a Cold War jeremiad on atomic fallout. The music is ominous, the narration overbearing, the graphics cheesy and anachronistic. "The following program was produced by the Central Intelligence Agency," says the narrator at the outset, with more pride in ownership than seems right for any government agency, let alone a secret one.[10]

The narrator explains that there have been three major theories as to what brought down TWA 800: bomb, missile, or mechanical failure. Of particular concern to investigators were reports "from dozens of eyewitnesses" who saw objects in the sky usually described as flares or fireworks. "Was it a missile?" asks the narrator. "Did foreign terrorists destroy the aircraft?" The answer is quick in coming. No, "what the witnesses saw was a Boeing 747 in various stages of crippled flight."

To clarify the issue, the narrator embarks on a lengthy narration about "sound propagation analysis." To help the audience understand the concept, he uses lightning and thunder as a model. That the analysis manages to be both confusing and condescending at the same time is a testament to its sophistry. In any event, the CIA wants the audience to come away with one understanding. And this is underlined, literally, on-screen:

<u>The Eyewitnesses Did Not See a Missile.</u>

CIA analysts argue that given the time it takes sound to travel, and given their calculations, all the sightings of "greatest concern," those of ascending or streaking objects, "took place after the aircraft exploded." To reinforce this point, the analysts imply that all key witnesses heard the same initiating sound, a sound that can be precisely gauged.

The truth is that many key eyewitnesses heard nothing at all. They were either on planes or helicopters or boats or were blocked by the sounds of the ocean or were simply out of range. One FBI 302 after another reaffirms this point. Witness 468, for instance, was out fishing when he saw the explosion. According to the FBI, "No sounds, smoke or other activity alerted him to the crash."[11] Witness 503 saw a flare come off the horizon. "Suddenly the flare expanded into a much larger fireball. There was no sound heard at this point." Pivotal Witness 649, Joseph Delgado, "heard no noise." Witness 562, on a boat three miles east of the Fire Island inlet, watched as a flare "rose 'straight up' from the ocean and was in flight for approximately ten seconds." But 562 "did not see an airplane nor did he hear any sound associated with the fireball." For key eyewitness Dwight Brumley on US Air 217, the first explosion was "very noticeable and easy to see." But Brumley "did not observe a launch site, nor did he hear any sounds associated with what he saw." There are scores more accounts just like these.

As unreliable as sight is, sound is notoriously more so. Moreover, for obvious reasons, there could be no hint that the first sounds heard by some witnesses might well have been that of a missile launch or even a sonic boom out of the range of the cockpit voice recorder. Worse, all these calculations are pegged on a "loud noise" recorded on the cockpit voice recorder just before it stopped. As shall be seen, the custody issues surrounding the black boxes raise sufficient questions to doubt their reliability as a gauge of anything.

Just what that "loud noise" was, however, troubled the NTSB witness team, as is clear from the transcript. The CIA had told the team that this first explosion was powerful enough to shake a seventy-ton bridge eleven miles away. "You could feel the concussion like a shock wave," reported witness Mike Wire, who was on the bridge.[12] "The problem I'm having a little bit," team member Dennis Roderiques asked the analysts, "is that the center tank explosion is categorized as a low-order explosion." A low-order explosion would not shake a bridge a mile away, let alone eleven.

Dodging the question, Analyst 1 for the CIA countered—correctly— that an explosion of a missile warhead was "not nearly loud enough to do that sort of thing." Robert Young of the witness group was not satisfied. He had researched the issue on his own. He concluded from his research that "to produce the kinds of sound we're talking about, would be a minimum of 1,000 pounds of TNT at that many miles." He said incredulously, "I don't see how we can get a center tank to make that sound."

As is evident in the tone of this and other exchanges, witness group members lacked any real authority, and they knew it.

Like Roderiques, Young asked his question deferentially. When no one picked up this train of thought, the conversation drifted away. Neither side chose to ask the one even more salient question—if neither a missile warhead nor an exploding fuel tank could come close to making that sound, what could? If pursued, this question had the potential to break open the entire investigation, but it was years too late for that. More on this point will be discussed later.

There was a second, related problem with the sound that the NTSB did not take up with the CIA. According to the video, the "loud sound" captured on the cockpit voice recorder represented the beginning of the "onboard explosion." Although the CIA's sound propagation analysis is pegged precisely to that initiating sound, the force behind that sound does not breach the fuselage until it blows off the front third of the plane "four seconds" later. As shall be seen, those four seconds would take on a life of their own.

Fortunately for the CIA, these concerns did not trouble the major media. The CNN report that follows captures the essence of the video and the complacency with which it was received in November 1997.

The FBI said the 14-minute tape showed how all 244 witnesses to the crash saw the breakup of the Boeing 747 in the seconds after it exploded over the Atlantic Ocean, and not the explosion itself.

What some witnesses thought was a missile hitting the plane was actually burning, leaking fuel from the jet after its front part had already broken off, FBI officials said.[13]

The video encompasses two trompe l'oeils: the burning fuel and the ascending plane. CNN runs with the O'Neill theory, that witnesses saw burning fuel that only appeared to be ascending. The CNN report ignores the ascending plane theory altogether, apparently led in that direction by the FBI. What makes this particularly curious is that the video only implies the leaking fuel theory. It talks of "a trailing cascade of flames" falling to the horizon and shows as much, but never says that this was what the witnesses saw. The ascending plane, by contrast, was the video's showstopper. "Just after the aircraft exploded it pitched up abruptly and climbed several thousand feet from its last recorded altitude of about 13,800 feet to a maximum altitude of about 17,000 feet," says the narrator in that dramatically re-created stretch of the video.

As the narrator explains, the significant, sudden loss of mass from the front of the aircraft caused the rapid pitch up and climb. "The explosion, although very loud," continues the narration in a breathless bit of *chutzpah*, "was not seen by any known eyewitness." *Not one*. Supposedly, what they saw instead was a rocketing, noseless 747 trailing fire. It was this very light that the eyewitnesses had "repeatedly described as an ascending white light resembling a flare or firework." This claim needs to be emphasized. According to the CIA, not a single known eyewitness had seen the initiating explosion. The video also notes that many of the witnesses who thought they had witnessed a missile strike were "puzzled" because they had not seen Flight 800 itself. The plane should have been visible, the CIA argues. "The eyewitnesses almost certainly saw only the burning aircraft without realizing it."

To show the deep and utter dishonesty of these arguments one need only read the FBI summary of Witness 73, which the CIA analysts had at hand:

> She never took her eyes off the aircraft during this time. At the instant the smoke trail [of the ascending object] ended at the aircraft's right wing, she heard a loud sharp noise which sounded like a firecracker had just exploded at her feet. She then observed a fire at the aircraft followed by one

or two secondary explosions which had a deeper sound. She then observed
the front of the aircraft separate from the back. She then observed burning
pieces of debris falling from the aircraft.[14]

This witness saw the aircraft, saw a distinct ascending object hit the aircraft near the right wing, saw several explosions, and then saw the nose separate. Every one of her observations proved accurate. The sound "at her feet"
was probably that of a missile's launch, the ascending object.

If the testimony of Witness 73 can be challenged given her lack of expertise
in weapon systems, the testimony of helicopter pilot Maj. Fritz Meyer cannot.
"What I saw explode in the sky was definitely military ordnance," he said. "I have
enough experience with it to know what it looks like. I saw one, two, three, four
explosions before I saw the fireball. So the fuel in this aircraft eventually exploded.
But the explosion of the fuel was the last event, not the initiating event. The initiating event was a high-velocity explosion, not fuel. It was ordnance."[15]

Nor are these two witnesses exceptional. Scores of witnesses reported seeing bright white explosions before they saw the fireball. Several saw the nose
break off before investigators knew that this had even happened. Exactly how
many eyewitnesses saw the ascending plane was in some dispute. The CIA
cites only 21 of the 244 witnesses. But it became clear, as the questioning of
the CIA wore on, that there were fewer still. Roderiques sighed in frustration,
"If it's only one or two of them, it's not representative of all of them."

Analyst 1 pulled out his trump card, his key witness, the man who had
seen everything: "That [the ascending plane] is something that a few eyewitnesses saw. The guy on the bridge saw that."

ON the evening of July 17, 1996, when Mike Wire quit the switch gear
room on Beach Lane Bridge for a breath of fresh air, he had no idea he would
be strolling onto center stage of the most explosive political cover-up in
American history.

The union millwright from suburban Philadelphia had been working all
that day on this Westhampton bridge. At day's end, he leaned his burly six-
foot-six-inch frame against the rail on the southwest end of the bridge and
looked out towards the sea beyond the house line. At that moment a white
light caught his eye. On July 30, 1996, during a ninety-minute interview at
his Pennsylvania home, he told an FBI agent exactly what he saw. Here is
how the agent recorded the conversation on his 302:

Wire saw a white light that was traveling skyward from the ground at approximately a 40 degree angle. Wire described the white light as a light that sparkled and thought it was some type of fireworks. Wire stated that the white light "zig zagged" [sic] as it traveled upwards, and at the apex of its travel the white light "arched over" and disappeared from Wire's view . . . Wire stated the white light traveled outwards from the beach in a south-southeasterly direction.[16]

After the light disappeared, the 302 continues, Wire "saw an orange light that appeared to be a fireball." This description, by the way, matches the description Wire gave the FBI a few days earlier by phone. At the end of the 302, the agent added the now ironic notation, Wire "wishes to cooperate in any way he can and can be recontacted at any time."

Wire did not parrot these details. He had left Long Island for home the next morning before any story might have circulated. Had a coworker not alerted the FBI to what Wire had seen, Wire would have played no role in the drama to follow. After his interviews, Wire, the happily married father of three grown daughters, returned to his workaday life in Pennsylvania. Having little interest in politics and less in the Internet, he did not follow the controversy swirling around the crash. Wire did, however, see the CIA re-creation of the flight presented by the FBI in November of 1997, at least the abbreviated version shown on the news. He presumed this to be some temporary scheme to pacify the public and was fully unaware of his own role in it.

As Analyst 1 implied, the CIA chose to build its case squarely on Mike Wire's testimony. "FBI investigators determined precisely where the eyewitness was standing," says the CIA narrator of Wire in the transcript, while the video shows the explosion from his perspective on Beach Lane Bridge. "The white light the eyewitness saw was very likely the aircraft very briefly ascending and arching over after it exploded rather than a missile attacking the aircraft."

To be sure, this version of events does not at all square with Wire's detailed 302 from July 1996, recorded when his memory was at its freshest. For starters, Wire "heard the first of four explosions," only "after the fireball descended behind the house."

The discrepancies only mount. The CIA animation converts Wire's "40 degree" climb to one of roughly seventy or eighty degrees. It reduces the smoke trail from three dimensions, south and east "outward from the beach," to a small, two-dimensional blip far offshore. It places the explosion noticeably to the west of where Wire clearly remembers it. Most noticeably, it fully ignores Wire's claim that the projectile ascended "skyward from the ground" and places his first sighting twenty degrees above the horizon, exactly where Flight 800 would have been.

Curiously, however, the CIA narrator repeats Wire's claim that the projectile "zig zagged," although neither the CIA nor the NTSB animations show the crippled plane in anything but a perfectly smooth, elliptical ascent. The witness group picked up on this: "The airplane in crippled flight," said Roderiques. "I have a problem knowing how it would zigzag." Analyst 1's response: "He said the light is zigzagging or twinkling." But Mike Wire did not say "twinkling." It is not in his FBI 302 and it is not likely in his vocabulary. The analyst was simply improvising.

His studied indifference to facts helps answer the larger question of how the CIA could re-create events at such obvious odds with Wire's original and detailed 302. Here is what Analyst 1 reported to the NTSB:

> [Wire] was an important eyewitness to us. And we asked the FBI to talk to him again, and they did. In his original description, he thought he had seen a firework and that perhaps that firework had originated on the beach behind the house. We went to that location and realized that if he was only seeing the airplane, that he would not see a light appear from behind the rooftop of that house. The light would actually appear in the sky. It's high enough in the sky that that would have to happen.
>
> When he was reinterviewed, he said that is indeed what happened. The light did appear in the sky. Now, when the FBI told us that, we got even more comfortable with our theory. He also described, he was asked to describe how high in the sky above the house he thought that light appeared, and he said it was as if—if you imagine a flag pole on top of the house it would be as if it were on the top or the tip of the flag pole.

This may be the single most egregious and conscious bit of dissembling in the entire investigation, one that transparently rises to the level of obstruction of justice. Here's why: The FBI never contacted Mike Wire after July 1996. Someone made up this interview out of whole cloth. Persons within either the CIA or the FBI, most likely the CIA, knowingly and flagrantly corrupted the investigation into the tragic death of 230 innocent people. If there were a follow-up interview by the FBI, there should be a follow-up 302 complete with date, place, and name of agent. The NTSB docket includes all FBI follow-up interviews such as the one with Witness 73 described above. The last interview listed for Mike Wire was dated July 30, 1996. Wire says without hesitation that July 1996 was the last time he talked to the FBI.

Further, even if the FBI had decided to call back, Wire would not have changed his testimony. He has not changed it to this day. When he came back to Westhampton to be interviewed on camera by the authors, he told and showed us exactly what he told the original agent on his 302, though he had not seen that document himself.[17]

Wire has no reason to lie. In fact, he is fully aware of the potential consequences of telling the truth. Says Wire, "I understand the implications of dealing with the big guys." But the reserved, soft-spoken Wire, who served with the U.S. Army in Korea during the Vietnam War, still believes deeply in the concept of duty. "If we don't stand up for the country," he asks rhetorically, "who will?"[18]

The question remains: Why, of all the eyewitness accounts, did the CIA choose to focus on Mike Wire? Many others had seen almost exactly what he had seen, and some of them never claimed to see the streak of light come off the horizon. Their testimonies might have been easier to finesse. Best guess: The 302s contain information about occupation and residence. There is much the CIA can infer from them about income and media access. Most of the eyewitnesses on this, the affluent south shore of Long Island, viewed the events from their boats, from their summer homes, from their yacht clubs. One eyewitness, a humble mechanic from Philadelphia, saw it on his work break before heading home the next morning.

One must give credit here where it is due. The CIA almost got away with it. Wire spent the next four years fully unaware of what had transpired. Had it not been for an odd double slipup by the FBI, he might still be unaware.

On his 302, the interviewing agent from July of 1996 neglected once to capitalize "Wire." The FBI employee that redacted the 302s before their public release failed to black out "wire" since it was a common noun, not capitalized. The 302s also included Wire's hometown. Reed Irvine of Accuracy in Media, who has been diligently pursuing this case for years, caught the discrepancy, found Wire's name in the phone book, and called. This call did not take place until the spring of 2000.[19]

And the rest, as they say, is history.

DWIGHT Brumley is about as good an eyewitness as eyewitnesses get. At the time of the crash, the no-nonsense master chief had spent twenty-five years in the U.S. Navy and was still on active duty. An electronic warfare technician, Brumley was surface-warfare qualified, a qualified CIC watch officer, and had stood watch on an aircraft carrier. "I understand relative motion, relative bearing," says Brumley, "and I thought I would have been a good witness, the only witness with that level of expertise to look down on what turned out to be TWA 800."[20]

Brumley was such a credible witness that the CIA had to deal with his testimony one way or another, so the agency made him a witness in its own dubious cause.

On the night of July 17, 1996, Brumley was flying north to Providence aboard US Air 217. He was sitting on the right side of the aircraft, looking east when he noticed "a small private airplane that was flying pretty much at a course right at the US Air flight." He was able to track it, as it came towards the aircraft and it flew "pretty much right underneath," missing the plane by only "three hundred or four hundred feet." He followed it until the fuselage and the inboard wing cut off his field of view. "My first thought," says Brumley, "that was awfully close!"

To this point the CIA animation tracks with Brumley's story. The aircraft in the animated sequence appears to be more comfortably below US Air 217, but it does appear to be a small, private plane.

According to Brumley's 302, about "ten seconds" after the small aircraft passed, he noticed what appeared to be some kind of a flare rising up off the surface. But instead of pitching over and exploding, this object was "definitely moving pretty much parallel to the US Air flight and it was moving at least as fast, perhaps even faster." In other words, the object that Brumley saw, a "projectile" as described in his 302, was traveling largely north towards Flight 800, which was traveling largely east.

The CIA video, however, transforms that flare *into* Flight 800. In this version, Brumley sees the flare "almost exactly when the Flight 800 cockpit voice recorder detected an onboard explosion." The narration continues, "His statement that the flarelike object was traveling in an east-northeasterly direction agrees with the direction of Flight 800." Upon seeing the CIA animation, Brumley was not amused. "That is not in fact what I saw," he protested adamantly. "That was not even close to being an accurate representation of what I saw."[21] The object that Brumley observed was not moving parallel to TWA 800. It was moving almost perpendicular to the doomed airliner, right towards it.

To be sure, no one followed up with Brumley. The CIA did not show him the animation to see if it squared with his observation. In fact, the CIA did not interview him at all. Neither did the NTSB. The FBI had interviewed him once and then only cursorily. At the NTSB briefing in 1999, little attention was paid to Brumley's account. It was not until the very end of the session that someone thought to ask the CIA one of the few most critical questions in the entire investigation: What plane did Brumley see?

The CIA answer is a classic: "We think it's a P-3 and we think the P-3 was at an altitude of 20,000 feet and the US AIR was at an altitude of 21,700 feet."[22]

Think? A small aircraft nearly collides with a U.S. airliner at twenty-two thousand feet less than a minute before a second U.S. airliner is blown out of the sky, and the CIA "thinks" it's a U.S. Navy P-3. The CIA had access to Brumley's 302, in which he describes it as a "small airplane," one that "would seat approximately six people." The video refers to it only as a "small aircraft" and visualizes it as such, not at all like the lumbering, four-engine, ninety-five-foot-wingspan U.S. Navy P-3, which Brumley could never have confused with a six-seater.

Patricia Milton, echoing the FBI's version of events also in 1999, makes the following observation: "Radar pinpointed the coordinates of both US AIR 217 and the small commuter plane passing near it just before Flight 800 exploded."[23] Three years after the fact, the CIA and FBI were telling different stories as to which aircraft—the Navy P-3 or a commuter craft—buzzed dangerously close to US Air 217 less than a minute before Flight 800 exploded, and *neither story* makes sense.

IF CNN missed the gist of the CIA thesis, the *New York Times* got it down right. The article from November 19, 1997, sums it up:

> Twenty-one of the witnesses said they had seen something ascend and culminate in an explosion. But the C.I.A. determined that those people had almost certainly seen the flaming fuselage, without its cockpit and front section, as it pitched upward abruptly and erupted into a fireball just after reaching its maximum altitude of about 17,000 feet.[24]

In fact, all 244 eyewitnesses had seen a streak either in ascent or arcing in towards the plane, but at the time none of this information was public. Besides, the *Times* had paid almost no attention to eyewitnesses. It had only profiled one eyewitness to date, and that was a model eyewitness volunteered by the FBI, Michael Russell. According to the *Times*, "His sober, understated story was one of only a few that investigators have judged credible." The *Times'* account from August 17, 1996, bears repeating:

> At 8:30, just before they reached the dredge, "there was a glint, quick and sharp," in the right side of his field of vision, Mr. Russell recalled. He turned toward that part of the sky, which then remained dark for a few seconds. "It's hard to know how long," he said.
>
> Moments after that initial light, which had been as abrupt as a camera flash but not as bright, he said, a ball of brilliant orange light suddenly expanded around roughly the same spot and then "seemed to fall straight down," leaving behind it a spreading column of fire that did not follow like a comet's tail but hung in the air and unfurled from its now-plummeting source.[25]

This "sober, understated story" makes three points that could in 1997 only embarrass the CIA: (1) Russell saw the initiating explosion, (2) he saw it before he heard anything, and, more troubling, (3) the burning plane "seemed to fall straight down." It did not ascend in any shape, manner, or form.

Three days prior, on August 14, the *Times* had run the following graphic account of the plane's final seconds, supplied by a trio of investigators: "The blast's force decapitated the plane, severing the cockpit and first-class cabin, which then fell into the Atlantic Ocean. The rest of the plane flew on, *descending rapidly*, and as it did thousands of gallons of jet fuel spilled out of the wings and the center fuel tank between them" [emphasis added].[26] By this date, the FBI had access to the great majority of witness statements. The astonishing fact is this: Not a single one among them describes an ascending plane. This fact needs to be repeated. None of the seven hundred–plus witnesses reported that the plane ascended.

This inconvenient fact did not much faze CNN's Christine Negroni. She would write in her account of the crash, "Although the eyewitness information did not help determine the cause of the crash, it was extremely useful towards figuring out that the plane ascended after the initial explosion."[27]

Nor did it bother the *Times*. The day after the final FBI press conference, the newspaper ran a fulsome editorial, headlined "Conspiracy Inoculation," that speaks all too clearly about the state of American journalism in the Clinton years. "The stated reason for the Federal Bureau of Investigation's extraordinary news conference yesterday was to announce the termination of its 16-month criminal investigation into the 1996 explosion of T.W.A. Flight 800," says the editorial. "Its real purpose was to persuade skeptical Americans that the explosion was not a terrorist act . . . The F.B.I. has been justly criticized in recent years for erratic and often furtive behavior, first with the Branch Davidians in Waco and then at the Ruby Ridge standoff. This time it appears to have acted with admirable thoroughness and openness."[28] The Ruby Ridge standoff, in fact, took place a year *before* Waco. These were significant events. They resulted in an armed militia movement whose recruits numbered in the tens of thousands. That the editors casually confused their order shows how little attention the people at the *New York Times* were paying.

There is no room for euphemism here, no nice way to say what the CIA and the FBI had perpetrated—namely, the boldest and most flagrant lie ever visited on the American people in peacetime. More disturbing, not a single major medium, print or broadcast, challenged it, certainly not the *New York Times*.

Beyond the editorial offices of the *Times* and the other major media, there was little enthusiasm for the CIA's ascending-plane theory. "It was entertaining," Commander Donaldson told Director Freeh, "but like most cartoons [it] grossly abused universal laws of nature. Like: Newton's law of gravitation, Newton's first and second law[s] of dynamics, Newton's law of hydro-dynamic resistance and fundamental principles of aerodynamic lift, drag, dynamic stability and jet engine mechanics."[29]

Although the video narration claimed that the ascending-plane theory was "consistent with information provided by NTSB investigators and Boeing engineers," the engineers themselves vigorously dissented. "I brought [the Flight 800 documentary *Silenced*, which the authors produced] to work today and showed it during lunch to eight of my fellow Boeing workers," wrote one engineer, a man who had spent countless hours helping analyze TWA 800 on Boeing's Cray Supercomputers. "The room was deathly quiet the entire time." He continued, "My impression then was a missile strike and it is even more so today."[30]

The Boeing Company was no more enthusiastic. "Boeing was not involved in the production of the video shown today, nor have we had the opportunity to obtain a copy or fully understand the data used to create it," said the company in its immediate response to the CIA animation. "The video's explanation of the eyewitness observations can be best assessed by the eyewitnesses themselves."[31]

How did the eyewitnesses feel about the CIA animation? "That's what I call 'the cartoon,'" said helicopter pilot Maj. Fritz Meyer. "It was totally ludicrous."

> When that airplane blew up it immediately began falling. It came right out of the sky. From the first moment it was going down. It never climbed. The thought that this aircraft could climb was laughable . . . If you shot a duck with a full load of buck it came down like that. It came down like a stone.[32]

Consulting engineer Paul Angelides, who watched the disaster from his Westhampton deck, did not equivocate. "That bore no resemblance whatsoever to what I saw," said Angelides. "If they asked me, it didn't resemble it in any way."[33]

The NTSB witness group focused on another key eyewitness whose observations did not square with the CIA's. This was David McClaine, the pilot of an Eastwinds airliner flying south at sixteen thousand feet towards Flight 800's path. Flying about fifteen or twenty miles north when he saw the plane explode, McClaine told the NTSB witness group that he could see the plane explode and then "these two streams of fire came out the bottom and they came out together." McClaine told the group that he had watched the explosion from the beginning and insisted that no part of the plane ascended.[34] "If it had ascended," Robert Young of the NTSB witness group told the CIA analysts during his interview with them, "he would have been concerned because it ascended right through his altitude."[35] When a CIA analyst tried to deflect the question, Young continued. "I think [McClaine] would have noticed it," he argued. "Your analysis has it zooming to above his altitude."

"It's a very critical point that it's not critical precisely how high that plane went," Analyst 1 bluffed before pulling out his trump card once again. "Even if the plane went up several thousand feet on the ground there's maybe one witness that saw that, this guy on the bridge."

And how did the "guy on the bridge" feel about the CIA animation? "When I first saw the scenario I thought it was strange," remarked Mike Wire, "because it was nothing like what I saw out there."[36]

ON the fifth anniversary of the crash, retired United Airlines pilot and veteran flight investigator Ray Lahr watched a Fox-TV special on TWA Flight 800 with a wry smile. Although the government-friendly report showed select bits of the CIA animation, it did not show the heart of that animation, what Lahr calls "the ridiculous zoom-climb scenario."[37] The report did not even mention the zoom-climb. Lahr was not all that surprised. The zoom-climb had been quietly shrinking for years.

Four years earlier, the FBI had introduced the magical zoom-climb to great effect. It removed the most conspicuous obstacle to a government rewrite of the TWA 800 crash, the eyewitness accounts, and paved the way for a sustainable cover-up.

If the media were prepared to sign off on the most brazen propaganda trick in American political history, Ray Lahr was not about to. Like virtually every other aviator in America, he watched the CIA animation in stunned disbelief. This scenario was impossible, and he knew it. "Anyone familiar with this type of aircraft knows intuitively that when a third of the fuselage is blown away," says Lahr, "the aircraft will be so out of balance that it will immediately stall and fall out of the sky."

But Lahr was not one to rely on intuition. He was determined to get at the hard data used to create the flight-path study, a quest that was about to turn the mild-mannered pilot into an activist. Nor was he alone. Hundreds of aviators and engineers hammered away at the government scenario through all available channels and forced its agents into a gradual retreat, if not yet into a rout. In response to pressure, the NTSB would eventually release its own, much more modest, animated version of the zoom-climb.

"They got smart when the CIA got laughed out of town by aviators," observed Commander Donaldson. "The NTSB figured they'd get away with half of it. So they said it climbed 1,700 feet. It didn't."[38]

To be sure, the NTSB animation appears to address some of the concerns raised by the CIA version. Instead of showing a climb with the plane's wings level, the NTSB video shows the roll that would be expected from the loss of the nose. The NTSB's animated Flight 800, unlike its CIA cousin, corkscrews in the sky in great sweeping loops, then noses over and falls more or less straight down.

Still, these refinements and retrenchments did not pacify Ray Lahr. Indeed, they increased his concerns. If the data used were the same in both videos, if the process were scientific, the animations should have shown the exact same flight path. The only thing that might have changed was the camera angle. If, however, the videos were created merely to misdirect the media and the public, then their producers would have few qualms about altering them to quiet inquisitive aviation professionals like Ray Lahr.

Activism does not come easily to Lahr. Comfortably retired in Malibu,

Lahr had never before thought to challenge his government. Like many a veteran of World War II, he has long trusted the aviation establishment that has helped him prosper. When he began his private inquiries into the TWA 800 crash, he expected the government to reciprocate that trust. It has not. In fact, for all its storied "openness," the federal government has blocked Lahr and other independent investigators at every turn. This obstructionism has led to an increasingly exasperated series of letters from the NTSB to an impressively determined Lahr.

What Lahr has been requesting through the Freedom of Information Act are the calculations used by the NTSB to determine how TWA 800 could climb "several thousand feet with the nose blown off." Not surprisingly, the NTSB has rejected Lahr's request for information. Its agents cite the "proprietary" nature of the data and the NTSB's lack of authority to disclose Boeing "trade secrets."[39]

This, Lahr has argued, is nonsense. The NTSB had already released the pertinent data from Boeing, now part of the public record and no longer considered proprietary. According to the Boeing data, the aircraft weighed 574,000 pounds—before nose separation. The nose weighed 79,394 pounds. The center-of-gravity was at 21.1 percent mean aerodynamic chord (MAC) before nose separation. After nose separation it was at 57.8 percent MAC. This means that the center of gravity moved from about one foot in front of the center of lift to about eleven feet behind it, a profound shift, which created a huge nose-up torque of about six million foot-pounds. As Lahr notes, "It would be like putting both people on the same side of a teeter-totter."[40] The aircraft would have abruptly pitched upwards but could not have climbed more than two hundred feet before stalling at twenty-five degrees and going into free fall.

No, Lahr was not asking for any additional data from Boeing. As he told the NTSB, "The Boeing data already released demonstrates conclusively that it was impossible for TWA 800 to climb several thousand feet with the nose blown off."[41] Besides, Boeing had never been a willing participant in this whole exercise.

According to the CIA's own calculations, the plane ascended 3,200 feet in twenty seconds. Were the plane ascending like a rocket at a ninety-degree angle, as it appears to do in the video, its vertical speed would be roughly 109 miles per hour. As physicist Dr. Thomas Stalcup has pointed out, dramatic velocity loss is to be expected. He makes the analogy to a boy on a bike pedaling uphill whose energy conversion results in a loss of speed. Only one problem: "The radar data shows that the plane didn't slow down," says

Stalcup. "If it didn't slow down it didn't climb, if it didn't climb, the witnesses didn't see the plane climb, they saw something else."[42] The CIA based its flight-path mapping on "radar data and eyewitness reports." If its analysts could fabricate witness reports, radar data had to be a piece of cake.

Stalcup, in fact, has studied the radar data more carefully than anyone inside government or out. In that the NTSB has been more forthcoming with its analysis than the CIA, Stalcup chose to chart the NTSB's projected 1,700-foot zoom-climb against the available radar data. Having done so, he takes sharp issue with the NTSB claim that the climb "matched the JFK radar data." Says Stalcup, "No simulation in that report matches the JFK radar or any other data displayed in that report." He concludes, "The radar-recorded flight path of Flight 800 indicates that the aircraft immediately descended and turned left after losing power."[43]

Ray Lahr was led to believe that the CIA conclusions about the climb were based on a computer program. "If that is correct," wrote Lahr to the NTSB, "then there is a mistake in the computer program, or there was a mistake entering data into the computer program (garbage in—garbage out)." The method used to compute this climb, Lahr contended, was not revealed to the other parties to the investigation, nor at the public hearing, nor as a part of the written accident report. "That," contended Lahr, "is not an acceptable accident investigation procedure." Lahr should know. For many years, he investigated aviation accidents on behalf of ALPA, the Air Line Pilots Association. "The only way we can discover where the mistake was made," volunteered Lahr, "is to sit down and review the process."[44]

The NTSB has not taken Lahr up on his offer. Instead, its executives have stalled, bluffed, and passed him from one to another. Lahr's most recent correspondence has been with NTSB general counsel Ronald Battocchi. "You may wonder why I persist," writes Lahr in his opening. "The reason is quite simple. It was physically impossible for TWA 800 to make that climb."[45]

The absence of any reference to that climb, visual or audio, in the FOX report amused Lahr but did not appease him. He and others will continue to persist until the case breaks open.

"There is no need to make this a court case," wrote Lahr to Battocchi. "The answer is so simple. Let's get all of the interested parties, including Boeing, around a conference table, and let's hash this thing out."

The longer Lahr persists, the clearer the realization has become: There was no real "process." An agency that can manufacture an interview can just as easily manufacture data.

CHAPTER 10

BLACK BOXES

I think most citizens in our country are aware that the first thing, when we do have an aviation tragedy, that the Board tries to recover is the so-called black box.
—JIM HALL, NTSB CHAIRMAN

"TWA eight hundred, climb and maintain one five thousand," said the anonymous voice from Boston Air Traffic Control.

"Climb thrust," responded Capt. Ralph Kevorkian. Then he turned and said, "Ollie?"

"Huh?" said the twenty-five-year-old flight engineer, Oliver Krick.

"Climb thrust," said Kevorkian. "Climb to one five thousand."

"Power's set," Krick replied.

A few seconds later, at least according to the NTSB, the cockpit voice recorder picked up an unsuspicious mechanical movement, then one last unintelligible word, and finally, a sharp noise never before recorded in a cockpit. At the reported time of 2031:12 Eastern Daylight Time, all communication ended, and presumably nothing more was heard from TWA Flight 800—not a whimper, nor a bang.[1]

The audio references to an air disaster are as important as the visual ones, sometimes more so. As might be expected, there is a story here too. It began on the night of July 17, 1996, when Long Island Congressman Michael Forbes got word that a plane had crashed off the coast of his district. Sensitive to the political nuances, Forbes had a friend drive him to the crash site, and he arrived, in fact, well before the NTSB.

At an informal meeting on the morning of July 18 at 10 A.M., a Coast Guard officer told Forbes in the presence of two of his staffers that one of the black boxes had been found. There are two such boxes. One contains the cockpit voice recorder, or CVR, the other the flight data recorder, or FDR.

Shortly after learning of the find, Forbes casually passed this information live to a CNN feed: "I heard they got one box at least."[2] Forbes's claim should have surprised no one. The black boxes were the investigation's top priority, and finding them presented no great challenge in 130 feet of water. Earlier in that same year, for instance, the Navy had located both the CVR and the FDR at the crash site of a Turkish 757 within seven hours of the crash. For the record, the Turkish boxes had settled at 7,200 feet, more than fifty-five times deeper than Flight 800's.[3]

To make finding them easier, the "black boxes" are painted bright orange and are covered with reflective strips. Each box is also equipped with an underwater locator beacon (ULB), casually called a "pinger," which is activated by contact with the water. This beacon sends out an ultrasonic pulse easily detected by sonar and acoustical locating equipment. Pleasure boaters who had rushed to the scene were reporting the distinctive "pings" from the ULB almost immediately.[4]

No sooner had Forbes told CNN of the finding, however, than the cryptic Robert Francis of the NTSB publicly denied that the boxes had been found. "We don't know where they are!" he would tell the media over the next few days.[5]

Francis's cold denials left Forbes twisting in the wind. Embarrassed and angry, Forbes wanted to find out why he had been made to appear the fool. He assigned his chief of staff, Kelly O'Meara, to investigate the discrepancy. As the chief aide to the local congressman, O'Meara had access to government sources that other researchers were denied. The military had to at least respond to her requests, even if reluctantly and incompletely. What she learned stunned her.

AFTER considerable research, O'Meara concluded that the Coast Guard cutter *Juniper* took at least one of the boxes, and probably both, to the Brooklyn Navy Yard, seventy-five miles away, for discreet analysis. If O'Meara's account is accurate, this removal would have violated all protocol. The boxes were supposed to go directly to the computer labs at the NTSB.

On the day after the crash, when the only priority other than the boxes was the bodies of the victims, the *Juniper* made two trips to Brooklyn to off-load "debris." This was the only debris brought to Brooklyn in the course of the recovery. O'Meara has the documents to prove the *Juniper* made these trips, but as she acknowledges, "There is no record of what's on the offloads." O'Meara also admits that she has no hard proof that the boxes were among the cargo. The crew was not about to be interviewed. The *Juniper* left the scene after the second trip and never came back.[6]

The question needs to be asked: If the black boxes had been retrieved early on from the ocean floor, who did the retrieving? The answer may well be found, of all places, in the files of the Navy Public Affairs Library, where the Navy lists all of its support units in the TWA Flight 800 recovery efforts. These include:

- Special Boat Unit Twenty

- Special Warfare Group Two

- SEAL Delivery Vehicle Team Two

The Mark VIII SEAL Delivery Vehicle (SDV) is a mini-sub that carries the Navy SEAL team to its objective in a flooded compartment. It has its own compressed air or gas system to support the divers on the way and is typically launched and recovered from a host submarine.

The Los Angeles Class 688 Attack submarines can launch the SDVs from their horizontal launch tubes. The USS *Albuquerque* was in this class and was later confirmed to be in the "immediate vicinity" of TWA 800's flight path on the night of the crash.[7] The USS *James K. Polk*, the most likely host submarine, was based out of the Norfolk, Virginia, area in 1996, as was the Naval Special Warfare Development Group. Even if the *James K. Polk* were in port at the time of the crash, it could have made it to the scene by the next day.

In and of themselves, the Navy documents prove little, and this line of speculation might not be worth pursuing except for the odd involvement of one key individual, namely President Bill Clinton. On March 11, 1997, Clinton left his fingerprints on the case for the first and only time when he quietly signed Executive Order 13039. This was a job even Robert Francis could not do.

If the date of the order sounds familiar, it should. On the day prior, James Sanders and the Riverside, California, *Press-Enterprise* had launched a series of articles providing hard evidence that at least one missile had struck Flight 800 and that elements within the FBI and NTSB were covering up the same.

The executive order became effective, with unseemly haste, the very day after it was issued. On that same day, March 12, *Paris Match* published Pierre Salinger's claims of a missile strike and the supporting photos of the relevant radar.[8] The momentum from these disclosures might well have tempted those with critical information to come forward. EO 13039 made sure that would-be whistle-blowers thought hard before yielding to that temptation.

The summary of this highly specific executive order reads as follows: "Exclusion of the Naval Special Warfare Development Group from the Federal Labor-Management Relations Program." In essence, the order removed all federal whistle-blower protection from anyone, civilian or military, associated with U.S. Navy "special warfare" operations. Predictably, no reporter from the major media followed up on EO 13039 and its obvious implications.[9]

What lends all this admittedly circumstantial evidence added weight is the strange behavior of the U.S. Navy at the scene. As reported by *Newsday*, conventional Navy divers had been kept away from the crash site for several days after the plane went down. When the divers were finally ferried out to the site, they were not allowed in the water and would not go in for several more days.

The Navy offered several reasons for its reluctance. One was the weather. Capt. Stephen Bielenda, a local diving boat operator, wasn't buying that. "They should be down there diving," he told *Newsday*. "They said it was too rough out there, but my boat had 27 divers in the water on Saturday."[10]

Robert Francis didn't need a reason. "We'll send them down when we want to send them down, but we want to make sure it's justified," he told reporters on that same Saturday, three days after the crash.[11] Although the NTSB had been already shunted to the sidelines, and although Francis had no real authority to represent even the NTSB, he presumed here to speak for the U.S. Navy.

Francis would not have dared to do this on his own. Described as reticent and ineffectual by his colleagues, Francis lacked the natural bravado of a James Kallstrom. And yet here he was, providing instant information to the media on an incredibly sensitive topic, embarrassing a U.S. congressman in the process, and speaking out on behalf of the U.S. Navy. Someone had to have given him the authority to do this and the inside information with which to do it. That someone was almost certainly in the White House. It would be several days later, in fact, on the twenty-fifth of July, that Clinton Chief of Staff Leon Panetta would publicly bestow these powers on Francis, an unprecedented White House imposition.[12]

Even as the weather improved, government officials argued against sending divers down until the Navy's search technology identified key pieces of wreckage. This technology included an underwater sonar that looked like a sled, and a self-propelled robot bearing video cameras. As mentioned earlier, the selective editing of these videotapes—and the denial of that editing by the FBI—deeply troubled Jim Speer, an investigator on the scene. In the first few days after the crash, the Navy had also used a Pinger Locator System, a tube-shaped device with a sensitive microphone that was to listen for the distinctive "ping" from the recorders' underwater locator beacon. Capt. Chip McCord, chief of the Navy's diving operations on-site, contended that the sonar sled was necessary because the Navy's Pinger Locator System had failed in its mission.[13]

"The devices [pingers] are broken, destroyed or covered with sand or other material," McCord told *Newsday*. If a black box were to be found, "officials" again told *Newsday* that "the robot will be sent down to retrieve it because it can stay down longer and cover more ground. Divers would follow only if needed."[14]

A robot had some other advantages from the government's perspective. For one, it could not give interviews to the media. For another, it could not be injured or killed on a pointless mission. On the downside, robots lacked heroic appeal. With the president due to arrive in Long Island, drama won out over discretion. Fortunately, Kelly O'Meara managed to secure a video copy of the "Eureka" moment.[15]

With the cameras rolling, and the robots benched for the climactic moment, a diver found the one box sitting on the ocean floor as obvious as the hassock in his living room. In fact, he stepped on it. At the same time, and probably unintentionally, a second diver picked up the other box just as easily and only a few feet away. In their delight, the divers seemed genuinely oblivious to the likelihood that these recorders had just been dumped there. From all accounts, the Navy crew members on the ship above were likewise unaware of any mischief.

"There they were in their bright orange casings," notes Patricia Milton with her trademark credulity, "the size of shoe boxes, partially buried beneath sand, muck and wreckage, which explained why their signals had gone undetected for several days."[16] In fact, the Navy video exposed the truth—the black boxes were sitting on top of the ocean floor, covered by nothing except salt water. These boxes were about as open and exposed as they could possibly have been, given their original position in the tail of a doomed airliner. Truth be told, they were much too open and exposed. Said Robert Francis on the day after their recovery, "They were down there in that environment looking, and the light from the remote vehicle apparently was, was on the recorders, and the divers saw them." Added diver Kevin Gelhafen, "Recovering the boxes was merely picking them up, setting them in the basket, and tying them down."[17]

The boxes may well have been put back at the site by the same operatives who had taken them in the first place, a conjecture that squares with the yes-then-no announcement about finding the boxes in the early hours after the crash. If this were so, EO 13039 assured that no one would know just who these operatives were. It all worked out for the White House. When President Clinton came to Long Island on July 25, he had some good news to deliver:

> Just last night the divers who were braving the waters of the Atlantic to search for answers recovered both flight data recorders. Our experts are analyzing their contents at this very moment. This is a major step toward unraveling the mystery of Flight 800. In the meantime let me again ask every American not to jump to conclusions. This investigation is moving forward with great care and even greater determination.[18]

"Just last night" indeed. With timing this fortuitous, who could doubt the "care" and "determination" that moved this investigation forward?

"AFTER an extensive search," the NTSB's Al Dickinson would state at the NTSB's first public hearing in December 1997, Navy divers recovered both the CVR and the FDR. A Coast Guard Falcon aircraft flew the recorders to

NTSB headquarters in Washington, where NTSB engineers immediately began to analyze them.

"Both contained good data," Dickinson would acknowledge, "and revealed a routine flight until ending within a fraction of a second of one another at approximately 12 seconds after 8:31 P.M."[19]

"Usually, something is going on before," the NTSB's Jim Cash would say of the CVR. "The crew will say something or there's other indications going on. In this one, everything was just perfectly normal, just the noise at the end and that's it."[20]

The NTSB learned something else about the recorders upon retrieving them—their pingers worked, at least the one on the CVR. As noted in the NTSB's "Factual Report" on the CVR investigation from October 20, 1997, "The Dukane underwater locator beacon that was installed on the CVR was slightly dented and scratched but operated normally when tested in the lab." Robert Francis, in fact, had made the same claim about the CVR the day after its recovery. "The underwater locator beacon was attached and operative," he told Betty Bowser of PBS's *NewsHour*.[21]

If this game playing with the retrieval of the recorders seems trivial, rest assured, it was not. In the great majority of cases, the recorders detail the cause of a plane's demise. In the case of TWA Flight 800, not surprisingly, the recorders offered no obvious clues.

The lack of clues, however, was suspicious in and of itself. As Terrell Stacey reported, no one at Calverton had a ready answer as to how a low-level explosion in the center wing tank or even an overpressure could produce enough energy to put the CVR and FDR out of action simultaneously. Indeed, all available evidence implied a catastrophic bomb or a missile. All electrical systems had stopped virtually at the same time. There was no cry of warning or apprehension by the crew. There was no indication that any instrument or piece of equipment malfunctioned before the crash. Jim Cash would tell Christine Negroni, "About the third day I had the recorder, it was obvious that I didn't have the golden nugget and probably wasn't going to have the golden nugget."[22] A "golden nugget" could blow open the investigation; an "inference" could not.

If there were no nuggets at the end of the cockpit voice recorder, there was at least a sound. According to Patricia Milton, the NTSB's John Clark and Bernard Loeb listened on earphones to the CVR the moment it came in to the NTSB facility. "There is just a little noise at the end," Loeb told his colleagues. He added that the "split-second sound" was almost identical to the one heard on the CVR of Pan Am 103 after a bomb exploded in its cargo hold.[23] Loeb obviously made this claim before the NTSB's message shifted from "no missile" to "mechanical." He lacked any scientific basis upon which to make it.

When the NTSB released the transcripts of the CVR in October 1997, that sound was described matter-of-factly as "similar to tape recording damage noise."[24] In its notorious animation released in November 1997, the CIA raised the ante, describing Loeb's "little noise" as a "loud noise." Added the CIA, "National Safety Board analysts concluded this sound is associated with the beginning of the destruction of the aircraft."[25]

By the time of its first public hearing in December 1997, the NTSB was having a hard time staying on message.

> The CVR also showed no anomalies until the last fraction of a second before power loss terminated its operation as well. During that last moment, the device captured a *high-energy* signal that was consistent with an explosion in the fuel tank, whose sound was transmitted to the cockpit area microphone through the aircraft structure [emphasis added].[26]

Only explosives can trigger a "high-energy" event. A spontaneous fuel-tank explosion is a "low-energy" event. The noise that investigators first suggested was a bomb in a cargo hold had been transformed into an explosion in the fuel tank with more than a few loose ends dangling.

NTSB brass had access to more precise information. Some nine months before its first public hearing, the board had quietly contracted with Stuart Dyne of Britain's Southampton University to analyze the information that the CVR conveyed, especially the "high-energy signal" at the end. Stuart Dyne knew his stuff. About this there was no dispute. He launched his TWA 800 study in England on March 3, 1997. He was confident that he could locate the point of initiation and identify which type of event—bomb, missile, or mechanical—caused the plane to explode. At the investigation hangar on Long Island, members of the official Sound Spectrum Group, ALPA representatives included, patiently awaited results of Dyne's analysis. They are waiting still.

Had the results favored a mechanical explanation—or even been neutral—the NTSB would have released the results in a heartbeat. The board had a history of leaking favorable information, even when inconclusive. While an argument from silence, given the board's history, it is not absurd to suggest that the study probably supported something unfavorable to the official story, possibly a missile hit.

An ALPA document filed with the NTSB's Final TWA Flight 800 Report makes no bones about the pilot group's ultimate feeling of betrayal:

> The NTSB and interested parties invested a significant amount of resources in supporting the cockpit voice recorder (CVR) sound spectrum activity. However, the Sound Spectrum Group has never met to review or discuss any of the testing that was conducted. The valuable data that was collected during those tests has never been published, nor has there been any group or Party opportunity to analyze the CVR from TWA Flight 800 in the light of the work that was done. Furthermore, the NTSB has not made the analysis of a third party's study on this subject available to investigators or the public.[27]

A member of the Sound Spectrum Group has told the authors that the Flight 800 CVR recorded a vibration traveling through the frame of Flight 800 in excess of two thousand feet per second. The group knew from prior research that a fuel-air explosion would send a vibration through the 747 frame at less than 350 feet per second.[28]

The implications of the two-thousand-feet-per-second finding must have troubled the NTSB. In 1997, the board withheld the mere existence of the Southampton tests from the press and public. The NTSB also inserted an odd bit of information into the record to discredit the findings of the secret Southampton report should they ever be revealed, to wit: "The amplitude of the [CVR] noise was not a reliable means of comparison because these noise events typically overload the CVR recording system when occurred [sic]."[29]

As it happens, the testing began one week before the *Press-Enterprise* had published its eye-opening articles about a likely missile strike. If the English study had pointed to a high-order detonation, not a low-order fuel-air event, it would have supported Sanders's missile-fire conclusion.

The sequence of events is critical. If the CVR tests had proved a missile strike before the articles appeared, key NTSB and FBI officials could have lived with the results. But the articles changed everything. They alleged not only a missile strike, but also a deliberate cover-up of the same. Up until this point, those few officials in the know had been protecting the White House. From here on in, they would be protecting themselves. Withholding the study results at this stage was less about discretion than obstruction.

And so the NTSB pressed on, squandering millions more on illusory scientific analysis towards an end that held no promise from the beginning. And to preserve the illusion, the Justice Department pushed through the arrest and conviction of "conspiracy theorist" James Sanders and his wife, Elizabeth, for the entirely ironic crime of "conspiracy."

IT was a year and a half after the crash that independent investigator Cmdr. William Donaldson first sensed that all was not right with the flight data recorder. In fact, he might not have noticed at all had retired TWA captain and engineer Howard Mann not alerted him.

When Donaldson attended the first open NTSB hearing in December 1997 as a reporter, he was handed an unwieldy packet of documents. The packet included the NTSB's "factual report" on the "tabular data" of Flight 800's flight data recorder. This report showed the data from all the recorded variables on the FDR grouped in discrete, one-second "data blocks."

What Donaldson overlooked, but what Mann noticed, was that the last data block on the report had literally been lined out. Next to the line was the casual notation in longhand, "End of Flight 800 data." Looking carefully, Donaldson was able to read through the redaction, inadequate as it was, and come to some understanding of what this last second of data revealed. It was eye-opening.[30]

The aircraft had been climbing at about 22 feet per second to 13,799 feet, when all of a sudden the altimeter registered a drop of 3,672 feet. Obviously, Donaldson realized, the airplane didn't suddenly fall nearly 4,000 feet, but rather something catastrophic happened to cause this seeming loss of altitude.

The next data column showed the airspeed dropping from 298 knots to 100 knots. In other words, it lost 198 knots in one second. Donaldson knew this could not have happened either.

These were real instruments, however, recording real data. The plane's altimeter functioned like a barometer. It sensed the pressure outside the airplane and converted it to a reading of altitude. The tremendous drop in the reading of altitude meant that the instrument recorded the level of pressure one would expect to find at ten thousand or so feet.

Donaldson calculated that the force that created this phenomenon had a real pressure of 1.32 pounds per square inch. Arbitrarily multiplying the known pressure of a center wing tank explosion by a factor of ten,

Donaldson realized that it still could not have generated the necessary force to create a sudden increase in pressure of this magnitude, an "overpressure" as it is called.

The other relevant sensor charted by the FDR was the angle-of-attack system. This system measured the exact angle at which the wind struck the nose of the aircraft. Immediately before the overpressure struck the plane, the angle of attack was three degrees. When the overpressure wave hit, the angle of attack shot up 106 degrees. A quarter second later it went back down to thirty degrees and a quarter second after that it was back down to three degrees, which is essentially the normal position. What these figures meant, claimed Donaldson, was that "this data is real."

The only event that could explain these three variables from the last data block was a violent detonation outside and beneath the aircraft, what Donaldson called a "near experience of high explosiveness." The resulting overpressure pushed the plane up to an almost vertical position and within seconds ripped off its nose. The overpressure also sent to the altimeter and the airspeed gauge a confusing mass of raw information that the instruments could not readily process.

Donaldson presented his conclusions at a press conference on January 9, 1998, at the Army/Navy Club in Washington, D.C. Lending support to Donaldson at the conference were Howard Mann and still another "conspiracy buff," Mark Hill, a retired Navy rear admiral. "It looks to me like there was a huge explosive warhead about sixty feet from the plane and blew the nose up and to the left," Donaldson claimed during the conference, which was sponsored by the Associated Retired Aviation Professionals and the watchdog group Accuracy in Media.[31]

The NTSB was not about to sign on. "We have absolutely no evidence that a missile struck the aircraft or that a fragment of a missile entered the aircraft," NTSB spokeswoman Shelly Hazle responded, craftily avoiding Donaldson's point that this catastrophic event took place near the plane. An NTSB "official" elaborated that the figures represented "junk data," an incorrect reading from the tape of an earlier flight, TWA 803, over which the Flight 800 data had been recorded.[32]

Soon thereafter, the NTSB removed the controversial data block from their posted data tables, the one with the allegedly blended 800/803 data. Now the last complete one-second data record block showed a set of engineering values totally in sync with the blocks immediately before it. The "not normal" signal content had disappeared.

An NTSB official, Dennis Grossi, awkwardly attempted to clarify this "confusion" at the board's final hearing in August 2000:

> And possibly the areas where confusion has set in is, in my report, I included data from Flight 803, which is the flight from the previous day. The way flight data recorders work, they produce a 25-hour record. But, in doing that, they write over the oldest information on the tape. And in this case, the information that was being written over by data from Flight 800 was the data from Flight 803 from the previous day.[33]

Grossi neglected to mention that at all times an approximately three-inch blank portion of tape separates the new data from old data. It is not possible to get the two confused. Nor did Grossi mention that the wandering line of information, if attached to the old data, would indicate that Flight 800 actually crashed the day before when attempting to land at JFK.[34]

If Donaldson and other investigators remained skeptical, it was with good reason. No investigation in aviation history had been plagued by so many things that didn't function quite right. The critical flight data were recorded over. The pingers on the black boxes were "initially" broken. The dog-training aids were leaking. The EGIS equipment gave false positives. The P-3 had a broken transponder. The satellites were malfunctioning. Heidi Krieger's camera lens was scratched. The FAA radar was on the fritz. These malfunctions shared one common denominator. Each one of them subtracted useful information from the investigation. Each one of them eliminated potential evidence of a missile attack on the airplane. Each one of them made the mechanical failure theory marginally more viable.

Donaldson understood, however, that he was arguing from a point of weakness. The opposition had both the evidence and the microphone. As in Sanders's case, officials could produce contrary theories, ridicule the people who challenged them, and remove their allegations from the public forum within a single news cycle.

To get at the truth of the black boxes, Donaldson and his fellow critics realized they would have to get their hands on the real data. They had one weapon to accomplish it, the Freedom of Information Act (FOIA).

Audio expert Glenn Schulze had been following the case closely. For the last thirty years he had worked as an independent consultant whose clients included the U.S. Navy and the Applied Research labs at the University of Texas among other high-profile clients. Just before the crash in 1996, his expert testimony in a Connecticut court persuaded a judge that the NTSB's ruling of "pilot error" in the case at hand was erroneous. The case shook Schulze's confidence in the NTSB.

When he read of family member Don Nibert's relentless quest for the truth, Schulze volunteered his services to Nibert for one dollar. He refused to accept the explanation for the confusion at the end of the FDR without more hard evidence. So Schulze joined Donaldson and other investigators in requesting that the NTSB provide not just the tabular data but the waveform charts from the last thirty data blocks before and after the erasure gap at the end of the FDR.

This information did not arrive for nearly a year. What the NTSB finally sent was a small and truncated two-block set of waveforms immediately preceding the erasure gap—about 3 percent of the requested information. Nor would the NTSB supply a reason why it had once again stonewalled its critics.[35]

Only the threat of legal action forced the NTSB to produce a full sixty-plus data-record block centered on the erasure gap. This time, however, the NTSB sent the information copied in reverse. The NTSB again offered no explanation for what seemed like petty obstructionism.

Despite significant distortion as a result of the tape reversal, Schulze was able to read the data. Only one problem, a large one: Each data block within a group of sixty-four such blocks ends with its own distinct number. The NTSB's tabular data ended with the number 6. Its waveform charts ended with the number 4. The NTSB could offer no satisfactory explanation for the discrepancy.

Schulze, however, knew exactly what the discrepancy meant. Among other things it meant that the problem with the FDR was, if anything, more serious than what Donaldson had originally thought.

ON December 12, 2000, Jim Hall, chairman of the NTSB, sat uncomfortably across from Don and Donna Nibert. There was good reason for his discomfort. The Niberts, from Montoursville, Pennsylvania, had lost their sixteen-year-old daughter in the crash of Flight 800 and had journeyed to Hall's D.C. office to find out why. Hall, the least qualified and most political chair in NTSB history, surrounded himself with his director of research and engineering, a legal adviser, and two FDR specialists.

As a family member, Don Nibert was able to exert pressure others were not. Not one to give up, he had involved himself in the fight to secure the FDR data. In his efforts, he had enlisted Schulze and retired pilot Howard Mann, "who," says Nibert, "knows more than any man alive."[36]

A college professor with a technical bent, Nibert was shocked by what the two men shared with him. "Both of them told me there were four seconds missing at the end of the tape," remembers Nibert. "We had four seconds edited and removed. These are crucial seconds. They occur right at the end of the flight."

What reason would the government have to remove the original four seconds? "Best guess," says Schulze, "they show something hitting the airplane."

Alarmed, Nibert secured the meeting with Jim Hall. Schulze attended at the Niberts' request. As the meeting unfolded, Schulze made a lengthy, highly technical presentation to the NTSB's top FDR experts. "The experts did not want to be there," says Nibert. "You could cut the air with a knife there was so much hate in the room."

Schulze paused briefly after explaining the first four of his five explanatory flip charts, looked squarely at the NTSB experts, and challenged them boldly: "Hard evidence extracted from the NTSB's own reports is consistent with the FBI and NTSB withholding the last four Flight 800 FDR one-second data blocks and over 3,000 data bits from the public."[37]

In a world with more honor, these would have been fighting words. By the year 2000, however, at least at the top rungs of the NTSB, honor was largely a memory. If the science here is complex and not easily transcribed, the reaction of the accused needs no explanation. As Schulze's notes reveal, "No NTSB staff member commented on or objected to the 4 missing seconds claim."

The charge Schulze had presented was devastating. He was claiming that the NTSB's final FDR report was missing—"at a hard minimum"—the last four actual seconds of data. By lining up radar and voice transmissions, someone had reconstructed the final four seconds to show a steady ascent and an uninterrupted flight before the recording ended abruptly and mysteriously at 20:31:12 EDT. As Schulze knew, however, the embedded FDR time code ended at 20:31:08. He believes that the reconstruction of the four seconds on the FDR at least would have taken longer than the week the black boxes went missing. If correct, this would implicate the NTSB in the corruption of the data.

Incredibly, Jim Hall did not protest the government's innocence. His first response was to complain about the wording used by Schulze in a letter to the Niberts. In the letter, Schulze had called attention to the properties of the CD waveforms sent by the NTSB. He claimed that they were "consistent with this CD being a crudely manufactured and bungled forgery of the actual TWA FL 800 FDR tape."[38] Hall had little stomach for straight talk.

Brushing Hall's complaint aside, Schulze presented more hard evidence to back up his charge that the CDs were forgeries. As he insisted, each CD released under FOIA should have provided one consistent set of FDR information. This was not the case. Instead, each CD had highly inconsistent data at the precise location on the tape where the four original seconds of data appeared to have been removed.

The NTSB experts offered no rebuttal to Schulze's presentation. They weakly offered the excuse that the spike marking the end point of data on the FDR was "normal and is the result of the erase head losing AC power." The experts could not, however, explain why this spike was removed from one of the three CDs the NTSB had fobbed off on the public.

"They really didn't explain anything," says Nibert. "They did not have an answer for the four missing seconds."

The only way to confirm or deny any tampering was to release the original FDR tape to an independent laboratory. Don Nibert asked Jim Hall to approve just such an independent test. Hall asked for the request to be put in writing. Nibert did as requested.

The NTSB was given ample opportunity to turn the original FDR tape over to an independent testing facility for analysis. This testing could have proved Donaldson and Schulze wrong, exposed them for the malcontents that they were alleged to be, and erased all suspicion that someone within the government had altered the tape. To date, the NTSB has refused to do anything of the kind. The board "completely ignored and failed to respond to Mr. Nibert's perfectly legal and proper request as a Fl[ight] 800 Family Member," Schulze has observed.[39]

Based on the evidence, including the NTSB's refusal to place its own data to the test, Schulze has come to a damning conclusion:

> It is my strong belief that the NTSB cannot release the FDR accident tape from FL 800 for the purpose of independent read-out and analysis without revealing their complicity in tampering with this most important piece of TWA FL 800 accident investigation.

As the father of a sixteen-year-old victim, Don Nibert has come to feel the betrayal on a much deeper level:

> I feel that we have not been told the truth. I feel that we have been lied to. I feel that we have been used, all the families have been, because [the authorities] stated to anyone who contradicts them that they shouldn't say this because of the additional pain they cause the family. We were used as pawns to stymie critics of the investigation.

A WEEK after this meeting, with two years left on his tenure as chairman, Jim Hall abruptly announced he was quitting the NTSB. He immediately took a job at a law firm where he would serve as a lobbyist for Chrysler-Daimler, a company that he had often praised and awarded in the previous two years.

This move was considered sleazy even by Washington standards. "There was no quid pro quo," Hall protested. "What I had to do as a safety board chairman, I did with integrity."[40] But by the year 2000, in the Washington of Jim Hall and Bill Clinton, the word *integrity* had no more substance than the word *is*.

CHAPTER 11

EXPLODING HYPOTHESES

There is a time-honored principle of logic known as "Occam's razor"—the simplest explanation is usually the best explanation.

Consider its application in the case of TWA 800: Hundreds of witnesses watch streaks of light head towards the plane; FAA radar picks up an unknown object merging with the plane; and the plane explodes catastrophically without a word from the cockpit.

On August 14, 1996, four weeks after the crash, Don Van Natta Jr. reported for the *New York Times* that "the pattern of the debris" persuaded investigators that "a mechanical malfunction is highly unlikely." Additionally, the *Times* article stated emphatically, "Now that investigators say they think the center fuel tank did not explode, they say the only good explanations remaining are that a bomb or a missile brought down the plane off Long Island."[1]

Occam's razor says, yes, missile, but the NTSB had little use for logic. If "senior investigators" were telling Van Natta that "the center fuel tank caught fire as many as 24 seconds after the initial blast that split apart the plane," NTSB "officials" were not so ready to concede.

"I don't think anything rules out anything at this point," said the NTSB's always-reliable Robert Francis in August 1996. Van Natta then added prophetically, "By keeping open the possibility of a malfunction, safety board investigators can continue to pursue all possibilities, no matter how remote."

Truer words were never spoken. The NTSB would explore a range of increasingly remote possibilities, and with each new test, its investigators would wander farther from the evidence. In the next four years, despite an extraordinary effort, they would not discover one new fact that would make a mechanical malfunction any more credible than it was within four weeks of the crash. Not one.

But as Van Natta noted, "While investigators, speaking not for attribution, said they have concluded that the center fuel tank did not explode, publicly they have refused to say that." They dared not. They understood the consequences. With the actual investigators silenced, the "officials" would control the microphone. In time, through sheer numbing repetition of their contrived hypothesis, they would establish it more or less as public consensus.

IN the beginning, NTSB officials could only say what did *not* happen to the plane. Over time, they would have to explain what *did* happen. At the very least, they would have to create a science-based, mechanical theory for the crash, one credible enough to satisfy the media's mild curiosity.

To make this theory work, the NTSB would need to establish at least two critical points. The first was that the fuel-air mixture in the center wing tank was sufficiently volatile that the least spark could set it off. The second was that the aircraft was capable of spontaneously generating that spark. The theoretical spark itself would require two separate causes of its own—a break in the insulation of the wiring and a breakdown in the system that limits the strength of the current through those wires. All these conditions were fully necessary to validate any mechanical theory.

No one disputes that the center wing tank (CWT), which sits in the fuselage under the passenger seats, erupted in flames. The only questions are when and how. Before mid-September 1996, the working presumption was that a bomb or a missile had caused it to blow. As the needs of the Clinton administration shifted, however, so did the story line. As discussed earlier, Jim Hall himself introduced the NTSB's new working hypothesis, namely "that the explosion could have been caused by a mechanical failure alone."[2] This dramatic shift away from terrorism was reinforced within twenty-four hours by the St. Louis dog-training story.

On the basis of its own calculations, Boeing argued at the time that there would not have been sufficient energy in a CWT explosion to bring the plane down. But NTSB officials were "unpersuaded."[3] It was at this mid-September turning point that Hall presented the NTSB plan to stage computer simulations and lab tests and maybe even blow up a 747 or two. As he must have known, this strategy would not provide the NTSB with any answers, but it would gain them time and plenty of it.

Soon after this shift in direction, the NTSB discreetly advanced the theory that one of the plane's three fuel pumps, the scavenge pump, shorted and ignited the fuel-air mixture in the center wing tank.

The fact that the scavenge pump would naturally have been in the "off" position did not deter the NTSB. Spokeswoman Shelly Hazle told *Newsday* that the agency was continuing to look at whether the flight engineer had "inadvertently" turned it on. "I don't think we can rule it out yet," she was quoted as saying in October 1996.[4] In fact, however, the switch had been in the off position when investigators recovered the engineer's panel three months earlier.[5] What they had not recovered, however, at least not as far as anyone knew, was the scavenge pump. Its absence gave the theory life. As long as the scavenge pump remained "lost," the NTSB could theorize as it wished.

In reality, however, the scavenge pump had been found early on. Among the documents Terrell Stacey turned over to James Sanders was a printout of the debris recovered within the Green Zone, the one farthest from JFK. Deep within that printout was listed the plane's one and only scavenge pump. That document remains classified.[6] Although seemingly lost, too much circumstantial evidence accumulated for the NTSB to keep the scavenge pump as a suspect. The NTSB's Bob Swaim summarized this evidence at the safety board's final hearing in August 2000:

> The CVR (cockpit voice recorder) did not reveal a cockpit conversation regarding activation of the pump. The switch for this pump was found in the off position in the cockpit wreckage, and testing found that the flame protection features of the pump were effective.[7]

The scavenge-pump theory pointed to a problem that plagued the investigation especially in its early days: namely that hard evidence could easily disprove certain theories. As the investigation evolved, NTSB officials would steer it to the realm of what scientists call the "unfalsifiable," the realm where theories can neither be proved nor disproved.

Throughout October 1996, the NTSB's always-cryptic Bernard Loeb advanced his theory of the exploding fuel vapors in the CWT more publicly and aggressively. Soon afterwards, and presumably by coincidence, attorney Lee Kreindler sued TWA and Boeing on behalf of twenty-five victims' families, arguing that the explosion of the jet's center fuel tank was the most likely cause of the crash.

In early November, Loeb went a step further. In an appearance on *60 Minutes,* he told Ed Bradley that static electricity from a faulty Wiggins coupler most likely triggered the explosion. Loeb neglected to add that there was no evidence that any Wiggins coupler was faulty. The FBI's James Kallstrom was reportedly furious at this indiscretion, but Chairman Hall reassured Kallstrom that the NTSB "has more leeway to speculate because we're not bound by criminal legal standards."[8]

With or without the Wiggins coupler, static electricity stood as Loeb's "pet theory." It remained so, as Patricia Milton notes, until "scientists at Wright Patterson laboratories had proved unable to produce a single scenario under which static electricity could have caused a significant spark."[9]

There is no hard evidence to suggest that Loeb had a back channel to the White House or that he actively conspired with Hall and Francis. His desire to spite the FBI, to stroke his own ego, to stake out the NTSB's turf and to appease his superiors only gave the appearance of political conspiracy. His performance throughout the investigation confounded and irritated almost everyone.

Given the narrow direction in which Loeb focused his energies, NTSB staffers came to more or less a consensus, namely that if a spark had managed to enter the CWT and ignite the fumes, the resulting flames would spread from compartment to compartment and create an "overpressure." This process was theoretically capable of blowing the airplane to bits.

To substantiate this theory, the NTSB had to investigate, in its own words, "the phenomena associated with flame propagation in multicompartment, interconnected, and vented tanks representative of the accident airplane's CWT."[10]

One serious problem with the NTSB thesis was that kerosene-based Jet A fuel does not ignite readily like, say, gasoline. Commander Donaldson performed some simple but telling experiments on this point. In one, he stuck a lit match into a tin of Jet A fuel. The fuel doused the match like so much water. According to the *Aviation Fuels Handbook*, as Donaldson observed, Jet A fuel would actually quench an open flame even when warmed as high as 127 degrees Fahrenheit.[11] "This fuel is so safe a maintenance employee could have taken a smoke break standing in the residual fuel of TWA's tank," wrote

Donaldson in a letter to Jim Hall, "and put out his lit match in the fuel without consequence at temperatures up to 126°F!"[12]

Donaldson demonstrated convincingly that the only way the fuel could be made volatile at this temperature was for it to become vaporized through a severe blow to the plane's fuselage. "Jet A-1 fuel used by FL800 is safer than all its predecessors," Donaldson would write to FBI Director Louis Freeh. "It cannot be made to explode in-flight unless the tank is first exposed to shock."[13]

After two years of exhaustive testing, the investigating scientists contracted by the NTSB came to much the same conclusion:

> The ignition of Jet A fuel in one bay of the scale model resulted in transmission of the flame through the bay passageways and vent stringers and ignition in neighboring bays, illustrating the behavior of multicompartment flame propagation. Flamefront quenching was also observed to be a characteristic of flame propagation.[14]

"Flamefront quenching" meant that if flames moved to a different compartment, the Jet A fuel would likely extinguish them. The tests told the NTSB that even if a spark could be identified, it would not likely cause the violent explosion that ripped apart the airplane.

But the NTSB did not give up. It contracted with two more research laboratories—Sandia National Laboratories and Christian Michelson Research—"to develop computer code models of the combustion process that occurs in a 747 CWT."

Although their reports were understandably tactful, these scientists likewise failed to find any reasonable way to justify the presumed NTSB scenario. In fact, the known phenomenon of flamefront quenching made it impossible for any honorable scientist to develop a scenario supporting the NTSB's:

> In all the computer solutions, conditions were calculated that indicated that quenching could have occurred in some of the vents and passageways of the full-scale CWT geometry . . . Incorporating the effects of quenching in the calculations appeared to significantly affect the differential pressure histories that developed across the internal CWT structural members.

The NTSB grudgingly admitted to losing this battle, but given its easy access to the taxpayer's wallet, the agency was not about to abandon the war.

By this stage it could not afford to. The safety board needed some semi-credible theory to justify its abandonment of the obvious missile or the less obvious bomb theory. The NTSB would have to win by attrition, to wear the public and the media down.

So the agency contracted with Combustion Dynamics "to evaluate the consistency between the computer calculations of the full-scale CWT combustion model and other information and evidence obtained during the investigation." The NTSB had hoped "that by conducting this evaluation . . . it would be possible to narrow the number of probable ignition location(s) within the CWT." This hope was in vain. The NTSB had to concede defeat yet again: "Therefore, the rules-based analysis did not provide a definitive determination regarding the probability that any given location within the CWT was the ignition location."

But the scientists at Combustion Dynamics did discreetly imply that if the NTSB were to expend a few million additional taxpayer dollars, the agency might walk away with at least some token of support from within the scientific community. With hope still alive, the NTSB headed for Bruntingthorpe, England, to blow up a 747 CWT and to pray that Combustion Dynamics' "rules-based analysis" would prove to be something more than a polite gesture by scientists dependent on future government contracts.

But by the time the dust had settled from the Bruntingthorpe explosion, the NTSB was forced to admit that rules-based analysis offered no easy out: "The Board observed that the test parameters used resulted in a significantly more dynamic and destructive explosion within the test plane's CWT than was indicated by the accident airplane's wreckage." The "rules-based" analysis had literally been blown away. With all of its investigative hypotheses reduced to rubble, the NTSB chose to reconstruct the results itself in a way more to its liking:

> Finally, analysis of the results of computer modeling of combustion in a full-scale CWT under conditions simulating those of TWA flight 800 indicated that a localized ignition of the flammable vapor could have generated pressure levels that, based upon failure analysis, would cause the damages observed in the wreckage of the accident airplane's CWT.

No outside scientific agency or person had made such a statement. In fact, all contracted testing and analysis ran counter to what the NTSB was now saying. Even Patricia Milton had to acknowledge that the CWT pieces retrieved and studied in the England test as well as another test in Arizona "bore no resemblance to those of Flight 800." She consoles herself, however, with the thought that the government was at least "proving negatives."[15]

These highly public explosive tests, however, served a purpose beyond the gathering of facts. ALPA investigator Jim Speer explains just what that purpose was:

> [The NTSB] asked [the researchers] to spice [the fuel] up a little more and they had a data tag on their little TV video of the event, and it said "simulated vapor." They explained to the group that it was equivalent to kerosene fumes, and they had spiced it up with propane and hydrogen. I think any of you who have seen the Hindenburg blow up don't agree that propane and hydrogen and kerosene fumes are equivalent to just kerosene fumes. That's what the government did. Then they put it on the evening news, and so now everyone has seen that the government's opinion is that this fuel tank of a 747 is easy to blow up . . . which is about as close to lying to the public as you can get.[16]

"Several concerns arose during these tests which suggested that the simulant fuel may be a questionable substitute for Jet-A fuel," admitted the authors of a later report by the Sandia Labs.[17] But no matter. By this point the NTSB had shifted its real focus from science to spin. These contrived tests using a concocted fuel mixture would leave a lasting impression in the public mind about the very real explosion of TWA Flight 800. The NTSB's public statements about these tests reinforced that impression.

> Accordingly, the Safety Board concludes that a fuel/air explosion in the CWT of TWA flight 800 would have been capable of generating sufficient internal pressure to break apart the tank.[18]

This conclusion bordered on fantasy. Jet A's lack of flammability, according to the exhaustive analysis conducted under contract for the NTSB, created a high probability that the liquid would have extinguished any flames ignited by any known internal ignition source. Nor could the NTSB find a hypothetical spark of sufficient strength to ignite Jet A.

To be sure, if an explosion in the CWT had occurred, it would have blown the CWT apart. This, no one denied. But no scientific foundation existed to explain just how such an explosion could occur by purely mechanical means.

Patricia Milton writes in detail about the one NTSB test "that proved a 'positive' at last." On July 14, 1997, the NTSB ran "an exact duplicate of TWA Flight 800" out of JFK at the same time of day with the same weight equivalent. The plane was rigged with testing gear like a heart patient on a stress test. As the plane rose to 13,800 feet, the temperature in the CWT crested at an average high temperature of about 120 degrees Fahrenheit.[19]

To her credit, Milton acknowledges that "this was not the answer to how Flight 800 had crashed" since the source of ignition was "still a mystery." But she ignores some equally compelling negatives.

For one, as Commander Donaldson observed, "The fuel temperature in TWA 800's center wing tank (CWT) was well below minimum flammability much less at explosive vapor temperatures." As he noted, Jet A fuel is capable of quenching an open flame even at 127 degrees Fahrenheit, let alone 120. For another, as Milton notes, the outside temperature at the time the trial plane took off from JFK was eighty-seven degrees, sixteen degrees higher than it was when TWA 800 took off. "Other than that," says Milton with a credulousness bordering on the comic, "everything was identical."

What is more, 747s had taken off literally tens of thousands of times from runways considerably hotter than JFK at its hottest, without one of them ever having blown up in midair. Why the fuel tank would overheat on what Witness 607 described as "a clear chilly night" mystifies the observer. As Commander Donaldson told FBI Director Freeh, "In the entire history of American turbine powered civilian air transport, there has never been an in-flight fuel tank explosion in any aircraft caused by mechanical failure!"[20]

If the NTSB were correct, the crash of TWA Flight 800 had been a unique event, a first in the seventy-five-year history of commercial aviation. One would think that such an event would have left a highly distinctive signature. Physical evidence would clearly have spelled out what specific conditions could have caused so singular a catastrophe.

The "emulation flight test," as it was called, yielded no such clues. Bernard Loeb told the *New York Times* that the tests "helped us far more than we ever imagined possible. It was a key step toward finding out the probable cause of this accident."[21] But what was that cause? All that the JFK flight test proved was that at 13,800 feet, the fuel in Flight 800's CWT would have been capable of quenching any fire that might have started there. Just as troubling, the test offered not a scrap of evidence about the second necessary condition, an ignition source.

Milton, to be sure, wasn't quite sure what these tests proved other than that unspecified "changes were in order for the fuel-air mixture in all 747 center fuel tanks."[22] The need to make changes based on nonexistent evidence would lead to a series of often contradictory recommendations that no one could really take seriously.

One recommendation that emerged from the emulation flight test, for instance, was that Jet A fuel be replaced, possibly by JP-5, a fuel used by the Navy. Why the need for a new fuel? Reported the *New York Times*, "Investigators believe that the little fuel inside the center tank of Flight 800 had been warmed as the plane sat on the runway, turning it into an explosive vapor."[23] But if anything, the emulation flight had proved the opposite. Even on a night sixteen degrees warmer than the one on which TWA 800 exploded, the fuel temperature had stayed well within a safe range. And for all the talk of heat-producing air-conditioning packs under the CWT, no one was about to recommend that planes sit on a runway without AC. This, the public would have noticed.

By the year 2000, the NTSB had exhausted just about all possible scientific testing that might reinforce its mechanical scenarios. The scientific community had too much integrity to validate desperate theories either about fuel volatility or ignition sources. Accordingly, the NTSB ceased scientific inquiry along these lines.

From this point forward the board would descend from modern science to old-fashioned alchemy and sum it all up in a fable worthy of Harry Potter. Titled "Factors Suggesting the Likelihood that a Short-Circuit Event Occurred on TWA Flight 800," this NTSB report focused on the second necessary condition for a spontaneous explosion, an ignition source.[24]

ONE is hard-pressed to identify a single fact in this tortured report. Guesswork and supposition run rampant.

"When powered," reads the report, "damaged wires would be vulnerable to short-circuiting." The report then admits that the accident and the recovery "probably" caused at least "some" of that damage. One would think so.

At its final hearing the NTSB went to great lengths to show how closely TWA Flight 800 must have resembled other planes whose condition "suggests that at least some of the damage to the wiring insulation of the accident airplane very likely existed before the accident."[25]

"We have similar photos from 747's, the A-300 that I showed you, DC9s, and other airplanes," the NTSB's Bob Swaim remarked at one typical juncture. "Drill shavings can be found even in new airplanes." The obvious question that the NTSB shies away from is why these planes didn't blow up and never have. The NTSB report continues:

> Evidence of arcing was found on generator cables routed with wires in the leading edge of the right wing, near the wing root. Although this arcing *might* have been caused by the breaking of the forward wing spar and subsequent fuel fire, it is *possible* that it *could* also have been caused before the explosion [emphasis added].

A pause here is in order. Consider the choices the NTSB presents as to what caused the arcing found on the generator: (1) the catastrophic breakup of the forward wing spar and the subsequent fuel fire, which did take place; (2) a "short circuit" in the wiring, which might conceivably have taken place before the explosion. An honest investigation would focus on the first explanation. The NTSB, however, focused on the second. To put this in perspective, it is as if the L.A. cops completely ignored O. J. and went after the "Colombian drug dealers."

The report then lists a series of anomalies that "could" or "might" "suggest" a source of the ignition.

> It is *possible* that one or more of these anomalies were a manifestation of an electrical event that resulted in excess voltage being transferred to the CWT FQIS wiring. On the basis *of this and other evidence* previously discussed, the Safety Board concludes that a short circuit producing excess voltage that was transferred to the CWT FQIS wiring is the most *likely* source of ignition energy for the TWA flight 800 CWT explosion [emphasis added].

One problem. No other "evidence" was "previously discussed." All that preceded was vague guesswork and supposition. The speculation continues: "Although no clear evidence of arcing was found inside TWA flight 800's CWT, fire damage along the route of the FQIS wiring was severe enough that it *likely* would have obscured any such evidence."

The report continues:

> Another *potential* source of ignition energy is resistance heating, which could have resulted from a thin filament being heated through contact with a wire, probe, or compensator exposed to excess voltage. Although *no*

clear evidence of a filament ignition was found inside TWA flight 800's CWT, such evidence *could* also have been physically lost or obscured by fire damage [emphasis added].

This aimless speculation goes on and on and on to the point of absurdity, considering the NTSB's acknowledgment that the computer modeling done by the two research laboratories—Sandia National Laboratory and Christian Michelsen Research—failed. "The results of that modeling could not be used to determine the most likely ignition location." The NTSB officials, in fact, knew the whole exercise was a failure. At the final NTSB hearing, staffer Joseph Kolly came to the following reluctant conclusion:

The search for the probable ignition location was pushed to the limits of current technology. An accounting of the scientific uncertainties was meticulously maintained throughout the entire experimental, computational, and analytic processes. In the end, the uncertainties were too great to permit the identification of the probable location of ignition.

Ironically, the NTSB ruled out a missile because of a supposed lack of "physical evidence." Despite a desperate effort to find physical evidence for a mechanical failure, the NTSB could not find a shred of it.

Nor was the NTSB the only organization to review the wiring. The International Association of Machinists and Aerospace Workers (IAMAW) did its own assessment. These workers had far less interest in the hypotheticals of how a plane might work than in the reality of how it actually does. Unlike the NTSB's, their analysis cut right to the chase:

We conclude that the existing wiring recovered from flight 800 wreckage does not exhibit any evidence of improper maintenance or any malfunction that led to a spark or other discrepancy.[26]

Within the aviation industry, TWA maintenance had long been recognized as among the best, if not *the* best, in the world. The IAMAW recognized this if the NTSB did not. What did cause the center wing tank to explode? The IAMAW does not mince words:

A high pressure event breached the fuselage and the fuselage unzipped due to the event. The explosion [of the tank] was a result of this event.

What the IAMAW was saying is that the initiating explosion occurred *outside* the plane, penetrated the fuselage, vaporized the fuel, and caused the CWT to explode. The CWT eruption did not cause the breach in the fuselage. It was the "result" of that event.

Not surprisingly, the NTSB was no more interested in hearing the truth from the IAMAW than it was from the scientific community. So it ignored the IAMAW report and the scientific data and generally bypassed the inconvenient step of first demonstrating that the explosion occurred from within.

IF motives of the NTSB officials were less clear, their actions were transparent. By August of 1996, they knew for a fact, as the *New York Times* reported, that "the initial blast that severed the plane occurred slightly forward of the spot where the wings meet the fuselage," not in the center wing tank.[27]

In fact, a narrow strip of the fuselage ahead of the right wing had been recovered from the area closest to Kennedy airport and was the first to have been blown off the plane. All evidence pointed to this fact, including the nearby missing seats and the ejected bodies. The *Times* may have been complacent, but it was rarely careless with its facts.

By the time of the December 1997 NTSB hearing, the story had begun to shift. Al Dickinson of the NTSB claimed that "the pieces of wreckage that exited the aircraft first includ[ed] some structure from the center wing tank and fuselage just forward of the wings."[28] Recall, too, that the debris-field maps that Stacey shared with Sanders showed 98 percent of the CWT in the zone farthest from Kennedy, not closest.

By August 2000, Loeb had made the fuselage strips along the right wing disappear altogether. "I would like to reiterate," he claimed, "that the physical evidence irrefutably indicated that the first pieces to depart the airplane were from the forward part of the center wing tank."[29] The investigators had found no new evidence to justify this change.

One missing piece could clarify this controversy. It is part of the center wing tank from the right side of spanwise beam number 2, a part that would have been directly in the path of a missile. This part was cut in two during a metallurgical test on August 9, 1996. It was not included in the Calverton reconstruction, nor has it been identified in any NTSB document released since. On August 23, 2001, the NTSB was FOIA'd to produce the still-classified metallurgical testing report from 1996. To date, the NTSB has not been forthcoming.

James Sanders observed the area of damage on December 22, 1998, in the course of his limited, criminal-trial discovery process. The courts had allowed him three hours to photograph the reconstructed plane and other debris from the crash at the Calverton hangar on Long Island. Despite occasional obstruction from hovering officials, Sanders was able to photograph and document the area from which the red residue trail had crossed the plane.[30] In comparing these photos with imagery recorded earlier in the investigation, Sanders came to an extraordinary realization: The most critical part of the airplane, the part of the physical evidence that revealed the most about the cause of the crash, had been dramatically altered.

A little background is in order. FBI Witness 648, on a boat just five miles from the crash, had given a statement to the FBI identifying in great detail perhaps the single most sensitive piece of debris from the stricken 747. He described the right wing and a portion of the right side of the center wing tank as it ripped away in one piece from the aircraft a few thousand feet above the ocean.

In the first week after the crash, the Navy used search technology to identify key pieces of wreckage. The Navy inexplicably kept its regular divers and the NYPD's divers out of the water and away from the debris field—but not all divers. CBS News learned that members of a Navy SEAL team were scouring a sensitive Red Zone area, the area of first impact. These divers recovered some highly sensitive debris. Other debris too large to bring up by hand was placed off-limits until a removal plan could be devised.

People who knew what damage from a missile hitting aluminum might look like were assembled to analyze the Navy videotape of the debris field. At this early stage of the investigation, they probably had no idea that the debris they identified would be forever concealed. Nevertheless, the sensitive areas of the videotapes were classified under national security and removed from the official investigation. This editing is what caused ALPA investigator Jim Speer to protest.

One enormous piece of debris particularly alarmed the screeners. It was the massive section of the entire right-side floor of the center wing tank still attached to the right wing. The thrust of the damage strongly suggested that a missile blast had ripped upward through the bottom of the right side of the center wing tank, continued through the right side of the passenger cabin by the wing, and blew out the top of the fuselage.

No imagery of this damage was expected to leave the hangar. But a Boeing engineer did manage to make drawings of it. Sanders was able to locate unedited TV news footage of some of this debris before it disappeared. And, most important, he also had secured FBI photos of the critical, massive right-side section. The photo showed the floor of the center wing tank, at the very bottom of the plane, to have been blown all the way upward. Were it placed in the reconstructed airliner as was, the floor of this tank would have thrust up into the passenger cabin.[31]

At the time the FBI photo was taken, all active talk of missiles was off the table. This piece of physical evidence, however, argued strongly for an external blast. It appears that by the second week of August 1996, someone ordered men with cutting torches to dissect it.

When Sanders visited the hangar, he was able to see up close the handiwork of those who had reshaped the plane. Sanders stood and literally touched the right side of the reconstructed center wing tank. The massive piece of flooring that the photo had shown sweeping upward had been mashed down. Someone had flattened the floor not just to its original level, but beyond that as if some mysterious mechanical force inside the tank had blown it downward—precisely the message the administration needed to send.

If this sounds far-fetched, it is not. The NTSB's Hank Hughes testified to a Senate subcommittee that an agent from the FBI with some experience in bomb investigations had been brought in from Los Angeles. Said Hughes, "I saw him in the middle of the hangar with a hammer in the process of trying to flatten a piece of wreckage." This was by no means standard behavior. "In investigative work," Hughes continued, "you do not alter evidence. You take it in its original state and preserve it. But I actually saw this man with a hammer, pounding on a piece of evidence, trying to flatten it out."[32]

Sanders's extensive photo analysis after December 22 revealed considerable alteration of the front and midspar as well, leading to the inescapable conclusion that the reconstruction had been tampered with in all key areas. Sanders would also use these photos to prove that critical seats had been removed and replaced and that the NTSB had merely smeared red dye on a sample before sending it to NASA in Florida.

While suppressing contrary evidence, NTSB officials hoped that somewhere along the line a scientific test would produce a hypothetical scenario in which a mechanical initiating event would enter the realm of the possible. A compliant media would then take this semi-credible speculation and turn it into a generally accepted fact. Unfortunately for the NTSB, that scientific hypothesis never developed.

But it didn't matter. All dissent had been marginalized. All dissenters had been denied a hearing at any serious forum. The game was over. The NTSB had won. Bernard Loeb brimmed with confidence at the final NTSB hearing in August 2000. Said Loeb in conclusion:

> A fuel air explosion with Jet A fuel was more than capable of generating the pressure needed to destroy the airplane. Together with the other physical evidence, this leads to the inescapable conclusion that the cause was a fuel-air break up in center wing tank.[33]

Loeb could be confident because by this juncture there was no one left to contradict him. The media had long since ceased any meaningful inquiry. After a year or so, for instance, the *New York Times* would routinely summarize the cause of the crash as follows: "An explosion in the plane's center fuel tank is believed to be the cause of the crash that killed all 230 people aboard on July 17, 1996."[34]

To her credit, Patricia Milton acknowledged the NTSB's failure to identify the source of the explosion, but she remained confident that the "likely suspect" would one day be found amid the plane's 150 miles of wiring.[35] It was that simple.

IN their relentless game playing, Bernard Loeb and other investigators seemed to lose sight of the fact that the great loss on July 17, 1996, was not an airplane.

One group of investigators never did. Indeed, of all the heroic work undertaken in the aftermath of the TWA Flight 800 crash, none was more exhausting, or more stressful than that done by the pathologists on the scene. By the day after the crash, police, military, and recreational boaters had recovered the ninety-nine bodies floating on the surface. Rescue workers then placed the remains in body bags and transported them by boat to a temporary morgue at East Moriches.

Initially, staff from the Suffolk County Medical Examiner's Office and the Suffolk County Police Department managed this overwhelming process. They assigned victims a medical examiner accession number, photographed them, and, when able, recorded the circumstances of their recoveries. They then placed the remains in a refrigerated trailer and transported them to the Suffolk County Medical Examiner's Office in Hauppage, New York.

In Hauppage, forensic pathologists from Suffolk County or from the State of New York performed autopsies on the victims while their families waited back at JFK, desperate for information. Although most victims were identified either by fingerprints or dental records, nineteen of the bodies were so severely damaged that they could be identified only through DNA.

In examining their remains, Suffolk County Medical Examiner Dr. Charles Wetli came upon an astonishing discovery: Two bodies shared the same DNA. Even more amazing, the bodies in question had arrived at the autopsy area two weeks apart. Perplexed, Dr. Wetli did further research and concluded that the two were a husband and wife who had been sitting next to each other when the aircraft exploded. So powerful was the blast that it fused the bodies together, right down to their DNA. Wetli had never seen or even heard of such a thing before. So unique was the event that Wetli was obliged to name it—"interbody implosion."[36]

This first instance Wetli shared with CBS producer Kristina Borjesson and Kelly O'Meara, who was then chief of staff for Congressman Michael Forbes. He told Patricia Milton of another horrific case, that of a man whose spine had been blown out of his body. Milton drew from Wetli's appraisal that this "took more force than even flying debris and 400 mph winds within the cabin could have produced."[37] But as is typical with Milton, she did not pursue it. Borjesson, however, questioned whether an event in the center wing tank could create such an extreme-pressure environment. "The experts I've spoken to," states Borjesson, "say no."[38]

Given the pressure under which the pathologists worked, not all salient information was documented. As the NTSB acknowledges, "The thoroughness of the forensic post-mortem examinations was highly variable."[39]

Understandably, the families cared far more about the identification of their loved ones than they did about the demands of forensic science. This haste, however, when coupled with the initial chaos of the first recovery efforts, would lead to an imprecision in forensic results. With more time, pathologists could have detailed any objects that had penetrated the bodies. There were many of them. An airline crash inevitably fills the air with lethal flying objects, and TWA 800's was more violent than most. "It was like a machine-gun nest in there," Dr. Wetli observed.[40]

One organization that remained vigilant even during the chaotic first days was the FBI. "Foreign material removed from the bodies was immediately released to an FBI technician," notes the NTSB's Final Report.[41]

On July 23, six days after the crash, CNN quoted White House Chief of Staff Leon Panetta as admitting that "chemical residues had been found on some of the bodies and plane parts." In those first few weeks, James

Kallstrom addressed the issue with an indirect affirmative: "I haven't said I haven't found it. I just haven't commented on it."[42]

The pathologists, however, were unable to keep up with the FBI. The autopsy reports did not document what the foreign material was or where it came from. Nor was trajectory information recorded. FBI officials had an exclusive hold on whatever knowledge could be gleaned from the objects. As soon became apparent, the FBI wasn't about to share this knowledge, not even with the NTSB.

In its Factual Report of October 17, 1997, the NTSB's Medical/Forensic Group made little reference to these foreign objects save to acknowledge the FBI's role and the limitation of its own research. Although the report contains a good deal of raw information, particularly in its data mapping, the authors decline to draw any real inferences from the mapping.

One data map, for instance, compared "victims with foreign bodies" and seat assignments. But as the report admits, "Foreign material penetrating the bodies of passengers is common in in-flight break-ups, severe impacts, and explosions." The report writers apologized for their inability to add any useful information about the location of the foreign bodies, their compositions, or their trajectories. Without this information, the data mapping was of little value.

The one data map that could have answered a lot of questions was scarcely explored at all: "Body Recovery Locations." Other than acknowledging that sixteen of the fifty-nine bodies identified by location were found in the Red Zone, the one closest to JFK, seven in the Yellow, and thirty-six in the Green, the report avoided any further comment on the subject.

The data map itself told a more interesting story. Of the victims eventually found in the Red Zone, all but one appear to have been sitting along and in front of the right wing. This would only make sense. As reported in the first weeks of the investigation, a narrow strip of the fuselage ahead of the right wing had been recovered from the area closest to Kennedy airport and was the first to have been blown off the plane. This was also the area where findings of explosive residue had been most concentrated.[43]

Col. Dennis F. Shanahan, M.D., a member of the medical forensic team, made an observation to Patricia Milton that shed more light on the issue. As he observed, forty-five of the ninety-nine bodies found floating on the surface had occupied rows 17 to 28, above the center wing tank, and yet they were not burned. Why they had "not incurred bad burns from the pressurized fuel tank explosion" remained, for Milton at least, a "mystery."[44]

This mystery could have been solved had the medical forensic team been encouraged to consider the larger picture and draw the likely inferences. Rows 17 to 27 along the right wing were the scene of the first and most specific damage to the airliner. Passengers sitting in those seats were the first blown out of the airline. Original, unedited estimates had the fuel tank erupting twenty-four seconds after the first rupture of the fuselage along the right wing. These passengers were not burned because they were no longer there to be burned when the fuel ignited.

The clothing of the victims presented another excellent opportunity for forensic analysis. Concerned by the FBI's failure to do such analysis, at least one family member privately had the shirt of her relative tested. She did this without telling the lab that he was a victim of TWA 800. The lab's report, "Analysis of Spattered Material on Shirt Fabric," offers some intriguing clues into the demise of TWA 800 but none that are fully conclusive. The results, however, suggest that an analysis of all the clothing would have established patterns for the dispersal of chemicals like aluminum, silicon, phosphorus, and chlorine that were found on this one victim's shirt, patterns that might have broken the case.[45]

If the FBI addressed these issues, it has maintained a strict silence on the subject. At its final press conference in November 1997, James Kallstrom made no reference whatsoever to the bodies, their condition, their clothing, or any foreign objects that might have been found within them. This subject was noticeable by its absence from the otherwise comprehensive list of research areas covered at the conference.

Frustrated by the FBI's failure to share such critical information, the citizen activists of FIRO, the Flight 800 Independent Research Organization, took the matter into their own hands. In September of 1998, the organization requested through the Freedom of Information Act (FOIA) a list of all foreign objects recovered from the bodies of the victims and the results of the forensic analysis of the physical characteristics of these objects.

Filing the action for FIRO was Graeme Sephton, an electrical engineer affiliated with the University of Massachusetts. When Sephton appeared later at the Sanderses' trial he caught at least one journalist's eye with a bumper sticker that read, "End Racist Death Penalty."[46] As was obvious, Sephton did not quite fit the media stereotype of the right-wing whack job.

Two weeks after Sephton filed the first FOIA request, the FBI turned him down cold. The FBI cited a law that exempted agencies from responding if FOIA compliance would "interfere with enforcement procedures."[47] The FBI, however, did not suggest what that interference might be, especially given that the agency had suspended its investigation a year earlier.

Not one to give up easily, Sephton filed an appeal with the Department of Justice challenging the FBI's refusal to release the relevant records. In October 1999, nearly a year after filing, Sephton finally heard back from Justice. To his surprise, the Department ruled in his favor. The FBI no longer had a reason for withholding the records and would immediately begin to process "those records that can be made available."

More than four months later, nearly a year and a half after his initial request, the FBI sent Sephton fourteen pages of records. Nowhere among them was any of the forensic data Sephton had specifically requested. Instead, the FBI sent him vague descriptions of the type of investigations undertaken by the NTSB and the FBI.

The saving grace of these documents was the acknowledgment of at least one key fact: FBI agents had not only secured the foreign objects found in the bodies, but they had also had them analyzed. Sephton learned that the FBI's New York office was "aware that all foreign matter found in or on the victim body was/were highly scrutinized by FBI bomb techs," that samples taken from simulated missile tests were compared "to actual fragments found in victim bodies," and, most tellingly, that the "investigation is continuing to identify FB's [foreign bodies] of unknown origin."

Despite this humble acknowledgment, Sephton was appalled by the FBI's transparent game playing. In July of 2000, he filed for an injunction to force the FBI to turn over seven additional pages of documents that it had deliberately withheld.

It would take more than a year and a change in administration before the FBI declassified a meaningful forensic report. The report, an analysis of spectral data recorded by the Brookhaven National Lab, revealed that twenty pieces of 0.2-inch-diameter round shrapnel had been removed from at least one of the victims' bodies.

The report noted that these pellets had been tested because of their "dissimilarity in appearance with TWA 800 debris." As to their source, the analysts could only conclude "unknown origin." For whatever reason, the FBI still refused to reveal whether other victims were similarly injured.

The pellets were composed of aluminum, traces of titanium, and "a little oxygen." Graeme Sephton immediately went to work to discover whether this "matrix" matched any known or proposed weapons system. What he concluded was that the only uses for such pellets "in our whole industrial society" was most likely in "munitions."

The FBI had this information, and probably a good deal more, while it was still actively involved in the investigation. To keep it from the NTSB, the media, and even honest investigators within the FBI, someone at the bureau had it "classified." Most agents did not know it existed, maybe not even Kallstrom. How else to explain Kallstrom's ringing declaration at the close of the FBI investigation that "the law enforcement team has done everything humanly possible" and still could find "no evidence" of a criminal act?[48]

If it was not ignorance, then it was obstruction of justice. There are no other choices.

ON Wednesday, August 8, 2001, an international panel of some seventy airline industry executives and federal officials rejected suggestions that U.S. airlines use a process called "inerting"—that is, the pumping of nonflammable gases into jet fuel-tanks to prevent explosions, like the one alleged to have destroyed TWA Flight 800.

The panel of aviation professionals told the FAA that the process was too costly for commercial use. They contended that the odds against a future fuel tank explosion were far too great to justify the price tag. The unspoken implication, however, was that the odds were too great for a fuel tank to have blown this way, including TWA 800's.

If the panelists had believed that a given 747 could explode because of a fixable problem, they would have fixed those problems in a heartbeat. To reject the FAA's recommendation, the panel had to ignore not only the NTSB's judgment on TWA 800, but also its judgment on other alleged fuel tank disasters in the past.

There were not many of them. Until recently, the only listed "fuel tank explosion" in the eighty-year history of airline disasters was a Philippine Airlines 737 that blew while the plane was backing from a Manila airport gate in May of 1990. And even this case was suspect.

The problems with the case began with its location, the benighted city of Manila, an international cesspool of Islamic terrorism and the home base of, among others, Ramzi Yousef. Yousef was the mastermind of the original World Trade Center bombing and the creator of the Bojinka plot, a plan to blow up eleven American jumbo jets in one day. More than just a schemer, Yousef was responsible for the bombing of Philippine Airlines Flight 434 on December 11, 1994.[49] Any explosion in Manila's airport would raise suspicion as to its origins, especially if it were the only explosion of its kind in the history of aviation.

A second problem with the Philippine Airlines explosion was the nature of the damage. Reportedly, the explosion blew the entire top of the center wing tank violently upwards. The upward blast in the case of TWA Flight 800 was clearly a localized event limited to a specific area at the right side of the center wing tank, concentrated between spanwise beams 2 and 3. The Philippine 737 may have blown up on its own, but if it did, it shed no light on the fate of TWA Flight 800.

When the aforementioned panel met in August 2001, it had another case to consider: a Thai Airways Boeing 737 that had exploded on the tarmac in Bangkok on March 3, 2001. This, too, was ruled a center wing tank explosion, but the panel had good reason to be suspicious.

The Associated Press report on the day of the Thai explosion was admirably straightforward. "A passenger jet Thailand's Prime Minister was to board exploded and went up in flames 35 minutes before its scheduled departure Saturday," noted AP.[50] Apparently, Prime Minister Thaksin Shinawatra was on his way to the Bangkok International Airport when the plane blew up on the runway. "Thailand has a history of coups and violent overthrows of governments," AP reported. "The explosion came two days after Thaksin gave Thailand's Constitutional Court 21 boxes of documents as part of his defense against a corruption indictment that could evict him from office."

According to AP, the Thai Airways president had said there was "a loud noise that sounded like an explosion" before the fire started. AP paraphrased the plane's captain as saying, "It was impossible for the plane to explode from an internal malfunction if the engines had not yet been started. The fully loaded fuel tanks, located in the plane's wings, were intact . . . indicating that burning fuel was not the cause of the explosion."

The *New York Times* was even more specific. "Minutes before Prime Minister Thaksin Shinawatra was to board a Thai Airways jet this weekend, an explosion from beneath his assigned seat blew apart the plane."[51]

On March 5, CNN added more telling details. One was that "the blast ripped through the floor and ceiling," a likely sign of a bomb in the passenger section. The second was the identification by Thailand's defense minister of the composition of the bomb as "definitely C-4."[52]

Nor was this the first time that a Thai plane had blown up. On October 29, 1986, explosives planted in a lavatory of a Thai International Airways Jet sent the plane plunging twenty-one thousand feet before the plane could make an emergency landing. The plane was on its way to Osaka after a stop—where else?—in Manila.[53]

But the investigation in March 2001 followed a pattern not available fifteen years earlier. This time the explosive residue, like all other evidence of a bomb, disappeared in a hurry. On April 11, the NTSB issued a press release that reads like a crude parody of the TWA 800 investigation:

> Physical evidence has been found that the center wing tank exploded. *The accident* [emphasis ours] occurred at 2:48 p.m. on a day with temperatures in the high 35 degree Celsius. The initial explosion of the center wing tank was followed 18 minutes later by an explosion in the right wing tank. Air conditioning packs, which are located directly beneath the center wing tank and generate heat when they are operating, had been running continuously since the airplane's previous flight, including about 40 minutes on the ground.[54]

Note the apocryphal TWA 800 scenario now transposed to a 737 on a Thailand tarmac: the heat, the overactive air conditioning, the center wing tank explosion, even if this was a 737, not a 747, and only nine years old at that. The parody grows cruder still:

> Although chemical traces of high-energy explosives were initially believed to be present, samples have been submitted to the FBI for confirmation by laboratory equipment that is more sensitive than equipment available in Thailand. Although a final report has not yet been issued, the FBI has found no evidence of high explosives in any of the samples tested to date.

How or why the NTSB and the FBI both got involved in a Thailand explosion was not at all clear. What was clear, however, was the dissembling. "Sensitive" equipment finds more explosive residue, not less. Once again, the FBI made the explosive residue go away—the only thing missing was the fabled careless cop spreading residue for a bomb-hunting dog. Again, the NTSB imposed its patented center wing tank scenario, this time not in four years but in four weeks. Again, a forty-minute layover on a ninety-five-degree day was made to seem unusually perilous. Again, the explanation held off the media.

The *New York Times* headlined only its second piece on the Thai Airways crash, "A Similarity Is Seen in 2 Plane Explosions." The headline infers both the NTSB strategy and the *Times'* passivity.[55]

CNN did no better. "Investigators are also looking at any role heat-generating air conditioning units may have played in the Thai blast," observed CNN's on-line service after the NTSB changed its story. CNN noted that these units were also a "contributing factor" in the explosion of TWA 800.[56]

That no member of the major media expressed even the faintest bit of skepticism reveals all too much about the state of American journalism. It was, of course, possible that the Thai Airways explosion did occur by accident; it was just not likely. Clearly, the panel of aviation experts gave it and TWA 800 little credence.

The American involvement in the Thai case was too quick and expedient. Still unable to identify an ignition source for TWA 800, the NTSB needed a parallel explosion to justify its miscellaneous rulings on that doomed flight.

As to the Thai prime minister, the one who was about to indict his buddies in a corruption scandal, the one who was about to board the plane, he would welcome an alternative explanation, one that would make him look less vulnerable and victimized. After all, accidents can happen to anyone, can't they?

CHAPTER 12

SHOW TRIAL

The first formal testimony in the legal assault on James and Elizabeth Sanders would be given in December of 1997. A week later, President Bill Clinton would give his sworn testimony in the Paula Jones suit. That testimony represented the first time the name Monica Lewinsky entered the public record.

The Sanderses entered their not-guilty plea in federal court on January 20, 1998. This just happened to be one day after the Monica story broke nationwide.

The whirlwind created by the Clinton-Lewinsky scandal would suck the air out of every newsroom in America. The administration's Byzantine legal assault on the Sanderses would play out in the vacuum left behind. With a lively sex scandal to divert them, the media paid little heed to what would prove to be one of the darkest chapters in the history of American free press.

THE day after the Sanderses' arrest in December 1997, James Sanders's source, "Hangar Man" Terrell Stacey, rendered his sworn plea allocution. A reluctant witness, Stacey stated the following:

When I was given an opportunity or when I—when Mr. Sanders offered to me or the fact I learned that he could help in the investigation through contacts and people he had in labs, then I on my own volition took the two small pieces and gave them to him to have them analyzed.[1]

Stacey could not have been clearer. He removed the residue samples "on my own volition." But at this stage such a revelation carried little weight. The wheels of Justice were grinding, and no imaginable mass of evidence could block their way.

Four weeks after Stacey's plea, the Sanderses were formally indicted. The charge was that they violated and conspired to violate 49 U.S.C., Section 1155, by importuning Stacey to provide those small pieces of material.

The Sanderses' attorney at the time, Jeremy Gutman, argued during discovery that the government had retaliated for one specific reason: James Sanders had exercised his constitutionally protected right to promote a theory about the cause of the Flight 800 disaster that challenged the "official" version. The retaliation was designed to dissuade Sanders, Gutman argued, "from further efforts to investigate and communicate facts in support of that theory." "Intent" of course, would be no easier to prove through direct evidence than in any instance of government wrongdoing, especially where no insider had broken ranks. Imagine Watergate, for instance, without John Dean. Gutman acknowledged as much. His trump card was "the chronology of events."

Gutman moved through the chronology day by day, month by month. Yes, the investigation was launched only after the *Press-Enterprise* article appeared. Yes, the government responded to the article by discrediting Sanders's theory. Yes, its agents followed that with the active harassment of Sanders and his wife. Yes, the government disregarded its own rules on media subpoenas, feigning ignorance of the "journalistic nature" of Sanders's work. Yes, the government threatened to indict both Sanderses if they failed to reveal James Sanders's confidential source.

Gutman was just getting warmed up. He continued that when the Sanderses refused to roll over, the government harassed their friends and coworkers and subpoenaed the Sanderses' phone records. When the Sanderses were arrested, the FBI issued a major press release accusing them of lying about the lab results.

This Kafkaesque show climaxed, of course, when the FBI agents paraded the humiliated couple before the media—and thus the Long Island jury pool—with their hands cuffed tightly behind their backs. And all of this, Gutman concluded, for an "obscure victimless crime."

This much the prosecutors expected to hear. Gutman surprised them, however, when he charged the FBI's James Kallstrom with committing the same crime of which the Sanderses stood accused. Apparently, Kallstrom had removed an American flag found among the debris and presented it as a souvenir to a relative of one of the victims. "It does not appear," Gutman noted ironically, "that Mr. Kallstrom has been subjected to criminal prosecution as a result of this act."

Gutman wanted to remind the federal judge that the law in question had been enacted to discourage souvenir hunters, not reporters like Sanders or concerned NTSB investigators like Stacey. Congressional intent was clear in the drafting of this one criminal section of Title 49, 1155(b):

> The Board [NTSB] witness testified in the hearings that numerous instances have occurred where souvenir hunters thoughtlessly and, on many occasions, maliciously carried off parts of aircraft wreckage which are vital to the accident investigation. Criminal penalties proposed in this bill will assist materially in alleviating this problem by providing a reasonable and effective deterrent.

Worse, Gutman continued, the Justice Department hid "this compelling evidence of selective prosecution" when it had an obligation to share it with the defense.

The case, Gutman concluded, "smacks of an effort to penalize the defendants for the perceived harmfulness of the contents of their communications, rather than for any harm arising from their conduct per se." The Sanderses were entitled, he believed, "to full discovery," whereby they would be privy to much information about the case kept tightly under wraps but which might exonerate the couple. Needless to say, the prosecution thought otherwise.

The Justice Department countered with two basic arguments. One was that its officials had no knowledge that Sanders was a journalist. Try as they might, they could find nothing within the *Press-Enterprise* articles even suggesting he might be one. "The March 10, 1997, article," claimed Justice, "did not clearly identify [Mr. Sanders] as a member of the media." The second, and less critical, was that James Kallstrom was exempt from the federal criminal code. If he wished to become a souvenir hunter at a crash site, such was his right.

After digesting the Justice Department's opposition to full discovery, the defense team prepared a response, confident that the government had stepped far beyond the envelope of truth and reasoned debate. The response was compelling.

If the government was not prepared to concede that the Sanderses were engaged in actions protected by the First Amendment, what, Gutman asked, could their motive possibly have been? The government suggested no other alternative. Quite the contrary. The Justice Department's own press release on the occasion of the Sanderses' arrest contended that Sanders "misrepresented" the results of his lab tests in media reports. In that same press release, Kallstrom admitted the following: "These defendants are charged with not only committing a serious crime, they have also increased the pain already inflicted on the victims' families."[2]

Short of a signed confession, there could hardly have been clearer proof that Justice prosecuted Sanders because of his opinions. Kallstrom's reference to the families' "pain" had nothing to do with the removal of material from the airplane wreckage. Of course not. The imagined pain derived from the shattering of the families' faith in the government's theory and their trust in Kallstrom himself.

During the broadcast of the *NBC Nightly News* that same day, December 5, 1997, correspondent Robert Hager called Sanders's efforts "a plot to rewrite the history of TWA 800" and cited Kallstrom as his source. Sanders's real offense was not theft; it was writing history or, worse, rewriting it.[3]

The claim that the *Press-Enterprise* articles did not clearly identify Sanders "as a member of the media" struck Gutman as "preposterous." He noted that the article referred to Sanders in its second paragraph as "author and investigative reporter James Sanders." Three paragraphs later the article described Sanders's two previous nonfiction books of investigative journalism.

As to the charge of theft, the defense team argued that "Sanders' conduct does not warrant prosecution under 49 U.S.C., Section 1155 any more than that of James Kallstrom, whom the government acknowledges removed a flag from the wreckage."

To be sure, the government implied that Kallstrom's removal was "authorized," but it did not cite any statute that gave Kallstrom that privilege while denying it to Terrell Stacey. This argument had to drive Justice to distraction. How dare the defense team compare Kallstrom's noble act to Sanders's thievery? This argument left Gutman a huge opening, and he drove right through:

If the government means to suggest that Kallstrom's conduct does not warrant criminal prosecution because it served a high-minded and worthy purpose, the Sanders' conduct is equally blameless. In seeking to uncover and disseminate the truth about the causes of the Flight 800 disaster, the Sanders were acting in the tradition of the First Amendment, which recognizes the importance of an "untrammeled press as a vital source of public information."[4]

To this point, the arguments were all presented in writing. Now that Judge Joanna Seybert had the arguments in front of her, she had a decision to make. As was obvious to all parties, the government could not tolerate full discovery. Its actions to date, so often indefensible, needed judicial protection if they were to avoid exposure and review.

In a nation that adheres to the rule of law, justice mandates a level playing field. At this stage of the proceedings, the judge could dictate just how level that field would be by how much discovery she allowed.

On the day oral arguments were scheduled, Judge Seybert walked into the courtroom, sat in the high-back leather chair, turned to prosecutor Benton Campbell and said words to the effect of, "Excellent brief." She offered no such kindness to Jeremy Gutman, the Sanderses' attorney. She then proceeded to issue a ruling that cut right to the chase. There would be no discovery beyond the legal minimums. The trial was to begin in less than two months.

If this account seems one-sided, it is so only because the proceedings were. Seybert's intent may be elusive and beyond proof, but the emotional impact of her rulings was palpable. The Sanderses were left stunned and unnerved.

It was in this chilled environment that the Sanderses' team soon received Seybert's written explanation for her denial of additional discovery. She began by alleging that Justice's conduct amounted to only "incidental limitations on [the Sanderses'] First Amendment freedoms." The judge then took a page out of the Justice Department playbook and inserted a spurious argument to justify her ruling:

The indictment charges much more than a simple relay of a message from Sanders to Stacey; rather, the indictment charges that the Sanders actively conspired to have the fabric removed from the hangar and delivered to James Sanders.

The judge had to know this charge was false. The portion of the indictment dealing with this issue is presented to remove any doubt as to who was presenting fact and who was presenting something less:

> In or about December 1996, JAMES SANDERS asked Terrell Stacey to remove some of the reddish residue from the seats that had been recovered from TWA 800 so that JAMES SANDERS could test the residue for the presence of missile fuel exhaust.
>
> In or about December 1996 and January 1997, ELIZABETH SANDERS spoke to Terrell Stacey and asked him to remove a sample of the residue from the seats that had been recovered from TWA 800.
>
> In or about January 1997, in Calverton, New York, Terrell Stacey attempted to scrape a portion of the reddish residue from the seats of TWA 800. Being unable to scrape off the residue, Terrell Stacey cut a portion of fabric from the seats on which the reddish residue could be seen.[5]

The indictment states only that James Sanders once "asked" Stacey to remove a sample of the residue for the specific purpose of testing. Elizabeth Sanders was also accused of having "asked." Nothing in the indictment even hints at an active conspiracy to remove fabric—part of the physical plane.

The court then addressed the second element in the selective prosecution "test." Namely that "the prosecution was motivated by a desire to chill the defendants' exercise of rights protected under the First Amendment." In addressing this issue, the judge changed the Sanderses' chronology of federal acts against them. Some of the court's changes minimized defense accusations of government wrongdoing and embellished the Sanderses' alleged acts.

As to the defendants' charge that the government's prosecution was "in retaliation for their efforts to publicize their theory that a Navy missile was the cause of the Flight 800 explosion," Judge Seybert was equally dismissive. She ruled that the defendants "failed to establish a substantial and concrete basis sufficient to allow further discovery to overcome the presumption of regularity on the part of federal prosecutors."

The legal playing field had been dramatically altered. In essence, the judge announced that she was pulling for the home team. The effect was to give the government a distinct advantage in its effort to silence its accusers.

In the course of preparing for trial, James Sanders came to a disturbing realization. The prosecution was repeating his work product, sometimes word for word. He soon learned why. The Justice Department had seized his computer, the one he had left in storage in Kansas City, and had done so without a warrant.[6] Elizabeth Sanders had other worries. If she could barely understand what was happening to her and Jim, how difficult it must be for her elderly mom to understand, especially given her uncertain grasp of the language and culture. How difficult and embarrassing.

The trial began on April 5, 1999, at the modern, unimposing United States District Court in Uniondale, Long Island. In attendance, wrote the *New York Times* dismissively, were "nearly a dozen conspiracy theorists." They were convinced that the Sanderses "were being prosecuted as part of a Government cover-up of the cause of the crash."[7]

If the conspiracy theorists were convinced, the media were conspicuously not. The *Times* described James Sanders as a "self-styled freelance investigative journalist,"[8] a gratuitous dig at a reporter whose most recent reportorial book had sold more than one hundred thousand copies in the last year. Even more patronizing and inaccurate was the Associated Press, which dismissed Sanders as "a self-styled accident investigator."[9] In other words, Sanders was not one of them. He did not deserve the media's support or their sympathy.

After the jury was selected and before opening arguments, prosecutors attempted to convince Judge Seybert that the warrantless seizure of a journalist's computer was within the law. Given the judge's responsiveness to this point, they had no reason not to be optimistic.

Then an odd thing happened. Seybert came alive to the case in front of her. If her rulings on discovery, vindictive prosecution, and the First Amendment had seemed to the defense team pro forma—perhaps even part of some sinister game plan—her performance as the case moved forward seemed altogether more balanced.

Balanced as it may have been, Seybert's rulings would not prove overly brave. Although she did rule against the government seizing Sanders's computer and its work product, she would not acknowledge how that seizure corrupted the entire case. She could not bring herself to deny or even question the legitimacy of the government's intent.

The prosecutor, David Pitofsky, was a studied dramatist. As he launched his opening argument, he turned and pointed to the Sanderses and let the jury know just who was on trial.

"You will hear testimony about the investigation," he told the jury, "but this case, in this case you will not be asked to decide anything about how that investigation was conducted." Of course not.

The pretrial rulings enabled Pitofsky to put NTSB and FBI brass on the stand. They would casually flatter themselves with tales of a thorough, legal investigation. But the defense would not be allowed to challenge their contentions. Case in point: On one occasion, Pitofsky called senior FBI agent Ken Maxwell. Pitofsky had one purpose for calling Maxwell. He wanted to draw a specific inference that circumvented the truth.

In reality, the Flight 800 investigation had never officially been declared a crime scene.[10] It was legally a "crash scene." By law, the NTSB was the lead agency. By law, the FBI had an inferior position. Maxwell admitted this on the stand. Pitofsky, however, casually began to use the phrase "crime scene," suggesting a higher level of seriousness. Maxwell soon caught on and began to parrot Pitofsky. The repetition had to weigh on the jury.

On day two, the trial's one critical witness, Terrell Stacey, took the stand. On direct examination, Pitofsky led Stacey through his work at Calverton Hangar, his first meeting with Sanders, and their ongoing relationship. Pitofsky then introduced the issue of the reddish-orange residue trail that could be seen across the backs of the seats in rows 17, 18, and 19.

> *Pitofsky:* Returning to your telephone conversations during this period, what sort of conversations did you have with Jim Sanders about the existence and importance of this reddish coloring on the seatbacks?
>
> *Stacey:* That from the standpoint of the investigation he was doing, that it would be, that it would be very important, or nice to have that—I remember him using the term once, that that would slam dunk, if it came out positive for explosive residue, then it would slam dunk as far as being absolute proof that some outside force affected the airplane.
>
> *Pitofsky:* What, if any, discussion did you have about what you might do with regard to this red coloring?
>
> *Stacey:* Well, he being an investigator, former investigator with the police department, indicated to me we would just need a very small sample of it. To just take a pen knife and scrape off a little of it on to an envelope, and it would just take a very minute sample to have analyzed.
>
> *Pitofsky:* And how specific were your discussions about what would be done with the sample once you obtained it and sent it to Mr. Sanders?
>
> *Stacey:* That they would be taken to a private lab to be analyzed.

Stacey's honesty here accomplished little for the prosecution. He did not say that Sanders had coerced him into getting a sample. Nor did he even say that Sanders asked him for a sample. Sanders had simply made it clear he would gladly accept a sample and have it tested. Stacey's testimony did not begin to describe a conspiracy.

Pitofsky then went to the heart of Stacey's story—his reluctance to obtain the residue. Had he not been reluctant, the government would have lost the rationale for the alleged conspiracy, even by the tortured logic of this case:

Pitofsky: And what was your reaction to the idea of removing the sample?

Stacey: Well, I was concerned about it, or leery about it because I knew we had been warned many times to maintain a confidentiality of the investigation and we knew we weren't supposed to take anything out of the hangar.

Pitofsky: Do you recall, what if any discussion did you have with Mr. Sanders over the phone about those types of concerns?

Stacey: Each time I talked with Jim I relayed to him what we were doing had to be in the strictest confidentiality. And my being jeopardized, my position with the company being jeopardized as well as my position in the investigation, as well as the company's position with the investigation . . .

Pitofsky: Approximately how long did it take you to decide whether to get involved in this scheme to remove the evidence?

Stacey: I would say three weeks, or approximately so. I was vacillating back and forth in my mind as to whether or not to take this step.

It was this "vacillation," this alleged hesitance on Stacey's part, that required the supposed coercion and provoked the conspiracy. On December 8, 1996, in the midst of Stacey's alleged vacillation, he and Sanders talked on the phone, a call that Sanders routinely tape-recorded. The pair discussed several issues from inside the investigation, but the issue of the residue did not surface until the last few minutes when Sanders began to sign off:

Sanders: In any case, I won't keep you anymore here; I wanted to check with you. So I'll just anxiously await the residue and whatever else . . .

Stacey: Whatever else I can scrounge.

Sanders: Yeah. Exactly. Yeah. I can either come up and get it or, which is ever more convenient, I can either come up and get it, or mail it. But it's a little easier for me now normally because Liz lands at her apartment this evening. She's driving up there right now.

Stacey: Oh my.

Sanders: Then she ends up next week going right back to St. Louis for five days. Then from the twentieth through the end of the year she's flying or at least on call to fly.

Stacey: Does she get the holiday off, or Christmas off?

Sanders: No. No. She's working both that and probably, assuming they grab her for a flight—she said the thirtieth but I presume she meant the thirty-first. Unless her schedule is—unless that's when they end her schedule. I don't know if they do them in thirty-day cycles or what.

Stacey: I think this one ends on the thirty-first.

Sanders: So if they grab her for one of those, where she's halfway through a flight on the thirty-first, she's working on the first too. In any case, I'll have easier access to places to stay and cars and that kind of stuff. I also have a forensics expert online to analyze it very quickly so we don't have to stand in line at a crime lab somewhere, probably out on the West Coast, and wait for a month while they get around to it.

Stacey: I'll make that my top priority, because that group, like I say, Les and them were talking about finishing up, so that place ought to be fairly secluded in a few days. There won't be a lot of people.

Sanders: Oh, outstanding, good.

Stacey: OK.

Sanders: OK. Well, give me a buzz whenever and we'll figure out how to do a handoff on it and go from there. I appreciate all the help.

Stacey: OK. Very good.

Sanders: OK. Talk to you later.[11]

This tape recording reflected the true status of Stacey's thoughts at that time. There was no hesitation, no coercing. Obtaining the residue was, he volunteered, his "top priority," along with anything else he could "scrounge."

The tape also accurately reflected the journalist-source relationship. They were comfortable discussing all issues related to the Flight 800 investigation. When Elizabeth Sanders's name came up, there was no reference to her participation in any manner in this journalist-to-source relationship, even as a liaison or courier. Yet it was acknowledged that she had an apartment just thirty miles west of the Calverton Hangar and was driving there that very night.

Stacey was not a reluctant source. He was an enthusiastic participant who volunteered to obtain the telling residue sample despite the obvious risks. Within twenty-four hours, the existence of this tape would be revealed to the jury.

But on this day inside the courtroom, the prosecution did not know about the tape or the truth it contained. So Pitofsky continued to lead Stacey through a story shaped by the government's desire to nail the Sanderses, and by Stacey's desire to avoid ruin.

Pitofsky: During that time did you speak to anyone else about the idea of obtaining a sample from the Calverton facility?

Stacey: Yes.

Pitofsky: Who was that?

Stacey: Liz Sanders.

Pitofsky: Under what circumstances—first of all, how many conversations did you have with Liz Sanders on this particular topic?

Stacey: On this particular, only one.

Pitofsky: You testified that after the initial conversation with Jim Sanders it took about three weeks to make your decision. Where in the two or three-week period while you were trying to make your decision, did the telephone call from Liz Sanders occur?

Stacey: All I can say is it occurred during that time. I couldn't recall if it was the beginning of it, the middle or end. I honestly don't know.

Pitofsky: What do you recall having been said by both yourself and herself in as much detail as you can recall?

Stacey: Just the thing that I remember about it is she just indicated to me that it would be nice to have that sample, or we really needed that sample . . .

Pitofsky: Did there eventually come a time when you decided whether or not you would obtain this sample?

Stacey: Yes.

Pitofsky: And did you in fact decide that you would obtain the sample?

Stacey: Yes.

Pitofsky: Why did you decide to go ahead and take the sample from the Calverton facility?

Stacey: Again, there was a heavy burden with the investigation, frustration with the investigation, the lack of sharing the information by the NTSB and, of course, the FBI. Many theories going around and NTSB people trying to prove the theories; being away from the family; constantly being involved in the investigation of the wreckage and so forth. I thought this would be a means of me obtaining some more information, more analysis to find out the cause of the accident of Flight 800.

Stacey's instinctive honesty once again derailed the prosecution. When asked why he had decided to take the sample, he did not cite the Sanderses' coercion but his own frustration with the course of the investigation. When the prosecutor heard this answer, he knew he was in trouble. A follow-up question, if answered incorrectly, could destroy the government's case. Pitofsky halted the questioning.

The Sanderses' attorney, Bruce Maffeo, eagerly began his cross-examination of Stacey. He immediately zeroed in on Stacey's alleged reluctance to remove the residue.

Then Maffeo shocked Pitofsky. He calmly walked over and dropped the transcript of Stacey's taped interview with Sanders onto the prosecutor's table. Pitofsky leafed through the pages and soon read Stacey's highlighted words: "I'll make that my top priority."

Maffeo had saved the transcript for cross-examination. Had he introduced it into evidence at the beginning of the trial, the prosecution would have reshaped Stacey's testimony around it. On cross-examination, however, the tape could be used to impeach the testimony Stacey had already given. The moment had arrived. Maffeo now gave Stacey a copy of the transcript and asked him to read it.

Maffeo: Have you had an opportunity to review it, Captain Stacey?

Stacey: Yes.

Maffeo: Having had an opportunity to review it, does it refresh your recollection that you told Sanders in December 1996 that you would make removing the residue your top priority?

Stacey: No, sir.

Maffeo: Does it refresh your recollection at all?

Stacey: No, sir.

Maffeo: Do you recall telling Sanders in the same conversation that you would have to wait until the people who were working in that area of the hangar completed their job and wait a couple of days?

Stacey: No, sir.

Maffeo: No recollection of it at all as you sit here today, sir?

Stacey: No.

Maffeo: Isn't it a fact, Captain Stacey, that you removed the red residue of
   your own volition and to find out the cause of the accident?

Stacey: Yes.

Maffeo was on a roll. Stacey was precariously close to abandoning the
script the prosecution had carefully prepared. Maffeo pressed hard:

Maffeo: My question to you, Captain Stacey is this: At the time that you
   snapped off these two three-inch samples of seat fabric, you didn't
   believe at the time that you were compromising the ability of the
   NTSB or the FBI to conduct an investigation [with the] remaining
   samples left in the cabin; is that correct?

Stacey: Correct.

Maffeo: In fact, Captain Stacey, is it not true that at the time that you performed those actions, you did not believe that you had violated or that
   you were breaking the law?

Pitofsky: Objection.

THE COURT: Overruled.

Stacey: Repeat the question, please.

Maffeo: At the time you snapped these two samples off, Captain Stacey,
   you didn't, in fact, think you were breaking the law?

Stacey: That's correct.

Other than an admission that the Justice Department had coerced
Stacey, there was nothing else the defense could have hoped to get out of
him. Within minutes, court was adjourned for the day, and a very happy
defense team walked out the front door.

In 1999, consciously or otherwise, the major American media had
moved fully into a pro-administration mode. The *New York Times* went so
far as to distort Stacey's testimony to justify its bias.

As the "paper of record" reported, "[Stacey] told the jury that Mrs.
Sanders had pleaded with him to help provide evidence for her husband's
investigation into the crash."[12] Stacey took the residue, the *Times* wrote on
another occasion, "at the repeated insistence of the Sanderses."[13] Terrell
Stacey never made these claims under oath at the Uniondale Court House.
The *New York Times* contrived them for its own purposes.

Newsday published a story suggesting that the defense team's failure to
mount a First Amendment defense showed its agreement that Sanders was

not a journalist. Intentionally or otherwise, the reporter had ignored the judge's ruling against a First Amendment defense.

"Years ago," wrote the discerning Phillip Weiss in *Jewish World Review,* "there was glory in rewriting history and talking about Government cover-ups, but the discourse is now so complacent and sophisticated that Mr. Sanders' beliefs seem in bad taste." The consequence, Weiss continued, is that "no one in the press community has embraced him despite the obvious First Amendment issue."[14]

THE morning after Stacey's nearly disastrous testimony, Pitofsky had one last chance to get him back on message. His answers the previous day had badly undermined the prosecution.

The prosecution cannot talk privately to a witness while he remains under oath and can potentially be recalled to the stand. But Pitofsky had a legal excuse: Stacey had to listen to the audiotaped conversation the defense had introduced only on cross-examination. By law, Pitofsky could discuss only the audiotape with Stacey. But the government had yet to allow the rule of law to restrict its efforts, and it wasn't about to start now. Pitofsky's questions when court resumed argue strongly for witness tampering:

> *Pitofsky:* Good morning, Captain Stacey. I will remind you are still under
> oath. Do you recall, Captain Stacey, yesterday you were asked by Mr.
> Maffeo on cross-examination whether you removed the red residue,
> and I quote, of your own volition, and to find out the cause of the
> accident? Do you remember being asked that question?
> *Stacey:* Yes.
> *Pitofsky:* And you remember your answer to that question was yes?
> *Stacey:* Yes.

The next question would never have been asked had Pitofsky not known in advance what the answer was going to be. Someone had to have coached the witness before he entered the courtroom on day three:

> *Pitofsky:* Would you please explain to the jury what that phrase means that
> you acted of your own volition in this matter?

This question was far too open-ended. Stacey could have taken it in any direction he wished. His response to that question the day before had stopped the prosecution dead in its tracks. At the time, Pitofsky dared go no further. But on this day he asked the question with confidence.

> *Stacey:* That—was to—it was during the time that I came and appeared before Judge Pohorelsky, and I was accepting responsibility for my actions, as well as making certain that it was clear that no other TWA or investigative personnel at the hangar had assisted me in taking the material.

This was pure concoction. The day before Stacey had all but exonerated the Sanderses. Now, he was claiming to have cleared his coworkers who were never under suspicion in the first place.

Pitofsky continued the line of questions:

> *Pitofsky:* I just want to make clear that it is your testimony this morning that what you meant when you used that phrase at your plea hearing and what you meant when you answered yesterday, had to do with whether any TWA or other hangar persons had assisted you or worked with you on this matter?
>
> *Stacey:* That's correct.
>
> *Pitofsky:* Did you mean you didn't receive influence from anyone in this matter?
>
> *Stacey:* No.
>
> *Pitofsky:* And did you receive influence from persons in this matter?
>
> *Stacey:* Yes.
>
> *Pitofsky:* And who did you receive influence from persons in this matter?
>
> *Stacey:* From Jim and Liz Sanders.

Less than twenty-four hours before, Stacey had inferred that Elizabeth Sanders had had no influence on him. To the defense team, it seemed apparent that the current answers had been rehearsed. Now, it was Maffeo's turn. On re-redirect, he honed in on the facts, and Stacey again began to wander off script.

> *Maffeo:* You had an opportunity to listen to the tape that was just played to the Court today, sir?
>
> *Stacey:* Yes.
>
> *Maffeo:* You listened to it, to it before you came to court this morning?

Stacey: Yes.

Maffeo: You recognize your voice on that tape?

Stacey: Yes.

Maffeo: It is your voice saying you will make getting the residue your top priority?

Stacey: Yes.

Maffeo: Your voice saying you will get anything else you can scrounge up, right?

Stacey: Yes.

Maffeo had reestablished for the jury Stacey's eager participation in the plan to remove a residue sample. This was Stacey's "top priority," not necessarily Sanders's. It was Stacey, too, who volunteered to "scrounge" for other telling evidence.

He continued.

Maffeo: And specifically, do you recall being asked this question by the judge and giving this answer, on page 17. Question by the Court: Mr. Stacey, can you describe briefly in your own words what you did in connection with the crime charged? Answer: I was assigned to the investigation immediately after the accident and started working on it. Well, first off I brought that plane back from Paris the day before and had flown the airplane three times in the previous week. And I was assigned to the investigation. We had been there for many long months. I was away from the family, under [a] lot of pressure and emotional stress to try to find out the cause of the accident. And when I was given an opportunity or when Mr. Sanders offered to me, or the fact that I learned that he could help in the investigation through contacts and people he had in labs then I on my own volition took the two small pieces and gave them to him to have them analyzed.

Maffeo: Do you recall giving that answer to that question posed by the Court in your plea appearance?

Stacey: Yes.

Maffeo: And anything in your statement to the Court under the oath on December 10th about Jim or Liz Sanders pressuring you to take the residue? Did you say anything like that to the Court on December 10th, 1997?

Stacey: Say the first part of the question?

Maffeo: During the course of your allocution before the Magistrate Judge on December 10th, 1997, did you tell the judge that you had been pressured by Jim or Liz Sanders to take the samples of the red residue?

Stacey: No.

Bruce Maffeo then wrapped up the re-cross-examination and Jeremy Gutman took over. Being Liz Sanders' attorney, Gutman changed the focus somewhat:

Gutman: Captain Stacey, you testified yesterday under oath to this jury about one telephone conversation with Liz Sanders that touched on the subject of residue; is that correct?

Stacey: Correct.

Gutman: And you couldn't remember when that took place?

Stacey: That's correct.

Gutman: And you really couldn't—let me read your testimony to you. You testified, just the thing that I remember about it is she just indicated—indicated to me that it would really be nice to have that sample or we ral [sic] needed that—really needed that sample, correct?

Stacey: Correct.

Gutman: Your testimony, yesterday?

Stacey: Yes.

Gutman: You don't remember the exact words you said in that?

Stacey: No.

Gutman: And is that the conversation that you believe influenced you to remove the residue?

With this question, Pitofsky leaped out of his chair in objection. Any answer to that question would hurt his case. As Stacey admitted earlier, he had had only one phone conversation with Elizabeth Sanders. If Stacey answered yes, the defense could reveal that this one call had taken place on January 9, 1997, *after* Stacey had taken the samples from the hangar. If Stacey answered no, the jury would be left wondering when exactly this "influence" took place.

After some legal wrangling, Judge Seybert called Pitofsky and Gutman to the bench. Finally, she allowed the question.

Gutman: Were you referring to that partially remembered bit of conversation when you said on your redirect testimony just a little while earlier this morning that you were influenced by Liz Sanders?

Stacey: No. Specifically, no.

The case against Elizabeth Sanders was shot—or so it seemed. In his opening statement Pitofsky had told the jury that Stacey would reveal how Elizabeth had coerced him. Instead, Stacey continued to testify that their one conversation had not influenced his decision to take the residue.

Pitofsky's case against James Sanders was also wavering. As successful as Pitofsky had been in stacking the deck, especially in removing the First Amendment, he still had too weak a hand to win. Pitofsky did, however, have one card up his sleeve, and he proved devious enough to play it.

Pitofsky: Captain Stacey, I want to focus on the events of your plea of guilty in this case. There was some question as to what occurred there. Sir, what did you understand to be the issue before the Court during that hearing? Let me ask you this way: Whose guilt or innocence did you believe to be in issue on that day?

Stacey: Mine.

Pitofsky: And did you believe that the guilt or innocence of Liz and/or Jim Sanders was in issue on that day?

Stacey: No.

Pitofsky: And did you believe what was in issue that day was your guilt or innocence and your willingness to accept your responsibility for your participation in this conduct?

Stacey: Yes.

Pitofsky: And were you charged with a conspiracy in this case? Did you plead guilty to a conspiracy count in this case?

Stacey: No.

Pitofsky: The count you pled guilty to was focused entirely on you; is that correct?

Stacey: Yes.

Pitofsky: And you were also asked questions about what you said about Liz Sanders and her influence or lack of influence during your plea allocution. Do you remember during your plea allocution you were asked questions about Liz Sanders, or you gave information about Liz Sanders, that you mentioned Liz Sanders during your allocution?

Stacey: No, not that I recall.

Pitofsky: I will read you the question and answer and you tell me if it is accurate to your recollection. Do you recall the *Judge* asked you, during this period did you speak to anyone else about obtaining [t]his red residue? And you answered, yes, Liz Sanders called me. And the *Court* then asked you, how did that conversation go? And you answered, she just indicated we really needed to get that sample in order to find out what happened. Does that refresh your recollection as to whether you mentioned Liz Sanders during your plea allocution? [emphasis added]

Gutman: Can we have a page reference, please?

Pitofsky: I am sorry, page 34, lines 17 through 23.

Stacey: You lost me, and I was thinking of plea allocution, so let's start over, please.

Pitofsky: Let me represent to you what I just read.

As he leafed through the pages of the plea allocution, Maffeo realized what Pitofsky had done. He could not believe it. "Objection," he shouted. Gutman had caught on too. "Objection, objection, objection. Can we approach?" When they were invited to do so, Gutman called Pitofsky's bluff.

Gutman: Your honor, this is grand jury testimony. I move for a mistrial.
    This is an inadmissible statement.

Pitofsky: Then I made a mistake.

A "mistake?" Pitofsky was an experienced attorney. He had been exposed to tens of thousands of pages of transcript from trials, depositions, and grand jury testimony. The formats are distinctly different. Transcripts taken outside the courtroom setting have the witness name at the top of each page and the transcriber's company name and phone number at the bottom of each page. Transcripts generated inside the courtroom do not have either. No experienced attorney, no second-year law student, could confuse grand jury testimony with a plea allocution.

What is more, whenever a judge makes a statement, the transcript reads "THE COURT." If an attorney asks a question, the transcript reads "Q." Pitofsky was reading from a page that had "Q" before each question. Still, he had attributed these questions to the court. Besides that, he had to search through a number of pages to find the precise quote. Each page flashed like a neon sign saying, "This is not an allocution plea. This is inadmissible grand jury testimony."

What was Pitofsky's motive? Panic, possibly. But Pitofsky had been around the block. He understood juries. All this jury would see were two slick defense attorneys trying desperately to suppress some presumably damning bit of evidence.

The Sanderses' attorneys understood Pitofsky's game. They moved for a mistrial. They believed that Pitofsky had deliberately contaminated the jury. This judge, however, had felt the pressure of this case from the beginning. If she had any one goal, it was to finish the case quickly. She would tell the jury to disregard Pitofsky's last gambit. That would fix everything. No need for a mistrial. There was nothing the defense team could do to repair the damage that had been done.

The defense elected to call just one witness, Jeff Schlanger, the Sanderses' attorney in 1997. As a lawyer, and therefore an officer of the court, his sworn testimony carried significant weight, particularly if not rebutted by the prosecution.

Schlanger testified that the Justice Department promised to "target" Liz Sanders as of April 14, 1997, almost two months before they interrogated Stacey. The Justice Department was doing its targeting with absolutely no evidence, real or imagined, to implicate Elizabeth. In administrations that honor the rule of law, this does not happen.

Pitofsky could not find anyone within the government who had been at that meeting willing to rebut Schlanger's testimony. Not even the ubiquitous FBI agent Jim Kinsley, who attended the April meeting and now sat at the prosecution table next to Pitofsky, was willing to go that far. Schlanger went unrebutted.

As is typical in a criminal trial, the prosecution got the last word. "A conspiratorial government going after these people?" Pitofsky scoffed. "And, to what end? What is the government's motive? Ask yourself that. What is the government's motive to falsely implicate these people?"

One can hardly fault the jury for not knowing. They heard nothing about corruption within the investigation. They did not know about James Sanders's First Amendment right to expose that corruption or that his attempt to assert that right had been denied.

All they knew was that these two likely thieves may or may not have conspired to steal evidence from a crime scene. And why believe these "conspiracy theorists"? The establishment media obviously didn't. Besides, what reason did their government have to "falsely implicate these people"?

The jury returned after less than two hours of deliberation. Elizabeth clutched her husband's hand, almost too anxious to speak. She hoped for the best, but feared the worst. The worst is what they got.

"Guilty as charged," both Sanderses, not only for conspiracy, but also for aiding and abetting in the theft of the fabric. The audience gasped in disbelief. Even Judge Joanna Seybert looked stunned. The Sanderses faced as much as ten years in prison.

The jurors quickly left the courthouse by the back exit. Said the one juror who could be coerced into comment, "All I want is to get home."[15]

David Pitofsky beamed in delight. "The jury understood," he said, spinning nonsense even in victory, "that no responsible reporter would believe they could break into a place to get a story."[16]

At this sad moment of truth, as she wept softly, one thought flashed through Elizabeth's mind: "What will my mother think?"

CHAPTER 13

IMAGINARY FLAGPOLES

The skilled propagandist has a ready stock of tricks. One of them is to create detail so specific that it enhances the credibility of a lie and yet so commonplace that no one would think to contest or even check it—a detail like, say, a flagpole.

In fact, a flagpole would prove to be the one image that linked the two public airings of eyewitness information. The first citation of a flagpole occurred in connection with the CIA-produced animation of November 1997, the second at the final NTSB "sunshine" hearing in August 2000. In each case, the flagpole would serve as a critical, visual reference to negate the possible sighting of a missile. And, in each case, the flagpole would be imaginary.

"IT is difficult to put into words the enormity [sic] of this investigation," said Jim Hall during the December 8, 1997, NTSB hearings.[1] To read about Jim Hall is one thing. To see him in action is another. Imagine Floyd the Barber from Andy's Mayberry now as chairman of the NTSB: kindly, bumbling, full of empty bromides, in so far over his head one cringes on his behalf. (For the record, the primary meaning of "enormity" is "outrageous or heinous character." For once, Hall was on the mark.)

Now picture Howard Sprague, Mayberry's officious, self-deluding town clerk. Imagine him a little more unctuous and a little less charming, and you have the hearing's best supporting actor, Dr. David Mayer, acting chief of the NTSB's Orwellian-titled "Human Performance Division." From appearances, it would seem that Mayer's one and essential task at the August 2000 NTSB hearings was to discredit the eyewitnesses.

"As you well know," Mayer piously informed the NTSB Board, "the work of the committee is under the party process. If we would interview witnesses, we would form a group and the group would interview the witnesses."[2] Please note the words *if* and *would* and the following clarification by Mayer's boss, Dr. Bernard Loeb: "In this particular case, some of these witnesses we did not get to because the FBI initially interviewed them. That is a slight difference."

"Some of the witnesses"? Despite the clear directive of Title 49 that the NTSB be the "priority" agency on the crash scene, no one in the NTSB had interviewed a single civilian eyewitness on the ground. Ever. As Mayer observes, the NTSB's witness group "conducted about a dozen interviews," all of them with military personnel or airline pilots. By his own accounts there were 736 eyewitnesses total, well more than seven hundred of them civilians. A "slight difference," indeed! As Hall acknowledged more than once, "I would like to emphasize normal procedures were not followed."

Ironically, the absence of the eyewitnesses at the hearing made Mayer's job simpler. As propaganda experts attest, it is much easier to dissemble when one does not know the person about whom one is dissembling, and easier still if that person is not in the room. This is one likely reason why no eyewitness was allowed to testify at either NTSB hearing.

"In fact," said Mayer, "the witness reports were the first and only evidence or indication of a missile attack." Not exactly. The FAA radar was the *first* evidence, the evidence that stirred the White House Situation Room on the night of the crash. The eyewitnesses, however, were the only "evidence" that could speak for themselves, the only evidence that could not be corrupted, compromised, or lost. And unlike military personnel or government employees, the eyewitnesses could not easily be silenced. Allowing them to testify would throw open a Pandora's box that might never again be shut.

And so in August 2000, as at the NTSB's first public hearing in December 1997, no eyewitness was allowed to testify. By this stage, they would have only caused problems for the NTSB, whose mechanical thesis was now drafted in blood. "As I have already explained," the NTSB's Bernard Loeb pontificated early in the session, "the physical evidence indicated indisputably that a missile did not strike the airplane."

At this second NTSB hearing, however, investigators did at least discuss eyewitness testimony. As it happened, the discussion would reveal a good deal about the investigation, all of it inadvertent.

Mayer began to invent in his very first paragraph. "The FBI began interviewing witnesses on the evening of the accident and, within a week had contacted over 500 witnesses," he told the board. "During this time, safety board investigators reviewed the many witness accounts the FBI was documenting."

This was only marginally true. One NTSB representative was allowed to review the raw FBI interviews for three days before being mysteriously summoned back to Washington on July 25, 1996. He could not take notes or make copies. His only documented comment was that the reports were "generally similar."[3]

Otherwise, the NTSB was ignominiously shut out of the process in those first weeks. As Mayer himself would acknowledge, the NTSB formed a witness team only "later," five months later, November 12 to be precise. At the time of the chairman's report of November 15, 1996, the NTSB had just started the process of reviewing the "more than 450 witness accounts" that the FBI had sent over. Mayer's casual approach to the truth cautions the knowing observer to take nothing for granted in his or Loeb's testimony.

Mayer proceeded to enlighten the board on what a witness would have seen based on the NTSB's understanding of what happened to the plane. "As the accident airplane was flying near the Long Island Coast," Mayer stated authoritatively, "an explosion amid center wing tank had occurred. About three to five seconds later, the nose section departed and began to fall to the water." Despite the near-total lack of physical evidence, there is no longer any conjecture in the NTSB's position. The initiating event was "amid center wing tank," an odd locution, but an inescapable conclusion.

Mayer then added a new, confirming detail: "The center wing tank explosion occurred inside the intact airplane, so it's unlikely that witnesses would have seen this explosion."

Mayer's description of breakup is as clear as the NTSB provided, but it raises more questions than it answers. The analysis that follows is not simple, but it is critical to understanding the utter impossibility of the NTSB scenario:

- First, the center wing tank "explodes," but not so violently as to rupture the fuselage.

- Mayer consistently talks of an "explosion," while the other members of the NTSB team talk of an "overpressure." (For simplicity's sake, the term "explosion" will be used throughout this discussion.)

- The explosion is violent enough, however, to kill the two recorders but not before the CVR "captured a high-energy signal that was consistent with an explosion in the fuel tank." This, according to John Clark of the NTSB in the December 1997 hearing.[4]

- This signal represented the "fraction of second of loud noise" around which the CIA based all its second-by-second calculations for its infamous video. The production purports to show the physical marking of the signal, so critical is it to the CIA's theory. The CIA claims in the video that the "National Safety Board analysts concluded this sound is associated with the beginning of the destruction of the aircraft."[5]

- In other words, the initiating explosion was powerful enough to rattle a seventy-ton bridge ten miles away, but it was not powerful enough to breach the fuselage.

According to the CIA, there are about "four seconds" between the initiating explosion and the explosion that blows off the nose. Presenting his case in August 2000—after the "missing four seconds" had become an issue—Mayer proved more coy, estimating the time at "three to five seconds." Note, too, that in Mayer's prim retelling, "The nose departed." It is not blown off. That would require another explosion still.

In reality, given that the first explosion was not immediately catastrophic, the CVR would have picked up a loud noise, followed by a few seconds of explanations and expletives before the second catastrophic explosion shut down everything and blew off the nose. It wasn't the expletives that would worry those altering the data. It was the explanations—and the sounds of the final catastrophe. This is surely one reason why those four seconds had to disappear.

In Mayer's version of events, when the nose fell off, the rest of the fuselage continued on. "During the crippled flight," he claimed, "it is likely that a fuel-fed fire would've been visible to witnesses some distance away. Such a fire would've looked as a small light or streak."

But where did the fuel come from that caused "such a bright light that it can be seen 40 miles away"? Mayer had sat in on the briefing in April 1999 when the NTSB had asked the CIA this very question a year earlier. At that time, the CIA analyst cited the "residual fuel in the center wing tank," but the two honest NTSB team members weren't buying it. They pointed out that there were only fifty gallons of fuel; that, with the nose up, the fuel would have only rushed back into the rear of the tank, invisible even if burning; and that the fuel burned less visibly in any case. At this point Bernard Loeb had to intervene, as he and Mayer often did. "He's already said that's something he's not going to analyze," said Loeb, cutting off the conversation.[6]

In constructing his own scenario for the August 2000 hearing, Mayer kept the burning-fuel streak and ignored the unanswerable questions raised by his colleagues. "If a witness saw this entire sequence," said Mayer, "what we would expect him or her to see, was a streak of light followed by a fireball, which might split into more than one fireball as it fell."

The only explosions an eyewitness would have seen in this version were the fireballs that occurred when the wing tanks broke apart, some time after the eruption in the fuel tanks. Mayer cited some corroborating examples. One was Paul Angelides, the engineer who watched the events from his deck in Westhampton. Here is how Mayer described what Angelides saw:

> According to the FBI witness document, he noticed a red flare descending; it was on a slight downward arc from west to east. There was a thin, white smoke trail following a red dot. He watched the red dot for three or four seconds and then he saw a fireball erupt. This witness may have seen some of the last stages of the structural breakup of the airplane.

Now, here is how Angelides remembers the event, a recollection that has not changed from day one. Indeed, he gave the FBI sketches of the same:

> A red phosphorescent object in the sky caught my attention. The object was quite high in the sky, about 50-60 degrees, and was slightly to the west and off shore of my position. At first it appeared to be moving slowly, almost hanging and descending, and was leaving a white smoke trail . . . I quickly realized that the object was too large and then began moving too fast to be a distress flare. I followed the object as it moved out over the ocean in the direction of the horizon. I lost sight of the object, as it was about 10 degrees above the horizon. In the same area of the sky out over

the ocean, I then saw a series of flashes, one in the sky and another closer
to the horizon.[7]

Mayer's use of Angelides as a witness for the defense is a sign of some des-
peration. To be sure, Mayer had never talked to him. He dared not. Angelides
first picked up the object overhead, heading away from shore. He cites the figure of fifty to sixty degrees above the horizon. TWA 800 was flying at about
twenty degrees above the horizon. The object only "appeared" to be descending because it was moving out away from shore. Like virtually all other witnesses, Angelides describes a white smoke trail and a pair of flashes, one
higher then the other, and only after these the fireball and the quick descent
to the sea. Nothing climbs anywhere. As Mayer himself admitted on several
occasions, "There is remarkable consistency among the witness accounts."

Angelides was one of the many eyewitnesses who did not pick the object
up rising off the horizon. By Mayer's own account, fifty-six witnesses did claim
that "the streak originated at the surface or behind the horizon and/or that it
traveled straight up or nearly so." To be sure, this number had been adjusted
downward, inexplicably so, from the figure of ninety-six such witnesses that
the NTSB cited after reviewing only two-thirds of the witness statements in
1997, but it still left Mayer with a good deal of explaining to do.

"We weren't surprised to find some accounts that didn't seem to fit,"
Mayer noted cheerfully, adding, "It's possible that, for some witnesses, as the
airplane maneuvered in crippled flight, it appeared to fly nearly straight up."

Although Mayer made no mention of the CIA's magic 3,200-foot climb
in his own initial description of events, nor any climb at all, he fell back on
this canard to solve an unsolvable problem—the ascent from the horizon.
Note, too, how he distanced himself from the CIA's analysis. In this retelling,
the plane didn't fly straight up. It only "appeared" to and then only to "some"
of the witnesses.

By this stage in the investigation, no one at the NTSB wanted any more
part of the CIA's zoom-climb than they did the FBI's dog training. Consider
this eye-opening exchange between Hall and Mayer, offhandedly injected
midway through Mayer's testimony.

Hall: Now, if you could show that the airplane did not climb after the nose
departed, will [sic] that change your analysis?
Mayer: No sir, although we believe that the airplane did climb after the
nose departed.

"We believe"? The federal government had spent millions convincing the American people that the eyewitnesses saw an ascending plane and not missiles, and now the NTSB was expressing serious doubt that the plane ascended. Added Mayer of the zoom-climb, "Our analysis is not actually dependent on that."

James Kallstrom of the FBI, however, would stick to his guns. In November 2000, he told Andrea Stassau of Channel 8 in Connecticut that "the plane climbed—3,000 feet or so and it was spewing flames." As to those eyewitness like Major Meyer and Master Chief Brumley who claimed otherwise, Kallstrom could only mutter, "I have no idea why these people say what they say. It's nonsense. It's stupid. It has no basis in fact at all."[8]

To help explain away the "relatively small number" of eyewitnesses that could not be shoehorned into his explanation, now just fifty-six, Mayer trotted out two other excuses. One was that the FBI documents "contain incomplete information or are vaguely worded." In fact, it was only this vagueness that allowed him to exploit the testimony of someone like Paul Angelides. The second was the "well-documented" phenomenon of memory error, a phenomenon that he summarized for a confused board member:

> The point of what I'm saying is that witnesses had many opportunities to be exposed to information that could have been incorporated into their memories before they were interviewed. No one has perfect recall. Even memories that we are sure of can contain errors. And this is one possible explanation why a relatively small number of witnesses provided information that doesn't seem completely consistent with physical evidence.

In other words, all fifty-six—or ninety-six—eyewitnesses that saw the streak come off the horizon had suffered memory error, all in the same fashion. Yet, as Mayer admitted, the FBI did some five hundred of its interviews within the first week, when memories were at their freshest.

Board member George Black ventured still another reason why witness memories were unreliable: "their condition . . . at the time they made these observations." He then referred to the several witnesses who observed the event at a yacht club. "I suspect," Black said with a chuckle, "I know what some of their conditions might have been." To be fair, this comment made even Jim Hall squirm.

AT this point, Mayer explored the testimony of several key witnesses. The first was Mike Wire, the millwright from Philadelphia and "the man on the bridge" in Westhampton.

Mayer had to have held his breath on this one. He knew something that had so far escaped every single representative of the major media, namely that the CIA based its animation squarely on Wire's testimony. He also must have known that Wire's alleged new testimony was contrived. There was no man more important to silence and keep silenced than this soft-spoken mechanic from Philadelphia.

"According to FBI documents," said Mayer, "he said that he saw what appeared to be cheap fireworks coming off the beach about 4 or 5 houses west of the bridge. It was like a white spark that went up and arched across the sky."

If there were one telling moment in the entire four-year investigation it was this one, and yet no one caught it. Mayer had just wiped from the collective memory the final alleged FBI interview with Mike Wire, the single most critical piece of eyewitness evidence in the investigation to that date. It is useful here to recall the CIA conversation with the NTSB from a year earlier. Said CIA Analyst Number 1:

> Let me say something else about this eyewitness [Wire] because I think this is interesting. He was an important eyewitness to us. *And we asked the FBI to talk to him again, and they did.* In his original description, he thought he had seen a firework and that perhaps that firework had originated on the beach behind the house. We went to that location and realized that if he was only seeing the airplane, that he would not see a light appear from behind the rooftop of that house. The light would actually appear in the sky. It's high enough in the sky that that would have to happen.
>
> When he was reinterviewed, he said that is indeed what happened. The light did appear in the sky. Now, when the FBI told us that, we got even more comfortable with our theory. He also described, he was asked to describe how high in the sky above the house he thought that light appeared, and he said it was as if—if you imagine a flag pole on top of the house it would be as if it were on the top or the tip of the flag pole.[9]

The CIA statement cries out for explication. Just how high is a flagpole? Who puts a flagpole on the roof of his house? In fact, no one does or even imagines such a thing. This interview never took place. The flagpole detail was added to ground the report, give it the illusion of reality. As shall be seen soon enough, however, the only detail from this interview that appealed to the NTSB was the flagpole.

The NTSB, which had already disowned the zoom-climb, now disowned the very interview on which the zoom-climb was based. Mayer did not refer to this key interview at all. In fact, he based all his calculations on Wire's real interview from July 1996, working from the assumption that Wire did see something come up from the horizon "4 or 5 houses west" of the bridge.[10] If Wire had first seen the plane twenty degrees above the horizon, as the CIA attested, all of Mayer's geometry would have been pointless.

It proved pointless in any case. Mayer's conclusion was just as specious as the CIA's. "He saw a streak and a fireball," said Mayer of Wire, "moving just like the accident airplane would have moved. His report is fully consistent with the breakup sequence of the accident airplane."

To understand just how brazen a bit of nonsense this is, one only needs to read Wire's original 302:

> Wire saw a white light that was traveling skyward from the ground at approximately a 40 degree angle. Wire described the white light as a light that sparkled and thought it was some type of fireworks. Wire stated that the white light "zig zagged" [sic] as it traveled upwards, and at the apex of its travel the white light "arched over" and disappeared from Wire's view . . . Wire stated the white light traveled outwards from the beach in a south-southeasterly direction.[11]

Gone in Mayer's new account were the forty-degree ascent, the white smoke trail, the movement outward from the beach, the disappearance, and the telltale zigzag. Only in the purest of informational vacuums was Mayer able to advance his thesis.

Mayer next challenged the testimony of Dwight Brumley, the Navy electronics warfare specialist on US Air 217. "It sounds like this witness saw some of the breakup sequence of Flight 800," Mayer mused, "but some people would suggest that he saw a missile." Mayer's next revelation was again stunning:

> We used radar data to study this sequence. First, here's the track of US Air Flight 217 which was at about 22,000 feet. We determined the identity of the airplane that this witness saw pass underneath Fight 217 and used it as

a reference point. The other airplane was a US Navy P-3 Orion operating at about 20,000 feet.

Here too Mayer resorted to a fact-free series of analyses to prove that the flarelike object Brumley saw rise up off the surface of the ocean "is consistent with his having seen the latter stages of the breakup of Flight 800." But there is a larger issue at stake in this scenario, the small plane that Brumley saw.

Although the CIA animation in 1997 showed a small airplane much like the one Brumley described, by the time of its briefing with the NTSB in 1999 the CIA was claiming that Brumley's plane was, in fact, the P-3.[12] Mayer attended that meeting. When his turn came at the NTSB's August 2000 hearing, he echoed the CIA line that Brumley's "small, private plane" was the P-3. In fact, the P-3 is neither small nor private. It has four engines, a ninety-five-foot wingspan, and enough Navy regalia about it to alert a twenty-five-year Navy vet.

It is also inconceivable that a P-3 would pass so narrowly under a U.S. airliner if on a routine mission. "My first thought," said Brumley, "that was awfully close!" Brumley estimated three hundred to four hundred feet.[13] The FBI 302 stated the distance as "approximately 500 to 700 feet."[14] Mayer argued for two thousand. Brumley is likely correct. The FBI was likely mistaken. And Mayer is simply flailing. He had to say something: A P-3 on a routine mission would never fly that close to a commercial airliner.

This apparent confusion raises a question that will prove central to the mystery of what happened on the night of July 17. Based on the radar data, it appears, in fact, that the P-3 is tracking the small plane, a concept that will be developed in the next chapter.

Mayer next challenged Maj. Fritz Meyer and Capt. Chris Baur on the Air National Guard helicopter, citing only Meyer by name and ignoring Baur's testimony. Again, he used radar data and other Goldbergian calculations to reiterate a point that to the knowing observer seemed increasingly delusional:

The helicopter crew began flying to the accident site about 43 seconds after the explosion of the center wing tank. In other words, late in the breakup sequence, long after any missile would have been fired. They saw a fireball and they flew out to where the airplane would've been in final seconds of breakup sequence. They didn't see a missile.

In fact, they were practicing landings when both Baur and Meyer reported seeing the streaks that led to the two white flashes. That they were able to comprehend what they had seen and respond that quickly is a testament not only to their experience but also to their visual acuity.

Ironically, the witness that presented Mayer the most trouble was one known at the hearing only by his number, 649, but identified by Patricia Milton as school principal Joseph Delgado.[15] Mayer did not mention him in his original presentation but only in response to a question from Chairman Hall. The question was most likely scripted and rehearsed—there had been a full dress rehearsal for the hearing—and it came in reaction to a full-page ad placed in the *Washington Times* by watchdog organization Accuracy in Media.

"Witness 649," said Mayer in an unusual burst of candor, "described events that certainly do sound like a missile attacking the airplane."

The NTSB had some sense of what a missile attack might look like. In April 2000, the NTSB had conducted a missile visibility test. The purpose was *not* "to determine if Flight 800 was struck by a missile." Added Mayer, "We've known for a long time that it wasn't." How the NTSB could have hoped for an unbiased result given its predisposition beggars the imagination, but that is the least of the issues involved.

As Mayer explained, the NTSB conducted this test to determine what a missile launch would look like to observers at known distances from a launch point. The test was conducted at Eglin Air Force Base near Ft. Walton Beach, Florida, reportedly in about the same visibility conditions as those on Long Island at the time of the accident.

The NTSB positioned observers at known locations up to fourteen miles from the launch site. After each launch, the witnesses were asked to describe what they had seen. "All of the observers," admitted Mayer, "saw the missiles and described them as a rapidly rising light." The missiles tested were all shoulder-launched.

At this juncture, the 2000 NTSB hearing, as it often did, grew bizarre and Clintonian. Consider Mayer's description of a "hypothetical missile attack." Based on the test, this is what the witness of a missile attack on TWA 800 could have expected to see.

> The rocket motor of the missile would be visible and it would look like a light ascending rapidly for about 8 seconds. Then the motor would burn out and the light would disappear for as much as 7 seconds.

To this point, Mayer was describing almost exactly what Wire, Delgado, Goss, and countless other witnesses had seen, right down to the brief disappearance of the missile. Mayer then added an absurd wrinkle that allowed him to dismiss these eyewitnesses.

> After this, a second streak of light, the airplane in crippled flight would become visible. It would be different from the first streak moving slower, then it would develop into a fireball.

The NTSB "carefully reviewed the witness accounts" to determine if anyone had described such a scenario but could find none that did. It's not surprising. Mayer's scenario weds two self-excluding events. The first streak of light represents a missile as eyewitnesses would have actually seen it, but the second streak of light represents a plane streaking upwards because of an internal eruption of the center wing tank as only the CIA could have imagined it.

In a darkly humorous moment, the audience at the NTSB hearing might have been tempted to think, *What horrible luck! First the plane blows up spontaneously and streaks upward, and then it gets hit with a missile.* No other reading of Mayer's testimony makes sense.

For all that, Delgado, like many others, had presented the FBI with a drawing so specific and so suggestive of a missile strike Mayer could not easily dismiss it. Other witness drawings might have proved even more awkward to explain away. But fortunately for the NTSB, the FBI was "unable to locate" at least thirty of those drawings.[16]

In fact, Delgado described almost exactly what the witnesses had seen in the NTSB test. He saw "an elongated object that had an oval head," which gave off a "bright white light with a reddish pink aura surrounding it." He saw the object ascend "fairly quick" and "vertically," then watched it "slow" and "wiggle," then "speed up" and get "lost." At the same time, Delgado observed a second object that "glimmered" in the sky, higher than the first. This was TWA 800. The ascending object continued on its way and, he believed, "impacted" with the doomed airliner. Finally, Delgado saw a puff of smoke, then another puff, and finally a "firebox."[17]

The "firebox" represented the explosion of the wing tanks. It was not the initiating event, as the NTSB would claim, but the culminating event. Like Meyer and Angelides and countless other witnesses, Delgado saw the two white flashes, one higher than the other. What he did not see—what no eyewitness reported seeing—was the 3,200-foot climb of a noseless air-plane portrayed in the CIA animation.

In short, Delgado presented a real problem for Dr. Mayer. His drawing had been precise and detailed, so Mayer could scarcely blame the FBI. He had been interviewed within forty-eight hours of the crash, so his testimony was unlikely to have been corrupted by "memory error." And he had been working out at a local track so his "condition" would have been acceptable even to board member Black.

Mayer solved his problem with flagpoles. Mayer claimed of Delgado, "He said that everything he saw occurred between these flagpoles." Mayer then used an illustration to show where those flagpoles were located at the Westhampton school and vectored Delgado's line of sight from between those flagpoles out to sea.

"So again," said Mayer, "it doesn't appear that this witness was looking in the right location to see where flight 800 would have been when it would have been struck by a hypothetical missile." If he were looking in the wrong direction, Mayer implied, none of his testimony could possibly matter.

One objection here. A huge one. In none of the FBI notes does Witness 649, Joseph Delgado, ever mention a flagpole, let alone two flagpoles. With good reason. There weren't any at this school.[18] Mayer—or perhaps some other agent who assessed the site—imagined flagpoles that did not exist and entered them into the official record. This is all easily verifiable, but who would bother checking a detail so commonplace and devoid of controversy?

FROM watching the NTSB hearing countless times, one senses that Mayer is a decent sort. If married, he is probably a dutiful husband and a doting father. One cannot help noting how eager he was to please.

Dishonesty could not have come easily to Mayer. For instance, he pref-aced his first introduction of the two flagpoles with a discreet "I believe." There are only two ways to explain the "I believe" comment. The first is that Mayer was uncertain about the details. Given that Delgado was among the most critical of all eyewitnesses and that Mayer had no more important function than to discredit this testimony, this explanation seems unlikely.

The second explanation is that Mayer wanted to leave himself wiggle room—"plausible deniability" in Beltway-speak—were he ever to be charged with obstruction of justice.

In any case, these flagpoles are hard to overlook. On two different occasions, government agents used a flagpole reference to distort or discredit eyewitness testimony in the TWA Flight 800 investigation.

This, of course, might have been a coincidence. It might also have been a coincidence that these just happened to be two of the three or four most critical eyewitnesses in the investigation. It might even have been a coincidence that neither of these eyewitnesses ever referred to a flagpole and that in each case the agents conjured the poles out of thin air.

But then again, maybe this wasn't a coincidence at all. Maybe the flagpole references suggest why the CIA was involved in the first place.

CHAPTER 14

FIRST STRIKE

At the final NTSB hearing in August 2000, Bernard Loeb spoke confidently and defiantly for the NTSB.

"As I have already explained," he declared early in the session, "the physical evidence indicated indisputably that a missile did not strike the airplane."[1]

Many of the top officials at the hearing echoed Loeb's refrain. "It was clear from the physical evidence," argued David Mayer, "that neither a bomb nor a missile strike had caused the explosion aboard Flight 800."

"Physical evidence is almost always the key," added board member John Goglia, "and unless there is physical evidence to back up the witness evidence, then it becomes very, very [sic] just a judgment call and you have really nothing substantial to hang onto."[2]

A few months later, speaking to a Connecticut news reporter, James Kallstrom of the FBI would add his own bit of absolutism: "There's not one scintilla of evidence that a missile hit the plane."[3]

If these senior personnel could not "find" any physical evidence, not even a "scintilla," there was a reason why. The evidence had systematically been lost, stolen, concealed, erased, deleted, denied, or simply ignored. This is not a matter of conjecture. This is a matter of fact.

No fewer than four serious professionals within the investigation made specific allegations of evidence theft or tampering: Linda Kunz and Terrell Stacey of TWA, Jim Speer of TWA and ALPA, and Hank Hughes of the NTSB. Their allegations were taken seriously. Kunz and Speer were suspended from the investigation, Kunz permanently. Stacey was arrested. And Hughes was denounced by the FBI's Kallstrom for his participation in a "kangaroo court of malcontents," namely a U.S. Senate subcommittee hearing.[4]

In a requested follow-up letter to that committee written on June 14, 1999, Hughes made the following observation:

> The absence of an evidence control log made it impossible to know what evidence had been removed from the hangers, what laboratory it had been sent to or by whom, what the nature and results of the tests were, and what the final disposition of the evidence was.[5]

Recall, too, that Assistant FBI Director Donald Kerr of the Laboratory Division had told Senator Grassley's subcommittee in a casual boast that "116 pieces of debris" had been sent to the FBI lab in Washington for further testing.[6] These pieces had all been screened and/or pretested at Calverton.

From day one, certain key officials had been systematically subtracting data from the investigation's information bank. As a result of this quiet calculus, officials were able to reduce 116 suspicious pieces of physical evidence to "not one scintilla" without attracting much attention. After four years of steady data embezzlement, Bernard Loeb could comfortably claim that an "overpressure event inside the center wing tank" brought down the plane and that "beyond any doubt that the overpressure was the result of a Jet A fuel/air vapor explosion in the center wing tank."[7]

By August 2000, in fact, subtractions had been made from *all* relevant forms of evidence, physical and otherwise. A summary here is in order.

1. Break-up sequence. In August 1996, investigators concluded that a narrow strip of the fuselage ahead of the right wing was the first to have been blown off the plane. In December 1997, the NTSB claimed that "the pieces of wreckage that exited the aircraft first include some structure from the center wing tank and fuselage just forward of the wings." By August 2000, Loeb would make the fuselage strips along the right wing disappear altogether, claiming that "the physical evidence irrefutably indicated that the first pieces to depart the airplane were from the forward part of the center wing tank."[8]

2. Satellite data. The CIA video claimed that the infrared sensor of an American satellite captured the breakup sequence, a claim repeated at the CIA's briefing with the NTSB. At the FBI's final press conference on the same day, the word *satellite* was not mentioned once. The NTSB told Don Nibert all three relevant satellites were broken. The satellite data today remain classified.

3. Radar data. On July 17, 1996, the FAA rushed the radar data to Washington. By the end of the next day, the data had become an "anomaly." In November 1996, the NTSB Chairman's Report acknowledged that a high-speed projectile had "merged with TWA 800," at least as it appeared on radar. The NTSB then leaned on the FAA to agree that it had not. In March 1997, the FBI seized pilot Dick Russell's copy of the radar. That same month Kallstrom claimed that the radar track was "a Navy plane flying with a defective transponder." By November 1997, he claimed that "what was depicted on the screen was normal air traffic and not a missile." In August 2000, the NTSB identified the track as a reflection of another aircraft, not the P-3.

4. Naval presence. Despite at least six credible sightings of a Navy warship off Long Island after 3 P.M. on July 17, the Navy insisted it had none within two hundred miles of the crash site. In November 1996 Admiral Kristensen claimed the *Normandy*, 185 miles south, was the closest ship. Right after the crash, the Navy P-3 crew told the FBI that the submarine *Trepang* was eighty miles south of the crash site. In March 1997, the P-3 crew told the NTSB that the *Trepang* was off the coast of Virginia two hundred miles south. That same month the *New York Times* reported that a sub was "near the flight path." By November 1997 Kallstrom cited the *Normandy* and now *three* submarines—*Trepang, Albuquerque,* and *Wyoming*—as being in the "immediate vicinity" of the crash site. How immediate? Within six miles.

5. Mystery ships. For five months the FBI denied the existence of a "surface vessel" that it would later identify as being three miles from the crash site, having a speed between twenty-five and thirty-five knots, and fleeing the scene. The FBI finally admitted its presence but never identified it. Kallstrom, in fact, said it was a helicopter. A few miles to the northwest of Flight 800, radar identified another surface vessel. The FBI has not identified this ship either.

6. The P-3. On July 17, the P-3 crew, one mile from the crash, allegedly saw and heard nothing. The pilot implied that clouds obscured his view even though it was a clear night. The surveillance equipment captured no images. While official Washington was in a state of near war, the plane was alleged to have run a routine sub exercise off the coast of New Jersey and/or Virginia. In addition, the plane's transponder was said to have been broken, allowing authorities to identify it alternately as the small plane that buzzed US Air 217 and the source of the mystery blip on the radar. Fully off message as late as March 1997, Admiral Kristensen was claiming that the P-3 was eighty miles south of TWA Flight 800 at the time of the crash.

7. Photographic evidence. The *New York Times* described Linda Kabot's photo image as a "cylindrical object with one end aglow." The FBI quickly took custody of the photos and the negatives and would not even share the original with the NTSB. According to the FBI, the object appeared to be "an aircraft" and was "not a missile." Heidi Krieger's photo of a likely missile-exhaust trail was "microscopically analyzed" and judged to be a "speck of dirt," a speck that appeared on only the one critical frame. NBC reportedly won a bidding war on a live video of the crash, which was promptly seized by the government.

8. Underwater imagery. The FBI made sure that investigators could not take an unabridged look at the ocean floor as videotaped by the Navy. ALPA investigator Jim Speer learned the hard way. "Look at the gaps in the time clock here," he told his FBI chaperone. "There is no reason for gaps to occur unless the tape has been edited. I want to see the unedited version." "No" was the agent's response.

9. Explosive residue. Traces of explosives were found inside the plane and out by EGIS technology at the Calverton site. The equipment had registered at least twelve confirmed hits for explosive residue, probably many more. One hundred sixteen pieces in all were sent to the FBI lab for confirmation. There, only residue traces inside the fuselage survived the second test. On September 20, 1996, the FBI released the specious St. Louis dog-training story, and all residue became irrelevant, including that on the victims' bodies.

10. Residue trail. Terrell Stacey identified a reddish-orange trail across the cabin interior in rows 17 through 19. James Sanders had a sample tested. Ninety-nine percent of its elements were consistent with those in an incendiary warhead. After the story broke, officials would tell the media that there was no residue trail and that Sanders's sample was actually a 3M adhesive. When tested independently, the adhesive in no way matched Sanders's sample. NASA refused to confirm the NTSB cover story. Years later, Sanders would obtain documents revealing that the original test results for the residue had been classified under "national security."

11. The scavenge pump. In late 1996, the scavenge pump was considered the prime suspect in the ignition of the alleged fuel-tank explosion. What made the pump so attractive was that it had not been found, at least not "officially." In time, the NTSB would exonerate the pump, but the pump's mysterious absence filled the information breach nicely for months. In fact, the pump had shown up on official documents early in the investigation. These documents are still classified.

12. The nose gear door. "Jet's Landing Gear Is Said to Provide Evidence of a Bomb," declared the headline of the *New York Times* on July 31, 1996. The doors had not yet been found. If they had been blown inward, officials could hardly deny an external explosion. As it turned out, they *were* blown inward. In the summer of 1996 these revelations would have blown open the investigation. And so, although logged in during the month of August 1996, soon after the *Times* article, the doors were ignored for more than a year and "rediscovered" only after public interest in the story had waned.

13. The right wing. ALPA investigator Jim Speer identified a leading edge wing-rib damaged in such a way he thought it merited testing for explosive residue. Maj. Fritz Meyer confirmed it. On July 23, 1996, *Newsday* added detail, reporting that "a chemical test showed traces of a rare explosive on a wing from TWA Flight 800." After being sent to the FBI lab, says Jim Speer, "The part has not been seen since for five years now."

14. Witness drawings. Inexplicably, the FBI have been "unable to locate" thirty of these drawings. This has proved to be the standard FBI and CIA excuse for the failure to release documents under the Freedom of Information Act that prove either too embarrassing or too incriminating.

15. Passenger seats. The seats had great evidentiary value. "Not to our surprise," the NTSB's Hank Hughes told a Senate committee, "we found that seats were missing and other evidence had been disturbed." TWA employee Linda Kunz and two New York state troopers caught certain NTSB officials changing tags on seat parts. Over TWA's protests, Kunz was removed from the investigation and threatened with prosecution.

16. Metallurgy. From the beginning, as investigator Jim Speer has attested, NTSB management attempted to interpret evidence in ways that denied the possibility of a missile, often to the point of absurdity.

17. Keel beam. At its final hearing, the NTSB claimed that the "forward portion of the keel beam" was recovered from the Red Zone, the area closest to JFK. As FBI documents show, however, and as the *New York Times* reported, the keel beam was among the last parts to hit the water, not the first. It was found deep in the C, or Green, Zone, the one farthest from JFK. Investigators crossed out C 061 and changed it to B 061 and then changed the designation once again from B to A, the zone closest to JFK.

18. Flight data recorder. The FDR was likely removed, examined, replaced, and reconstructed for one purpose: to suppress evidence of an external explosion. "The NTSB cannot release the FDR accident tape from FL 800 for the purpose of independent read-out and analysis," says audio expert Glenn Schulze, "without revealing their complicity in tampering with this most important piece of TWA FL 800 accident investigation."

19. Cockpit voice recorder. The Navy's Captain McCord had argued that both "pingers" had been "broken, destroyed or covered with sand or other material." When found, the CVR was sitting uncovered on the ocean floor. Its pinger was clearly neither broken nor covered. The NTSB also found it necessary to withhold analysis done on the CVR in England. A vibration traveling through the frame of Flight 800 in excess of two thousand feet per second could not be explained as a fuel-air explosion.

20. Medical forensics. As the Suffolk County coroner implied, the horrific injuries to certain passengers "took more force than even flying debris and 400 mph winds within the cabin could have produced." FBI officials took exclusive hold on whatever knowledge could be gleaned from the objects within the victims. After years of FOIA requests, citizen activists obtained documents revealing that at least twenty round pellets of "unknown origin" were extracted from at least one of the bodies. These pellets had a "matrix" found in "munitions," but not in commercial aircraft debris.

21. Climb analysis data. Retired United pilot and ALPA investigator Ray Lahr requested through FOIA the calculations used by the NTSB to determine how TWA 800 could climb "several thousand feet with the nose blown off." The CIA now says it can find no documentary evidence that any analysis of this subject was ever conducted by its employees. At its final hearing in August 2000, the NTSB quietly disowned the climb scenario.

22. The center wing tank floor. The massive piece of flooring that photos had shown sweeping upward as a result of a likely missile blast had been mashed down for the reconstruction of the plane. Someone had flattened the floor not just to its original level, but beyond that, as if some mysterious mechanical force inside the tank had blown it downward. Said the NTSB's Hank Hughes of one FBI agent, "I saw him in the middle of the hangar with a hammer in the process of trying to flatten a piece of wreckage."[9]

23. Eyewitness reports. The subtraction of eyewitness evidence is even more flagrant than that of the physical evidence. No eyewitnesses were allowed to testify at any NTSB hearing. The CIA attempted to remove all eyewitness reports from the realm of the credible with a single fifteen-minute showing of its animated video. The CIA reduced the 244 witnesses who had seen a streak to one, the man on the bridge, Mike Wire, about whom they fabricated a follow-up interview.

24. MISIC analysis. Analysts from the Defense Intelligence Agency's Missile and Space Intelligence Center (MISIC) arrived on the scene in Long Island just two days after the crash and interviewed a reported thirty-four key eyewitnesses. The MISIC analysis, however, has all but disappeared from the public record. In the FBI's report, it barely merits a footnote.

THE subtraction of the MISIC data, the subtraction of all manner of evidence for that matter, does not damn the investigation as clearly as the few "additions" to the evidence pool do. There were not many, to be sure, but they stand out by their crude and reckless contrivance.

During his generally appalling effort to discredit the eyewitnesses, for instance, David Mayer added one specific detail. Witness 649 could not have seen a missile, said Mayer, because "everything he saw occurred between these flag poles." There were no flagpoles. Mayer made them up.

The CIA imagined flagpoles to augment the testimony of Mike Wire, the man on the bridge. Worse, the CIA fully imagined Wire's entire follow-up interview, the one on which it based its animation. The interview never took place.

The FBI gets credit for one egregious addition as well, the alleged dog-training exercise. The FBI did not fully imagine the exercise. It did take place. The FBI simply added the most salient detail, the location of the exercise on board the plane that would become TWA 800. The exercise did not take place on this plane, the only one that mattered.

One could launch a successful criminal investigation into the corruption of the investigation with no other evidence than these simple "additions," one each by the FBI, the NTSB, and, most flagrantly, by the CIA. In combination with the subtractions, the evidence for a criminal obstruction of justice in the investigation of TWA 800 overwhelms the objective observer.

The comprehensive listing of this evidence should not strike the reader as extraordinary. There is a binary quality to any such investigation. Yes or no. Open or shut. Explosive device or mechanical failure. Internal explosion or external explosion. To transform an external explosion into a mechanical failure, someone has to alter or suppress every known variable.

In a relatively open system of government like America's, officials are obliged to share most of this information. If it were indeed "beyond any doubt" that an overpressure in the center wing tank destroyed the airplane, why should the government withhold any information at all?

Why conceal the Navy's presence in the area of an *accident* like TWA 800's? Why not share the satellite images of this accident taking place? Why not share the analysis done to establish the noseless plane's 3,200-foot climb? Why classify the residue tests if it is only a matter of "glue"? Why reshape the metal in the process of reconstructing the plane? Why withhold the CVR tests? Why not subject the FDR to independent testing? Why deny the public the results of the medical forensic testing? Why suppress the work of the MISIC analysts? Why fabricate critical interviews? Why add flagpoles that don't exist? Why falsify records of where a dog-training exercise took place? Why humiliate the police officer involved? Why withdraw whistle-blower privileges from the Navy's Special Forces? Why harass, why intimidate, why arrest, why indict, why incarcerate? Why?

The answer should be obvious. Mechanical failure did not cause the demise of TWA Flight 800. Said the IAMAW unequivocally, "We have not been a party to any evidence, wreckage or tests that could conclude that the center wing tank explosion was and is the primary contributor to this accident."[10]

If the physical and eyewitness evidence fails to convince the skeptic, the behavioral evidence surely must. Senior government officials do not act this deceitfully in peacetime unless they have something serious to hide.

Nor did a bomb blow up the plane from within. There never was any evidence that it did. From the beginning, the "bomb" was a red herring, one that distracted the media and even the investigators themselves.

Absent the DNA, absent the independent prosecutor, the Clinton administration felt an increasing freedom to spin this disaster any way they chose. "In the end there were no missiles, no bombs, no mystery fleet, no fleeing ships, no terrorists, no U.S. Navy involvement," wrote Peter Goelz, former Managing Director of the NTSB, in May of 2001. "It was just a tired old 747 with an empty, explosive center wing tank."[11]

BEFORE September 11, that's how easy denial used to be. But not afterwards. ALPA investigator Jim Speer, for one, came forward because he believed that the corruption of the investigation may well have led to the events of that tragic day.

Given the state of the world since, it is no longer enough to say what did not happen on the night of July 17, 1996. The time is right to say what did. Among the literally hundreds of citizen investigators who have reviewed the TWA 800 case there is very nearly a unanimous belief that an external force, most likely one or more missiles, blew the plane out of the sky.

The debate has raged among them, however, as to who was responsible. James Sanders, among others, has implicated the U.S. Navy. Commander Donaldson had looked to terrorists. New evidence, some of it available only after September 11, suggests strongly that both theories are partly right, but that neither is exactly on the mark. Yes, terrorists were involved, but the behavior of the U.S. Navy before and after the incident argues strongly against terrorist missiles—after all, why would its ships flee the scene? Yes, the U.S. Navy was involved, but no, the shoot down was not the result of a practice exercise gone awry.

As to what Navy assets were involved, some questions remain unanswered. The problem is that neither the Navy—nor any government entity speaking on its behalf—can be taken at its word as to where the relevant ships were situated, what capabilities they had, and what, if anything, they had fired on that night. On the subject of the Navy's presence, all relevant agencies have deceived the public all too often.

After sixteen months of denial, the FBI's James Kallstrom quietly admitted at the November 1997 press conference that the *Normandy* and three different submarines were in the "immediate vicinity" of the crash site.

FAA radar captured four unidentified tracks "consistent with the speed of a boat" within three to six miles of Flight 800's course at the time of its midair breakup. The fact that three of the radar tracks disappeared right after TWA 800 crashed argues strongly that these were the submarines that Kallstrom had identified and that they submerged almost immediately.

One "surface vessel" less than three miles from the crash scene was headed away from the area at thirty knots (34.5 miles per hour). In response to questions from a congressional subcommittee, the FBI's number two man on the investigation, Lewis Schiliro, claimed that "the FBI first noted the presence" of this ship in January 1997. According to Schiliro, the ship remained visible on radar from 8:11 P.M. to 8:45 P.M. Although the FBI was allegedly unable to identify this ship, Schiliro added the meaningless disclaimer that "based on our investigative efforts, we are confident it was not a military vessel."[12]

Commander Donaldson caught the irony of these admissions. In a letter to Louis Freeh, he grilled the FBI director as to why "the FBI took five months to examine the Islip ASR8 radar tape for surface contacts when witnesses were describing surface to air missile fire the first day." He wondered too how the FBI could drop its criminal investigation without identifying this ship, especially given the "extremely credible witness testimony that implicates that vessel as a probable missile firing point."[13] He received no good answer.

Radar also located a still-unidentified surface vessel northwest of Flight 800's crash site in the area of the ocean where Mike Wire saw a missile shortly after launch. This may well have been the *Normandy* or another ship of its class. At least six credible eyewitnesses had seen a Navy cruiser prowling up and down the Long Island coast on the afternoon and evening of July 17. None of the witnesses recalled ever seeing a ship of that size so close to shore before. This cruiser was not likely playing games. It was looking for something.

As to the *Normandy*, its capabilities included the Tomahawk and Harpoon missiles for land and ship targets, as well as Standard missiles for aircraft up to one hundred miles away. According to the Navy, none of the ship's eight Standards were fired that night, and it had no Tomahawk or Harpoon missiles on board. In that the Navy had systematically denied any relevant involvement from day one, all such denials have to be taken lightly. The *Normandy's* involvement remains a mystery.

Regardless of the exact number and location of military assets, July 17, 1996, was not an ordinary day. Two days before the opening ceremony of the Atlanta Olympics and three weeks after the Khobar Towers bombing in Saudi Arabia, the United States military was entirely vigilant. "Quietly," writes Patricia Milton, "President Clinton had placed the country on the highest state of alert since the Cuban Missile crisis."[14] Milton makes this claim even though it adds nothing to her contention that mechanical failure caused the crash. On the first anniversary of that same crash, *USA Today* casually made the same claim.[15]

Through the Freedom of Information Act, David Hendrix of the Riverside, California, *Press-Enterprise* learned more about relevant military maneuvers than any reporter in America. "July 17, 1996," he writes, "was a busy day in a busy week for the military along the Northeast seaboard."[16]

The Islamic Change Movement, which had taken credit for the Khobar Towers bombing, had issued a communiqué early on July 17 that, according to Yossef Bodansky, "laid the foundation for the downing of TWA 800." As Director of the Congressional Task Force on Terrorism and Unconventional Warfare, Bodansky knows the subject as well as any man alive.

The communiqué was chilling. "The mujahideen will deliver the ultimate response to the threats of the foolish American president. Everyone will be amazed at the size of that response," it read in part. "Their time is at the morning-dawn. Is not the morning-dawn near?"[17]

Dawn in Afghanistan corresponded almost exactly to dusk in New York. So powerful was the warning that by the night of July 18, the State Department had already swung into denial mode.

"While it's up to those leading the investigation to make a judgment on what this means," said spokesman Glyn Davies unconvincingly, "we think that this is a common type of political tract circulated commonly in the Middle East, and that the only connection is a vague chronological one— that this thing surfaced at this dreadful time."

Janet Reno and the Justice Department rejected at least two serious claims of responsibility after the crash as well. So carefully had the public been spared any worry of an Islamic threat, however, that CNN felt compelled to explain what one of the claimants meant by the word *jihad*.[18]

Yossef Bodansky was not impressed by the denials. He took very seriously a communiqué made by the Islamic Change Movement in Beirut on July 18, 1996, through well-established Islamic terrorist channels. It read in part, "We carried out our promise with the plane attack of yesterday."[19] Given his concerns, Bodansky raised the alarm that follows not after September 11, but two years before:

> The case of TWA 800 served as a turning point because of Washington's determination and to a great extent ability to suppress terrorist explanations and "float" mechanical failure theories. To avoid such suppression after future strikes, terrorism-sponsoring states would raise the ante so that the West cannot ignore them.[20]

After September 11, the idea of using airplanes to attack American targets no longer seemed far-fetched. In the way of omen, Islamic terrorist Ramzi Yousef was on trial in New York on the day of July 17, 1996, for his role in the Bojinka plot, an attempt to blow up eleven American airliners over the Pacific.[21]

One element of the Bojinka planning mirrored Yousef's most notorious crime, the truck bombing of the World Trade Center in 1993. If one could stuff a thousand pounds of explosives into a van, reasoned Yousef on the laptop seized from the apartment he shared with Abdul Hakim Murad, a Pakistani pilot, why not stuff a comparable amount in a small plane and strike real terror into the belly of the beast? The one target he reportedly cited was the CIA building. More important was the methodology. The following excerpt from a classified Republic of the Philippines intelligence report shows that al-Qaida had plans to use small planes as flying bombs as early as 1994:

> The document [from Yousef's computer] specifically cited the charter service of a commercial type aircraft loaded with powerful bombs to be dive-crashed by SAEED AKMAN. This is apparently intended to demonstrate to the whole world that a Muslim martyr is ready and determined to die for the glorification of Islam.[22]

September 11 mastermind Mohamed Atta also made plans to use small, private planes to launch an attack of some kind within America. During the spring of 2000, in a stunning bit of *chutzpah*, Atta visited a U.S. Department of Agriculture office in Homestead, Florida, and attempted to apply for a government-financed loan. USDA manager Johnelle Bryant described his unlikely (and happily unsuccessful) request for *ABC News*:

> He wanted to finance a twin-engine, six-passenger aircraft, that he could use as both a charter flight, and remove the, the [sic] seats. And he said he was an engineer, and he wanted to build a chemical tank that would fit inside the aircraft, and take up every available square inch of the aircraft, except for where the pilot would be sitting.[23]

Although Atta had no known connection to the destruction of TWA Flight 800, and his avowed interest was in "crop-dusting," his plans to reconfigure the plane seem to have come right out of the al-Qaida playbook. As it happens, Dwight Brumley described the plane he saw as a "six-seater."

On the night of July 17, 1996, very few Americans were concerned about such threats and those that went public with their concerns ran the risk of ridicule or worse. A victim of this reality-phobic zeitgeist was Steve Emerson, the producer of a 1994 PBS documentary, *Jihad in America*. Upon its airing, Emerson was chastised for "bigotry and misrepresentations" and "creating mass hysteria against American Arabs" by his media colleagues.[24]

When Emerson claimed that terrorists were responsible for the downing of TWA 800, he further alienated the mainstream. National Public Radio all but banned him.[25] *USA Today* cited Emerson a dozen times before September 1996, not once after.[26] The events of September 11 rehabilitated Emerson by noon of that tragic day. As of this writing, he is NBC's principal analyst on terrorism.

Given the complacency that reigned on that summer night, one can understand why Navy Master Chief Dwight Brumley did not think *terrorist* as he watched that small, private plane head right at US Air 217 at twenty-two thousand feet. And yet all understanding of what transpired that night begins with "Brumley's plane," the plane that he saw. What is surprising about his sighting is that no official denied it. No agency of government claimed that Brumley was seeing things. "Now you can go back and use the radar data," said a CIA analyst at the NTSB briefing in 1999, "and indeed there is a plane that flies below him."[27]

Brumley's plane clearly did not have its transponder on. If it had, secondary radar could have read the number and easily identified it. In the absence of such a reading, the government was able to improvise answers as to the nature of the plane and its location. The CIA analyst, when asked about the plane's identity, replied, "We think it's a P-3 and we think the P-3 was at an altitude of 20,000 feet and the US AIR was at an altitude of 21,700 feet."

The CIA video, however, refers to the plane only as a "small aircraft" and visualizes it as such, not at all like the four-engine, U.S. Navy P-3, with its near one-hundred-foot wingspan.

Patricia Milton, writing in 1999, argues the FBI case as follows: "Radar pinpointed the coordinates of both US AIR 217 and the small commuter plane passing near it just before Flight 800 exploded."[28] The small commuter plane? Which airline? How could it possibly have passed so close? Why were none of its crew or passengers interviewed by the FBI? No such airliner can be identified on the radar anywhere near TWA 800.

At the NTSB hearing in August 2000, David Mayer took the CIA line: "We used radar data to study this sequence. First, here's the track of US Air Flight 217 which was at about 22,000 feet. We determined the identify of the airplane that this witness saw pass underneath Fight 217 and used it as a reference point. The other airplane was a US Navy P-3 Orion operating at about 20,000 feet."[29]

If the CIA analysts were discreet enough to merely "think" the plane a P-3, Mayer was daring enough to be positive. As Mayer and the CIA both knew, however, the P-3 passed three-tenths of a mile behind US Air 217. Mayer, in fact, had tried to check the CIA analyst at the 1999 briefing when the analyst first volunteered that Brumley's plane was the P-3. "Not that you have a clear memory of . . . ," said Mayer. "It's been a year ago," said the CIA analyst, catching Mayer's drift, "I'm sorry."

Mayer and the CIA both corrupted a second variable to make their stories work. The P-3 crew had told the FBI that it was flying "at 22,000 feet." Although this crew had deceived the FBI on other details, its members had no reason to lie about their altitude. Mayer did. FAA radar places US Air 217 at 21,700 feet. Brumley did not see a plane fly over US Air 217 but under. Plus, in controlled airspace, there must be one thousand feet of vertical separation between planes.

The radar data tell the better story. The P-3 was flying in the same direction as the plane Brumley saw at roughly the same altitude and just a few miles behind it. P-3 crew members had reason to track a small plane flying with transponder off almost directly at a U.S. airliner. They likely shut off their own transponder to avoid detection.

The P-3 crew must have all breathed a deep sigh of relief, as Brumley himself did, when the plane passed under US Air 217 not by two thousand feet, but by "300 or 400 feet."

But neither the P-3 crew nor the crews of the Navy ships beneath them had time to relax. The small plane did something dramatic, something that caused the U.S. Navy to fire within ten to twenty seconds after the plane had passed under 217. One of these missiles Brumley saw rise up off the surface and head north. It most surely came from the still-unidentified "surface vessel" that would promptly flee the scene. At least one other missile rose up from the west, likely from the other unidentified ship, and headed southeast. This is the missile that Mike Wire saw from the bridge.

If eyewitnesses had a hard enough time spotting a 747 in the sky from eight or more miles away, spotting a small plane was more difficult still. Some, like John Riley and his wife at Smith Point beach, observed a "light aircraft" just before they saw the "flare." Others like Anthony Curreri "thought two planes had collided." Both of these brief reports came from the Suffolk County police before the FBI took over.[30]

FBI Witness 24, however, provides perhaps the most tantalizing clues. Surfing with a friend off Robert Moses Park, he saw "what he thought was fireworks" and saw the subsequent "fireball" to the east "trailing down to the horizon." But as the surfer told FBI agent John Kintzing, he "remembered seeing a plane with a light on the left wing, flying from west to east just before the fireworks." He was not talking here about Flight 800, as Kintzing made clear with the following detail: "[The witness] thought this was strange because news reports said there weren't any planes observed on radar at the time of the explosion."[31]

Kintzing's summary of this phone interview was fewer than sixty words long. The official NTSB docket shows no in-person, follow-up interview. The FBI should have followed up with a witness whose information was so critical and whose perspective was so clear. They should have also interviewed his friend. The slighting of Witness 24 raises questions as to whether other such reports were suppressed.

The evidence that carries the most weight comes from the government officials who were trying to conceal it. On March 20, 1997, officials of the FBI, Navy, and NTSB briefed the House subcommittee on aviation behind closed doors. According to *Newsday*, they told the committee that "a streak on a radar track that was purported to be a missile heading toward TWA Flight 800 was actually a Navy plane flying with a defective transponder."[32]

Newsday also mentioned Kallstrom's appearance the day before at the International Airport Chamber of Commerce in which he too implicated the P-3, stating that a malfunctioning transponder shows an airplane's track as a solid line. "If you're a school kid, you could say it looks like a missile, or a cigar, or a pencil."[33]

In fact, the path of the P-3 never merged with TWA 800 on the infamous FAA radar tape out of Islip. As these officials had to know, and as records obtained under a FOIA request reveal, the southwest-bound P-3 made a pass about three nautical miles from at least six thousand feet above the largely east-bound Flight 800 about fifteen seconds before the jumbo jet began to unravel.[34]

Kallstrom, however, had confirmed what retired United pilot Dick Russell had been saying about the radar track all along. "This was not an anomaly," Russell insisted. "It moved in a direct path, and that is a good indication there was something there."[35]

National Guard pilot Maj. Fritz Meyer adds another intriguing detail:

> After my picture appeared on television I received a phone call one night from an anonymous person—person just got on the phone and said: "You don't know who I am but I work for Sikorsky" . . . He said there is a tape— and I don't think it is a tape, I think it is a digital disk—there is a tape of the Sikorsky radar which shows two targets approaching TWA 800 before the impact—one a high speed supersonic and one subsonic.[36]

The Sikorsky radar is in Riverhead, just five miles north of Gabreski Field, to which Meyer had been flying. It is a remote site run by the U.S. Navy Virginia Capes Authority, which in turn leases the digital information to Sikorsky for testing purposes. The caller provided Meyer enough inside information to convince him of his legitimacy.

The morning after the call, in the wording of the unknown caller, the FBI "confiscated" the tape. When Meyer later went to Washington to talk to his congressman, Michael Forbes, an assistant showed him a list of all the documentation the FBI said it was holding. Meyer looked for this particular tape. It wasn't there. After interviewing Meyer, a congressional subcommittee asked for the tape by its specific name.

"The FBI admitted," says Meyer, "that they did have it in their possession, said it didn't show anything unusual, but refused to release it to anybody." When this radar data was finally released, as physicist Dr. Thomas Stalcup has attested, there was a real "anomaly." The last sweep of the

Sikorsky data showed four data points deleted in the area of the sky where Brumley observed a missile.[37]

"It's just like any investigation where evidence comes up missing there might be a reason or it might just have been lost," says Stalcup, "but when you have data that's not just missing but deleted that doesn't happen by itself."[38]

Despite its best efforts at concealment, the government revealed more than it meant to. According to Kallstrom, a malfunctioning transponder showed an airplane's track as a "solid line" or what Dick Russell described as a "direct path." This path was what showed up merging with TWA 800 on the notorious FAA radar tape out of Islip.

A similar path must have led the CIA and the NTSB to identify the plane that passed under US Air 217 as the P-3. The question must be asked, if the P-3 could be plausibly substituted both for Brumley's plane and the unidentified radar track merging with Flight 800, is it not possible that the small plane Brumley saw *was* also the unidentified track? Indeed, is it not highly likely that the same plane that narrowly missed US Air 217 made a hard turn and next showed up on radar "merging" with TWA 800? Could this track have been the "subsonic" reading on the Sikorsky radar?

With its cooperative engagement capabilities (CEC), the U.S. Navy was able to track this plane, record its maneuver, and respond in a vigorous, coordinated fashion. In short, all available evidence suggests that the Navy opened fire on "Brumley's plane." It had no real choice. Although modern missiles are designed to avoid radar and infrared detection, the Sikorsky radar did manage to pick up at least one "supersonic" hit, a likely missile track.[39]

In that fateful moment before the missiles found a mark, it might be useful to review just which elements were in the sky off the Hampton beaches:

- TWA Flight 800 heading east with a northerly bias, climbing through 13,700 feet

- US Air 217 heading north-northeast, soon to cross 800's path, eight thousand feet above it

- A small private plane that has passed under 217 heading southwest and is now descending rapidly and looping back east to "merge" with TWA 800

- A Navy P-3, trailing the small private plane in a southwesterly direction

- A missile heading north parallel to 217 but faster

- A missile heading southeast towards the converging planes

At the NTSB briefing of the CIA in April 1999, government officials offered one more significant clue as to what happened next. The issue at hand was how to explain an explosion that was powerful enough to shake a seventy-ton steel bridge ten miles away. When the NTSB observed that the "low order explosion" of a center wing tank did not have that capability, the CIA countered that the explosion of a missile warhead did not have the capability either. They were both right. Robert Young of the NTSB witness group had researched the issue on his own. He concluded that it would take "a minimum of 1,000 pounds of TNT at that many miles" to produce the effect in question. Young's analysis laid out the data, but no one at the hearing connected the dots.

The evidence suggests that the unknown, subsonic object seen merging with TWA 800 on the radar was a small plane carrying a thousand pounds or more of high-energy explosives. If so, at least one of the Navy's missiles caught up with it, but alas, just a little too late. The resulting blast stunned even Major Meyer. He described it as a "high velocity explosion of some brilliant white light," a light he could not identify.

Meyer's copilot, Capt. Chris Baur, saw the same explosion at the same time. Although Baur has been understandably reticent about sharing his observations, the testimony he gave to the NTSB in January 1997, cited in chapter 3, may hold a critical clue. Baur described "an object that came from the left. And it appeared to be like—like a white-hot. Like a pyrotechnic." Baur described this "incendiary device" as moving from east to west when "It made the object on the right explode." This "incendiary device" was almost surely the northbound missile that Brumley and Delgado watched, now correcting to the west. but the "object" it made explode in a "brilliant white light" could not have been TWA 800. TWA 800 would not visibly break up for another several seconds when the plane's fuel tanks began to erupt in what Meyer described as "yellow" petrochemical explosions. The plane would not explode into a yellowish "fireball" for perhaps another 20 seconds after that.

The redacted data from the flight data recorder suggested a comparable phenomenon. "This is either a train wreck in the sky, or an explosive device, mid-air, outside the plane," Commander Donaldson argued. "The measurements indicate there was an explosion, a big explosion, outside the cockpit."[40]

The Machinists and Aerospace Workers came to a similar, stunning conclusion through their analysis of the wreckage. "It appears to the

IAMAW that a major event may have occurred on the left side of the air-craft," said the IAMAW in the most honest report filed with the NTSB. "This event that may have happened outside of the aircraft in close prox-imity to the aircraft . . . It could have contributed to or been the cause of the destruction of Flight 800."[41]

The question is often asked, if so many Naval personnel observed what happened, why have none come forward? In fact, some have tried, haltingly, anonymously. Their message is the same: "We had no choice." None of these reports, however, have been substantial enough to build a case on. One rea-son for their reluctance to speak is that very few Navy personnel knew exactly what happened that night, including virtually everyone on the sub-marines. The second reason, of course, is that they were ordered specifically not to for national security reasons. A third reason is simply fear.

What follows is a dramatized account of what most likely did happen the night of July 17, 1996, at least as closely as one can imagine it without the testimony of a key conspirator. Only the thoughts of the two pilots are fully imagined; they are, however, based on comparable cases.

"TAWAKALT ala Allah (I rely on Allah)," the solitary pilot prayed in the tight, musty cockpit of his small but powerful plane.

The pilot, a devout Muslim and equally devout enemy of the United States, angled his small jet southwest toward the Long Island coast and repeated the prayer to buck up his courage.

"Tawakalt ala Allah."

The cockpit smelled of faded glory: old foam rubber, sweat, a whiff of hydraulic fluid, and just a hint of mildew. The rudder pedals were of cast alu-minum with the manufacturer's logo, now nearly illegible, having been worn smooth with thirty-five years of use. The leather seats were cracked and worn. The pilot, in fact, had thrown a sheepskin cover over his, not that comfort mattered, not now anyhow.

The control panel, which had intimidated him at first with its haphaz-ard mix of newer radios and flight gadgets and older controls, now seemed comprehendible. Despite his mission, he admired the love and ingenuity that had gone into keeping up this plane. He wished the Americans had not been so kind to him.

Infidels! Had not their soldiers—women among them—defiled the Holy Land with their presence and insulted his people with their arrogance?

They had said they were there to stop Hussein, but Hussein had been stopped, and they were still there.

And after Saudi Arabia, then Somalia—hunger relief, they called it. And then Bosnia—peacekeeping. All lies. Where would this usurpation stop?

The pilot's trusted leaders, the Ulema, did not care to find out. They had issued a fatwa that the Americans were to be expelled, violently if need be. The Khobar Towers bombing three weeks before had hurt the American infidel, but did not hurt him where he lived. *This attack would*, thought the pilot. *This one would.*

"Tawakalt ala Allah."

His martyrdom would be too visible to ignore. With a lethal cargo of explosives immediately behind his seat, he would provide a spectacle that the parasitical Jews and their craven fellow Americans up and down the Long Island shore would never forget. And his would be just the first martyrdom of many.

"Tawakalt ala Allah."

The pilot cruised now at more than twenty-one thousand feet looking for his prey. He marveled at the handling of this old high-performance aircraft. He felt it could go to forty thousand if it had to. The plane felt that strong. They had built it well.

Those fools! How lax these infidels were—trusting him, helping him. They had sold him the plane for less than $100,000 because its engines had been "run out"—their mileage exceeded a cost-prohibitive FAA-mandated overhaul—and then issued him a ferry permit to fly to the scrap yard. He laughed to himself. The last thing he worried about was an FAA inspector.

What he did worry about was attracting attention. Even with the transponder off, FAA radar could "skin paint" his aircraft, discern it roughly from its outline, send a plane to track him. He worried even more about the ADIZs all along the coast—Air Defense Intercept Zones guarded by military radar and backed up with fighter aircraft. He wasn't worried about dying. He worried about not completing his mission.

At 8:30 P.M., with the sun no longer in his face, he was confident that he could find a large plane, maybe even a wide-body, ascending out of Kennedy, thousands of feet below. These planes would be climbing slowly during the initial phase of the flight as they headed for Europe—or better yet, Israel. Much easier to intercept and strike now than later.

The pilot watched Long Island's south shore come into view as he angled towards JFK. Just south of the Hamptons, he spotted a commercial aircraft in the distance. It appeared to be at about his altitude. It was still too far away to determine its size, but it was flying northeast. With a little adjustment, their paths would intersect.

"Tawakalt ala Allah."

The pilot's aim was good. He drew closer and closer to the unsuspecting plane, still on target. As he neared, however, his prey began to take the shape of a small DC-9. In fact, it was a Fokker, US Air Flight 217, headed for Providence, Rhode Island. "No, no," he said to himself. "Not worthy."

Just at that moment, Dwight Brumley, a twenty-five-year USN Master Chief with a specialty in electronic warfare put down the book he was reading and looked eastward out the window of US Air 217.

"I noticed off the right side what appeared to be a small private airplane that was flying pretty much at a course right at the US Air flight," Brumley recounts. "I followed it until the fuselage and the inboard wing cut off my field of view. My first thought—that was awfully close!"

The pilot pushed forward on the steering column, flew under the airliner, and missed by only a few hundred feet. Even he was not sure whether he had dodged it out of strategy or fear. He prayed more intensely.

"Tawakalt ala Allah."

And Allah was indeed with him. Or so it seemed to the pilot. He looked down and saw a slowly climbing 747, a widebody, three miles to his right and about seven thousand feet below. What good fortune! He rolled about 110 degrees of bank towards the 747, pulled the nose down, and dived at a forty-five-degree angle towards the target.

Once established on the down line, he pushed the plane hard and right on an accelerating course—forty-five-degree dive and forty-five-degree course intersect, continuously adjusting both angles.

Unknown to this would-be martyr, the U.S. military was watching and waiting. A U.S. Navy P-3 Orion, a large, four-engine surveillance plane, was trailing only a few miles behind, seeking confirmation. With his run at the US Air 217 and his sharp plunge towards Flight 800, the pilot had tipped his hand.

The Navy had held its collective breath as the pilot had narrowly missed 217, but now there was no mistaking his target or his trajectory. The enemy had been found. He was inside the gate. This was no time for caution. Decisive action was required. Within seconds of the small plane's pass under US Air Flight 217, the trigger was pulled.

Brumley saw it first, about fifteen seconds after the small plane had flown beneath his. "I noticed what appeared to be some kind of a flare," he recalls, but Brumley realized quickly that this bright, burning object ascending off the ocean was no flare. "It was definitely moving pretty much parallel to the US Air Flight and it was moving at least as fast perhaps even faster."

A surfer, looking out to sea and unbothered by the lights on shore, saw the same plane Brumley did, now circling east, and then immediately saw what looked like fireworks heading skyward.

The terrorist pilot knew this was no flare or fireworks. He watched it arc over and almost hesitate as it sought out its target. He pressed down on the steering column and aimed his light plane in front of and slightly below Flight 800. The race was on.

As the small airplane plunged, and Flight 800 ascended slowly and innocently east along the Long Island coast, Mike Wire, a millwright from Philadelphia working on a Westhampton bridge, saw a streak of light rise up from behind a Westhampton house and head south, southeast away from shore. The cruiser had weighed in.

Vacationers Lisa Perry, from her Fire Island deck, and Paul Angelides, from his on Westhampton, both followed a southbound streak across the sky and then each saw the northbound streak, the one Brumley saw, rise off the horizon at the last moment. Angelides also saw what appeared to be a large ship right about where the streaks would converge.

From a Westhampton school parking lot, Joseph Delgado, "Witness 649," saw Brumley's missile as well. As he told the FBI, he saw an object like "a firework," ascend "fairly quick," then "slow" and "wiggle" then "speed up" and get "lost."

At 8:31, FAA radar operators out of Islip saw an unknown object head towards Flight 800. The Sikorsky radar at Riverhead picked up a subsonic object and a supersonic both headed towards TWA Flight 800. At the same moment FAA radar picked up something else unusual—a ship of good size nearly right under Flight 800's airborne position.

The pilot of the small plane knew exactly what these people were seeing: two missiles, hesitating, turning, zigzagging, eagerly seeking his aircraft. He leaned harder on the column.

"Tawakalt ala Allah."

Two National Guard pilots in their nearby helicopter now picked up the missiles in flight. Major Fritz Meyer, a winner of the Distinguished Flying Cross for his service over Vietnam, saw the southbound missile clearest. "It was definitely a rocket motor," says Meyer.

To attempt a head-on strike was to risk failure. Better to take advantage of the high-side attack, flash past the widebody on the low side, and flank the target on the left, the shore side. The Islamic pilot had made these classic "gunnery runs" before, but never for real.

"Tawakalt ala Allah."

After passing under and behind, the pilot quickly began to pull up and reconvert his speed to altitude. His hook confused the southbound missile. It corrected downward like an inverted Nike swoosh, then turned upward now into the belly of TWA Flight 800, passed through the center wing tank and into the passenger cabin on the extreme right side along the right wing, blowing debris out with it far and fast to the right.

"My God," said TWA Captain Ralph Kevorkian more calmly than he felt, "they're firing at us."

And that was it. The northbound missile overtook the terrorist plane just as it drew even with and slightly below Flight 800, slammed into it, and vaporized it in a blinding glare of white light, a blast so intense that it thrust a large beam violently into the cockpit, severed the recorders, bucked the 747 nearly upright, ripped the nose of it clear off and—incredible as it seems—fused the DNA of a husband and wife sitting closest to the blast.

"The first thing was a high-velocity explosion of military ordnance," says Major Meyer. "The second thing was another high-velocity explosion of some brilliant white light. I don't know what it was."

"You could feel the concussion like a shock wave," reports Mike Wire of the blast. Indeed, it shook the bridge on which he was standing in Westhampton even at ten miles distance.

And then chaos—a hellish, horrific chaos. "It was all confusion out there," says Angelides. "When that airplane blew up it immediately began falling," says Major Meyer. "It came right out of the sky. From the first moment, it was going down." At about seven thousand feet above sea level, as the noseless plane corkscrewed to the sea, the missile-damaged right wing and side began to tear away from the fuselage, rupturing the full right wing tank.

Now Angelides, Wire, Perry, Meyer, Brumley, Delgado, and at least 730 other witnesses watched as the tank exploded, and Flight 800 morphed into what Delgado described as a "firebox" and others as a "fireball."

"It got much larger, maybe four or five times as large," says Brumley, who was watching the explosion from overhead. "It was the same explosion. It just got bigger. My first thought was, 'Boy what was that?'"

The FAA did not hesitate. Its agents immediately forwarded radar data to the White House "situation room." It was in this room, "in the aftermath of the TWA Flight 800 bombing," as Clinton aide George Stephanopoulos inadvertently told Peter Jennings on that fateful September 11, that all key parties converged.

The critical decisions, however, were not made in that room. They were made upstairs in the White House family quarters. These decisions would shape American history in ways that no one present could ever have predicted or even imagined, in ways that all of them would live to regret.

A FEW days before the Olympics, in a presidential election year, an attack of this sort tested the mettle of the White House. A statesman would have accepted the responsibility and done what was right. A politician would have consulted polls and calculated electoral consequences before doing anything. Sometimes, a crisis can make a leader out of a politician. This time it did not.

This commander in chief was a consummate politician—among the best, or so they said. That, alas, is all that he ever was or would be. Two decades spent abusing the power with which he had been entrusted had permanently corroded his character—and the character of those around him as well. The president could not think but to calculate. And only a catastrophe, he quickly calculated, could prevent his reelection in November. He would not let Flight 800 be that catastrophe.

In those first few chaotic hours and days after the crash, all leads pointed in one direction. But no one was allowed "to go there." No government representative would openly volunteer information about a missile. There would be no public discussion of the troubling radar data sent to the White House, no mention of the scores of eyewitnesses that saw an object streak off the horizon towards TWA 800, no reference to the National Guard helicopter pilots who stared the missile attack in its face or the senior Navy NCO who watched it from above on US Air 217.

The air of normality would continue to reign in the run up to the August conventions and the November election. Clinton adviser Dick Morris, who regularly took the nation's pulse during this period, has since claimed on national TV that the president refused to impose sanctions on Iran even "when we had the Air 800, when we had the Olympics and when we had Saudi Arabia." In each case, added Morris, "There was decisive evidence that these were caused by terrorists."[42]

In the months that followed, in no small part to help raise campaign cash, the administration ruled out "bomb" as a possible explanation as well. The act of concealment would grow broader and more brutal each passing day, encompassing and corrupting every salient detail of the investigation. Before the charade was over, the government would spend more money and energy suppressing the truth than it would pursuing the terrorists responsible. Its agents would harass, humiliate, and intimidate scores of good citizens. And despite the enormity of the attack, the only people arrested would be a whistle-blowing pilot, his reporter liaison, and incredibly, the reporter's wife.

Instead of action, President Clinton gave America the illusion of peace and security. He had a talent for giving voters exactly what they wanted, and before September 11, illusion is all we asked for.

NOTES

UNDERSTANDINGS

1. Christine Negroni, *Deadly Departure* (New York: Cliff Street Books, 2000), p. 234.
2. Patricia Milton, *In the Blink of an Eye* (New York: Random House, 1999), "Acknowledgments."
3. William Langewiesche, "Dead End Story," *New York Times*, September 26, 1999.

1. FIRST IMPRESSIONS

1. "News Summary," *New York Times*, 17 July 1996.
2. In *The New Jackals* (Boston: Northeastern, 1999), author Simon Reeve speaks with American investigators in some detail about Bojinka, including the lesser-known details of the small plane to be filled with explosives to attack "the Great Satan" where he lives.
3. CNN.com, 26 June 1996.
4. Byron York, "Clinton Has No Clothes," *National Review Online*, 17 December 2001.
5. Robert Davey, "How Did TWA Flight 800 Blow Up?" *Village Voice*, 3 March 1998.
6. Lisa Perry, letter to Cmdr. William Donaldson, 17 October 1998.
7. Yossef Bodansky, *Bin Laden: The Man Who Declared War on America* (Roseville, CA: Prima, [1999] 2001), 180.
8. The fourteen men indicted for the bombing were members of Hezbollah. "Islamic Change Movement" was one of many shifting noms de guerre. Its leadership was mainly from Iran, although thirteen of those arrested were Saudis. One of the great mysteries of the Clinton years was the president's refusal to pursue this case. The indictments had to wait for the next administration.
9. The complete text of this communication can be found in Bodansky, page 182, and elsewhere. Text may vary with translation.
10. Dwight Brumley, interview by authors, videotape, September 2001.
11. FBI witness reports. Mike Wire, interview by authors, videotape, April 2001. Wire's account has never wavered.
12. Richard Goss, interview by Cmdr. William Donaldson at Accuracy in Media conference, 18 October 1997.
13. Lisa Perry, "Open Letter to the NTSB," *Dan's Papers*, 15 May 1998 (*DP* is a widely respected Long Island publication).

14. Paul Angelides, letter to Commander Donaldson, 12 July 1998. Paul Angelides, interview by authors, videotape, July 2000.

15. FBI witness summary 649, available through the NTSB. In her book, *In the Blink of an Eye* (New York: Random House, 1999), Patricia Milton identifies 649 as Joseph Delgado, 79.

16. "Divers Bring Up More Bodies from TWA Crash," CNN.com, 3 August 1996, and elsewhere.

17. Maj. Fritz Meyer, interview by Accuracy in Media, videotape; and by authors, videotape, on same occasion in August 2000. Also important, his videotaped presentation at the Granada Forum in California on 12 March 1998.

18. Brumley, interview. Also, Milton, 51.

19. Don Nibert, interview by authors, videotape, August 2001.

20. Flora Headley, interview by authors, videotape, September 2001.

21. There have been two mainstream books written on the subject of TWA Flight 800: Patricia Milton's *In the Blink of an Eye* and Christine Negroni's *Deadly Departure* (New York: Cliff Street Books, 2000). Negroni was a CNN reporter and is now working—no surprise here—for a trial attorney who specializes in airline disasters. Milton was and still is with Associated Press. Both were allowed extensive interviews with the government officials involved in this case. Some of the information they were provided is false or misleading. Much of it is straightforward and useful, as is Negroni's account of the FAA radar experience, 63–64.

22. Stephanopoulos's slipup would be one of many. Full text reported by Reed Irvine of Accuracy in Media, 19 September 2001.

23. Milton, 6.

24. Lawrence Wright, "The Counter-Terrorist," *New Yorker*, 14 January 2002.

25. Negroni, 39.

26. Milton, 28.

27. Negroni, 54.

28. Al Kamen, "Route to NTSB Runs Through Tennessee," *Washington Post*, 28 May 1993.

29. Negroni, 85.

30. Negroni, 60.

31. Milton, 131.

32. Negroni, 99.

33. Milton, 7. Her source is quite likely Tony Lake.

34. Milton, 7.

2. Lost Opportunities

1. George Stephanopoulos, *All Too Human* (New York: Back Bay Books, 2000), 437.

2. David Johnston, "Explosion Aboard T.W.A. Flight 800: The Theories," *New York Times*, 19 July 1996.

3. By all accounts, it was Hillary Clinton who insisted on a female attorney general, settling finally on the pliable Janet Reno. Shadowing Reno until his fall from grace was Hillary's former law partner, Webster Hubbell. At the time of the TWA Flight 800 disaster, Jamie Gorelick was functioning as the "political officer" of the Justice Department.

4. Interview by James Sanders, March 1997.

5. The authors have identified at least one of the editors and have been told his story through a highly reliable source. Efforts to interview the editor have been in vain.

6. Peter Jennings, ABC radio commentary, 14 November 1994.

7. A good summary of these various attacks on talk radio can be found in the Media Research Center's *Media Watch*, November 1995.

8. N. R. Kleinfield, "The Crash of Flight 800: The Overview," *New York Times*, 18 July 1996.

9. Patricia Milton, *In the Blink of an Eye*, 67.

10. Lewis Schiliro, testimony before Senate Judiciary Subcommittee on Administrative Oversight and the Courts, Washington, D.C., 10 May 1999.

11. Milton, 89.

12. Milton, 89.

13. Milton, 90.

14. Milton, 152.

15. Milton, 153.

16. This interview took place on 24 March 1997, as reported in the NTSB Group Chairman's Factual Report of Accident Investigation, 16 October 1997.

17. Milton, 153.

18. 24 March 1997 interview, NTSB Group Chairman's Factual Report, 16 October 1997.

19. Milton, 149.
20. Milton, 186.
21. Don Nibert, interview by authors, videotape, August 2001.
22. David Hendrix, "Two Years Later, Flight 800 Crash Questions Remain," *Riverside (California) Press Enterprise*, 17 July 1998.
23. Milton, 154.
24. It seems more likely that many high-ranking officers would have cooperated in the concealment of their assets if they did, in fact, believe that there was terrorist involvement and were waiting for the White House's response.
25. Don Nibert, interview by authors, videotape, August 2001.
26. Matthew Purdy, "Missile Theory Rebutted In T.W.A. Flight 800 Crash," *New York Times*, 12 March 1997.
27. FBI press conference, 18 November 1997, as transcribed in a press release of the same day. In his Senate testimony on 10 May 1999, Lewis Schiliro uses the same phrase, "their immediate vicinity to the crash site," and cites the same vessels.
28. James Kallstrom, interview with Reed Irvine, audiotape, reported in the Accuracy in Media newsletter, 14 September 1998.
29. Letter from FBI Acting Assistant Director Lewis D. Schiliro to Congressman James A. Traficant, 27 July 1998.
30. Letter, Schiliro to Traficant, 27 July 1998.
31. James Kallstrom, interview by Jim Lehrer, *NewsHour with Jim Lehrer*, Public Broadcasting System, 18 November 1997.
32. Christine Negroni, *Deadly Departure,* 138.
33. David Johnston, "Explosion Aboard T.W.A. Flight 800: The Theories," *New York Times*, 19 July 1996.
34. Johnston, "Explosion," *New York Times*, 19 July 1996.
35. Negroni, 140.
36. Dick Russell, interview by authors, videotape, September 2001.
37. Negroni, 140. Her claim of a ghost plane would be more believable had not the plane blown up precisely when the ghost merged with it.
38. Robert Kessler, "Streak ID'd as Plane, Not Missile," Newsday.com, 21 March 1997.
39. FBI press conference, 18 November 1997.
40. Hendrix, "Two Years Later," *Riverside (California) Press Enterprise*, 17 July 1998.
41. Milton, 169.
42. NTSB Board meeting on TWA 800, 22 August 2000.
43. Johnston, "Explosion," *New York Times*, 19 July 1996.
44. "Investigators Look at New Theory of Missile Fired from Boat," *London Times*, 22 July 1996.
45. Milton, 106-7.
46. Milton, 106-7.
47. Milton, 106-7.
48. Milton, 135.
49. Nibert, interview.
50. For all the secrecy involved, the CIA video, which aired only once on November 18, 1997, is readily available to the public for a small duplication fee.
51. Dan Barry, "Is That a Missile?" *New York Times*, 26 August 1996.
52. Barry, "Is That a Missile?" *New York Times*, 26 August 1996.
53. Milton, 234.
54. FBI press conference, 18 November 1997.
55. Milton, 234.
56. The contrast here is between what the *New York Times* reported in 1996 and what Milton reported in 1999. The NTSB lament on this subject testifies to the agency's overall futility. "Further analysis of the photograph was attempted by Safety Board personnel and no determination as to content could be achieved, partly due to the material being a copy." It gets sadder still: "A copy of the FBI analysis was requested on December 19, 1996, but has not been received."
57. FBI Press Release, 18 November 1997, as related at press conference of same day.
58. Milton, 234.
59. Milton, 234.
60. FBI Press Release, 18 November 1997.
61. Milton, 124.

3. FALSE DIALECTIC

1. Maj. Fritz Meyer, videotaped presentation at the Granada Forum in California, 12 March 1998.
2. Meyer, Granada Forum, also his interview by NTSB, 11 January 1997. As with Capt. Chris Baur, Meyer's statements are highly consistent from one interview to another.
3. Capt. Chris Baur, interview by NTSB, 11 January 1997.
4. Meyer, Granada Forum—this and subsequent Meyer quotes.
5. NTSB Group Chairman's Factual Report of Accident Investigation, 16 October 1997.
6. Jim Hall, NTSB hearing, 23 August 2000.
7. Christine Negroni, *Deadly Departure*, 150.
8. Negroni, 150.
9. NTSB Group Chairman's Factual Report, 16 October 1997.
10. NTSB Group Chairman's Factual Report, 16 October 1997.
11. Lewis Schiliro, testimony before Senate Judiciary Subcommittee on Administrative Oversight and the Courts, Washington, D.C., 10 May 1999.
12. Schiliro, testimony.
13. "The International Association of Machinists and Aerospace Workers: Analysis and Recommendations," submitted as part of the NTSB's final report, "In-flight Breakup Over the Atlantic Ocean, Trans World Airlines Flight 800," 10 August 2000. (Hereafter, "IAMAW Analysis and Recommendations") Although this damning formal report was submitted as part of the NTSB's official record, the NTSB brass all but ignored it.
14. Jim Speer, interview by authors, videotape, September 2001.
15. Negroni, 133.
16. Dwight Brumley, interview by authors, videotape, September 2001.
17. From a 1996 first-person account by Sven Faret and Ken Wendell.
18. Patricia Milton, *In the Blink of an Eye*, 142.
19. Milton, 87.
20. Milton, 235.
21. Milton, 236.
22. Milton, 77.
23. Negroni, 132.
24. Meyer, Granada Forum.
25. FBI Witness Summary, number 200.
26. Negroni, 134.
27. Negroni, 134.
28. "Former FBI section chief pleads guilty, admits destroying Ruby Ridge report," CNN.com, 22 October 1996.
29. James Bovard, "Ruby Ridge: The Justice Report," *Wall Street Journal*, 30 June 1995.
30. Although these incidents were widely reported, the most comprehensive source on the pattern of abuse is attorney David Limbaugh's *Absolute Power: The Legacy of Corruption in the Clinton-Reno Justice Department* (Washington, DC: Regnery, 2001).
31. Andrew Revkin, "To TWA Crash Investigators Not All Eyewitnesses Are Equal," *New York Times*, 17 August 1996—this citation and those that follow.
32. NTSB Group Chairman's Factual Report, 16 October 1997.
33. Testimony before Senate Judiciary Subcommittee on Administrative Oversight and the Courts, Washington, D.C., 10 May 1999.
34. Milton, 234.
35. These are the NTSB's own summarized numbers.
36. Witness Summary, NTSB Group Chairman's Factual Report of Accident Investigation, 16 October 1997.
37. Revkin, "To TWA Crash Investigators Not All Eyewitnesses Are Equal," *New York Times*, 17 August 1996.
38. Negroni, 98.
39. "The Fate of Flight 800: The Overview," *New York Times*, 26 July 1996.
40. James Bennet, "Clinton Sets Tough Rules for Tighter Air Security," *New York Times*, 26 July 1996.
41. White House, Office of the Press Secretary, press release, 25 July 1996.
42. Bennet, "Clinton Sets Tough Rules," *New York Times*, 26 July 1996.
43. Bennet, "Clinton Sets Tough Rules," *New York Times*, 26 July 1996.
44. Numerous Web sites attribute this quote to Kallstrom, one specifically on July 17, 1996, at 10:30

P.M. Newsday.com reported this same quote on July 27, 1996. He seems to have repeated the statement, or variations of it, in the first week or so of the investigation.

45. NTSB Group Chairman's Factual Report, 16 October 1997.

46. This raw footage purchased from ABC can be seen in the authors' video documentary, *Silenced*, produced by Jack Cashill and James Sanders and directed by Jack Cashill, 2001.

47. *Silenced*.

48. Jim Speer, interview by authors, videotape, September 2001.

49. Donald Kerr, testimony before Senate Judiciary Subcommittee on Administrative Oversight and the Courts, Washington, D.C., 10 May 1999.

50. Paul Quinn-Judge, "U.S. Sends Israel Bomb Detection Gear," *Boston Globe*, 5 March 1996.

51. Speer, interview.

52. Meyer, Granada Forum.

53. Meyer, Granada Forum.

54. Liam Pleven, "Hint of Bomb," Newsday.com, 23 July 1996.

55. Speer, interview.

56. Milton, 128.

57. "FBI Removes Four Crime Lab Workers, Including Whistleblower in OKC," Associated Press, 27 January 1997.

58. Negroni, 164.

59. Negroni, 99.

60. Negroni, 177.

61. Negroni, 154.

62. Negroni, 62, 197.

63. The source for this is an engineer assigned to the investigation. For fear of losing his job, he has chosen to remain anonymous, but he has proved useful in confirming and/or refuting information about the investigation.

64. Speer, interview—this and subsequent citation.

4. DOG DAYS

1. Patricia Milton, *In the Blink of an Eye*, 219.

2. Andrew Revkin, "A Bold Start Stretched to 16 Fruitless Months," *New York Times*, November 14, 1997.

3. Matthew Wald, "Jet's Landing Gear Is Said To Provide Evidence of Bomb," *New York Times*, 31 July 1996.

4. Wald, "Jet's Landing Gear," *New York Times*, 31 July 1996.

5. "Bomb Still Leading Theory in TWA Crash," CNN.com, 1 August 1996.

6. "Second Test Shows No Sign of Bomb Residue," CNN.com, 23 July 1996.

7. Don Van Natta Jr., "Luggage Spotted in Debris Trail Suggests an Explosion to Experts," *New York Times*, 6 August 1996.

8. Unedited footage, WABC TV, New York, 11 August 1996. Authors have footage in possession.

9. Van Natta Jr., "Luggage Spotted," *New York Times*, 6 August 1996.

10. Milton, 221.

11. Don Van Natta Jr., "Area Near Wings Is New Focus of Investigation," *New York Times*, 13 August 1996.

12. Milton, 183.

13. Milton, 184.

14. "Rough Seas Plague TWA Divers," CNN.com, 13 August 1996.

15. "Fuel Tank's Condition Makes Malfunction Seem Less Likely," *New York Times*, 14 August 1996—these quotes and those that follow.

16. These and other such quotes appear throughout Milton's book.

17. Kelly O'Meara, chief of staff to Long Island Congressman Michael Forbes, telephone interview by authors, December 2001. O'Meara would pursue this case deep enough to cost her job with Forbes.

18. Milton, 226.

19. From the beginning, by all accounts, Janet Reno played a largely ceremonial role in the Justice Department. She did not have the political confidence of the Clintons.

20. Mark Hosenball and Daniel Klaidman, "Desperately Seeking the Next 'Willie Horton,'" *Newsweek*, 3 June 1996. The piece claims that Republicans were hoping to identify liberal jurists of the sort who might turn loose another Willie Horton. While rejecting this kind of political mischief, the authors were predictably much more approving of politics Clinton-style.

21. The FBI's own documents and its daily maps issued in limited release attest to the same, as do the authors' sources within the investigation.

22. "Nose Gear Doors Baffle TWA 800 Crash Investigators," CNN.com, 5 September 1997.
23. "Nose Gear Doors," CNN.com, 5 September 1997.
24. The most complete account of this incident is David Hendrix's "TWA Crash Probe Turns to Damaged Nose Gear Doors," *Riverside (California) Press Enterprise,* 7 September 1997.
25. According to Sanders, the memo was just as likely to be a bureaucratic dodge as it was a conscious cover-up. Regardless, the memo is demonstrably false.
26. Milton, 226.
27. Milton, 227.
28. "Prime Evidence Found That Device Exploded in Cabin of Flight 800," *New York Times,* 23 August 1996—this quote and those that follow.
29. Milton, 227.
30. Milton, 221.
31. Henry Hughes, letter to Senator Charles E. Grassley, Chairman, Subcommittee on Administrative Oversight and the Courts Committee on the Judiciary, United States Senate, 14 June 1999, in response to Grassley's letter requesting additional information.
32. Sylvia Adcock and Michael Arena, "Probers Kept in Dark," Newsday.com, 24 August 1996.
33. Adcock and Arena, "Probers Kept in Dark," Newsday.com, 24 August 1996.
34. Maj. Fritz Meyer, Granada Forum, 12 March 1998—this quote and those that follow.
35. Christine Negroni, *Deadly Departure,* 185.
36. "Traces of Explosives Found on TWA 800 Crash Debris," CNN.com, 23 August 1996.
37. John Kifner, "Missiles Are Called Threat to Civil Aviation," *New York Times,* 25 August 1996.
38. "Ill-Fated TWA Plane Used for Troop Transport in Gulf War," CNN.com, 26 August 1996.
39. President Clinton's speech before the Democratic National Convention, 29 August 1996.
40. Andrew Revkin, *New York Times,* 30 August 1996.
41. Don Van Natta Jr., "More Traces of Explosives in Flight 800," *New York Times,* 31 August 1996—this quote and those that follow.
42. Milton, 184.
43. "Source: Traces of 2nd Explosive Found in TWA Debris," CNN.com, 30 August 1996.
44. Milton, 229.
45. Van Natta, "More Traces," *New York Times,* 31 August 1996.

5. RED HERRING

1. Walter Robinson and Glen Johnson, "Airlines Fought Security Changes," *Boston Globe,* 20 September 2001.
2. Matthew Wald, "White House Seeks $300 Million for Airport Bomb Detection and Other Safety Measures," *New York Times,* 6 September 1996.
3. Robinson and Johnson, "Airlines Fought Security Changes," *Boston Globe,* 20 September 2001.
4. Robinson and Johnson, "Airlines Fought Security Changes," *Boston Globe,* 20 September 2001.
5. Andrew Revkin, "Fuel Tank Crucial to all Crash Theories," *New York Times,* 19 September 1996.
6. Don Van Natta Jr., "Fuel Tank's Condition Makes Malfunction Less Likely," *New York Times,* 14 August 1996.
7. Revkin, "Fuel Tank Crucial," *New York Times,* 19 September 1996.
8. John Roberts II, "The Dissent of Flight 800," *American Spectator,* July 1997.
9. Revkin, "Fuel Tank Crucial," *New York Times,* 19 September 1996.
10. "Investigators: Test explosives set back TWA bomb theories," CNN.com, 21 September 1996.
11. Matthew Purdy, "Bomb Security Test on Jet May Explain Trace of Explosives," *New York Times,* 21 September 1996.
12. Don Van Natta Jr., "Setback in T.W.A. Crash Inquiry Adds Urgency to the Search for Evidence of a Bomb," *New York Times,* 22 September 1996.
13. Van Natta Jr., "Setback in T.W.A. Crash Inquiry," *New York Times,* 22 September 1996.
14. Van Natta Jr., "Fuel Tank's Condition," *New York Times,* 14 August 1996. The authors talked to Van Natta by phone in August 2001. He did not know that the dog-training exercise had been staged on another airliner.
15. Patricia Milton, *In the Blink of an Eye,* 231. The FBI claims that the date of the interview was September 20, but based on Milton's more specific timeline and CNN's claim that the FBI did not even learn about the exercise until the twentieth, the twenty-first seems more likely.
16. The activities of Officer Burnett are described in a lengthy letter signed by FBI Assistant Director in Charge James K. Kallstrom to Congressman James A. Traficant, dated September 5, 1997. All following FBI citations will be to this letter unless otherwise specified.

17. Herman Burnett, telephone interview by authors, August 2001.
18. This was reported by Dave Hendrix of the *Riverside (California) Press Enterprise* and published as a chapter, "St. Louis Canine Scheme," in James Sanders's book, *Altered Evidence* (Philadelphia, PA: Offset Paperbacks, 1999). Tom Shoemaker and Kay Pennington also did original research on the story as reported in the December 1998 and January 1999 *TWA Case Files Newsletter*.
19. The time sequence is based on TWA documents in force at the time, obtained by the authors.
20. Sanders, *Altered Evidence*, 72–80.
21. Tom Shoemaker, *TWA Case Files Newsletter*, January 1999.
22. Van Natta Jr., "Setback in T.W.A. Crash Inquiry," *New York Times*, 22 September 1996.
23. "Training Drill Possible Source of TWA Explosives Residue," CNN.com, 20 September 1996.
24. NTSB Chairman Jim Hall, letter to acting FAA Administrator Barry Valen, February 1997. The authors have reviewed this correspondence in its unedited form.
25. Milton, 231.
26. Milton, 231.
27. Burnett, interview.
28. Milton, 231.
29. Milton, 219.
30. Kallstrom, letter to Traficant.
31. FBI Agent Joe Cantamessa acknowledged at an early August press conference that there were at least ten EGIS-confirmed hits on the plane's exterior.
32. As will be explained in detail in chapter 10, the government has fought these FOIA requests every step of the way.
33. NTSB Chairman's Briefing/Status Report, 15 November 1996.
34. James Kallstrom, interview by Jim Lehrer, *NewsHour with Jim Lehrer*, Public Broadcasting System, 19 November 1996.
35. Milton, 320.
36. Milton, 319.
37. Milton, 319–20.
38. Christine Negroni, *Deadly Departure*, 185.
39. Negroni, 186. Unfortunately, Negroni's book, like Milton's, has no footnotes. The FAA comments seem to have been made shortly after the revelation of the dog training.
40. Negroni, 185.
41. FBI press conference, 18 November 1997.
42. Retired New Jersey police captain John Stankard, e-mail to authors, August 2001.
43. Robert Davey, "The FBI and Flight 800," *Village Voice*, 14 July 1999.
44. Robinson and Johnson, "Airlines Fought Security Changes," *Boston Globe*, 20 September 2001.
45. Victoria Cummock, telephone interview by authors, 12 September 2001.
46. Final Report of the White House Commission on Aviation and Security, 12 February 1997, provided to the authors by Victoria Cummock.
47. Victoria Cummock's dissent, 19 February 1997, provided to the authors by Ms. Cummock.
48. Cummock's dissent.
49. Tony Blankley, "High-Flying Politics," *Washington Times*, 6 September 2000.
50. *M. Victoria Cummock, Appellant v. Albert Gore, Jr., et al.*, United States Court of Appeals for the District of Columbia circuit, argued 22 April 1999, decided 18 June 1999. No. 98-5427.
51. NTSB hearing, 22 August 2000.

6. Decent Interval

1. Patricia Milton's *In the Blink of an Eye* provides convincing detail of James Kallstrom's genuine empathy.
2. Marge Gross, interview by authors, videotape, April 2001. Gross has made the same claim publicly at both the National Press Club and at an Accuracy in Media conference.
3. Hearing of the Senate Judiciary Subcommittee on Administrative Oversight and the Courts, 10 May 1999.
4. Milton, 262.
5. Senate Judiciary Subcommittee, 10 May 1999.
6. Milton, 348.
7. "IAMAW Analysis and Recommendations," 10 August 2000.
8. NTSB hearing, 22 August 2000.
9. Milton, 277.
10. Milton, 280.

11. Milton, 281.
12. Christine Negroni, *Deadly Departure,* 198.
13. Negroni, 205.
14. This particular investigator was informed of the tap by security officers at his place of employment. The investigator has been interviewed by the authors but has chosen to remain anonymous.
15. Jim Speer, interview by authors, videotape, September 2001.
16. These changes were noticed by James Sanders in the discovery phase of his criminal trial, during which he was allowed access to investigation photos and documents that others were not.
17. "IAMAW Analysis."
18. Speer, interview.
19. Linda Kunz is now Vice President for Flight Services of American Eagle. There is little dispute about the details of her firing. *Dan's Papers* discusses it in context in its 14 May 1999 edition.
20. Negroni, 211.
21. Jonathan Vankin and John Whalen, "How a Quack Becomes a Canard," *New York Times,* 17 November 1996.
22. This comes from William Langewiesche's lukewarm *New York Times* review of Milton's book (26 September 1999): "But it does contain accurate information and avoids the pitfalls of conspiracy mongering and gross speculation."
23. Milton, 269.
24. This incident is related in Kristina Borjesson's title essay, "Into the Buzzsaw," from her book, *Into the Buzzsaw: Leading Journalists Expose the Myth of a Free Press* (Buffalo: Prometheus, 2002), 110–11.
25. Milton, 269.
26. Borjesson, 111.
27. Pierre Salinger, letter to the editor, *New York Times,* 21 August 1997.
28. Confirmed by Dick Russell, interview by James Sanders, videotape, September 2001—this and information following from same interview.
29. Milton, 271.
30. Milton, 271.
31. Milton, 273.
32. FBI press conference, 18 November 1997, as transcribed in a press release of the same day. In his Senate testimony on May 10, 1999, Lewis Schiliro uses the same phrase, "their immediate vicinity to the crash site," and cites the same vessels.
33. James Kallstrom, audiotaped interview, reported in the Accuracy in Media newsletter, 14 September 1998.
34. Vankin and Whalen, "How a Quack Becomes a Canard," *New York Times,* 17 November 1996.
35. This story is related in Matthew Purdy, "Missile Theory Rebutted in T.W.A. Flight 800 Crash," *New York Times,* 12 March 1997.
36. Associated Press, 12 March 1997. The AP writer is Patricia Milton. Bacon's protestations come in response not only to Salinger's claims but also to AP reports that an "Air National Guardsman who witnessed the explosion of TWA Flight 800 repeatedly told authorities he thought a missile had struck the plane." The guardsman in question is not Major Meyer but Captain Baur. Reached at his home, "Baur would not comment."
37. Purdy, "Missile Theory Rebutted," *New York Times,* 12 March 1997.
38. NTSB interview with P-3 crew, 24 March 1997, as posted on NTSB Web site.
39. Purdy, "Missile Theory Rebutted," *New York Times,* 12 March 1997.
40. Written statement by Paul Angelides dated 12 July 1998.
41. The only major media exposure the story received was on TV's *Hard Copy.* The authors also spoke with radio commentator Peter Ford in August 2001 about Crocker.
42. Flight 800 Independent Research Organization president Dr. Thomas Stalcup, interview by authors, August 2001.
43. William S. Donaldon, Letter to the Editor, *Wall Street Journal,* 24 April 1997.
44. Milton, 342–45—this quote and those that follow.
45. Milton, 286.
46. Milton, 286.
47. NTSB hearing, 22 August 2000.
48. The FBI Trawler Operations Manual is posted on Donaldson's Web site, TWA800.com.
49. "Petition for the Reconsideration and Modification of the National Transportation Safety Board's Findings and Determinations of the Probable Cause for the Crash of TWA 800," submitted 20 May 2002, by FIRO president Dr. Thomas Stalcup.

50. "Petition for the Reconsideration," Dr. Thomas Stalcup.

51. Speer, interview.

52. Milton, 289.

53. Jim Hall's opening remarks, NTSB hearing, 22 August 2000.

54. Matthew Wald, "Clinton to Go Outside Aviation Circles for New F.A.A. Chief," *New York Times*, 2 May 1997.

55. Jim Hall, testimony before the House Aviation Subcommittee, 10 July 1997.

56. Andrew Revkin, "A Bold Start Stretched to 16 Fruitless Months," *New York Times*, 14 November 1997.

57. Speer, interview.

7. HANGAR MAN

1. James and Elizabeth Sanders were interviewed extensively on videotape by Jack Cashill in April 2001 for the documentary *Silenced*. Direct quotes come from these interviews.

2. Murray Weiss, "TWA Probers: Missile Witnesses Credible," *New York Post*, 22 September 1996.

3. Lewis Schiliro, testimony before Senate Judiciary Subcommittee on Administrative Oversight and the Courts, Washington, D.C., 10 May 1999.

4. NTSB Chairman's Briefing/Status Report, 15 November 1996.

5. NTSB letter to the FAA, 26 December 1996.

6. The FAA response to the NTSB request was written on January 9, 1997.

7. Stalcup speaks to this in the authors' documentary, *Silenced*, and elsewhere.

8. NTSB Chairman's Briefing, 15 November 1996.

9. McClaine's account is well documented in his interview with the NTSB, National Transportation Safety Board Docket Materials for Investigation DCA96MA070, TWA Flight 800, 17 July 1996, Witnesses, Appendix Z.

10. NTSB Chairman's Briefing/Status Report, 15 November 1996.

11. NTSB hearing, 8 December 1997.

12. NTSB hearing, 22 August 2000.

13. This actual physical alteration was well documented not only by Sanders but by the NTSB's Hank Hughes and others. Please see chapters 6 and 11.

14. The incident took place on or about December 15, 1996, and was captured on videotape. These and related quotes come from Sanders's contemporaneous debriefing of Mark Sauter and from the videotape and were reported in James Sanders's *The Downing of TWA Flight 800* (New York: Kensington/Zebra, 1997).

15. Hearing of the Senate Judiciary Subcommittee on Administrative Oversight and the Courts, 10 May 1999.

16. Robert Davey, "Flight 800: The Missing Evidence," *Village Voice*, 15 July 1998.

17. Howard Kurtz, *Washington Post*, 23 August 1999.

18. This episode is well documented in Kristina Borjesson's *Into the Buzzsaw: Leading Journalists Expose the Myth of a Free Press* (New York: Prometheus Books, 2002), 142–44.

19. The source was promised anonymity. His entire scientific career was in the missile and warhead industry. 3M 1357 glue was tested to determine elements and percentage of each. Stalcup analyzed the test performed at Florida State University. See chapter 8 for results.

20. The NTSB has access to an archive of CVR tapes from planes blown out of the sky by a bomb. The 340 fps figure came from this archive.

21. The bracketed information has been filled in by James Sanders from David Hendrix's notes. The parenthetical comments are Hendrix's own.

22. Multiple sources. FBI Special Agent Ken Maxwell, testifying at Sanders's criminal trial, under oath, confirmed the red residue was a hot topic.

23. James Sanders received these documents through the Freedom of Information Act.

24. Patricia Milton, *In The Blink of an Eye*, 306.

8. DAMAGE CONTROL

1. Loren Fleckenstein, "New Data Show Missile May Have Nailed TWA 800," *Riverside (California) Press-Enterprise*, 10 March 1997, 1.

2. Kristina Borjesson, *Into the Buzzsaw: Leading Journalists Expose the Myth of a Free Press*, 123–27. Borjesson's prepublication manuscript, shared with the authors, adds detail. Subsequent information is from this passage.

3. Bernard Loeb, testimony before the House Appropriations Subcommittee on Transportation, 11 March 1997.

4. All sources are investigators within the Flight 800 investigation. David Hendrix of the *Riverside (California) Press-Enterprise* independently found a source who confirmed Sanders's sources. All sources were on a "not for attribution" basis. The arrest warrant is quoted in detail later in this chapter.

5. Hearing of the Senate Judiciary Subcommittee on Administrative Oversight and the Courts, 10 May 1999.

6. Merrit Birky, NTSB Fire & Explosion Factual Report, published before the December 8, 1997, NTSB hearing.

7. Notarized affidavit signed by Charles Bassett, filed with the federal court as part of the Sanderses' criminal defense.

8. All TWA 747 seats are numbered. 19-2 is row 19, seat 2. The documentary *Silenced* shows the stark difference between Sanders's sample and the NTSB's.

9. Borjesson, 126.

10. Transcript, Dr. Merrit Birky, interview by Dr. Thomas Stalcup, audiotape, July 1998, shared with authors.

11. Transcript, Dr. Birky, interview.

12. Borjesson, 125.

13. Borjesson, 126.

14. Jeff Schlanger, sworn testimony in the Sanders trial, April 8, 1999.

15. James Sanders obtained FBI Special Agent James Kinsley's field notes during the course of the criminal case.

16. Kinsley, field notes.

17. This information comes from documents obtained under discovery during criminal case.

18. Kinsley, field notes. This and subsequent information.

19. Sanders learned of this through documents obtained from the phone company and Justice Department during the criminal proceedings.

20. Al Guart, "Evidence-Swipers May Face Fed Charges," *New York Post*, 19 November 1997.

21. Warrant of application for arrest, written by FBI Special Agent James Kinsley, December 5, 1997. Subsequent information is from this document.

22. Loren Fleckenstein, "New Data Show Missile May Have Nailed TWA 800," *Riverside (California) Press-Enterprise*, 10 March 1997.

23. The 140-page debris-field report was issued on December 3, 1996, and James Sanders received a copy soon after. He still has an original copy of the same.

24. Patricia Milton, *In the Blink of an Eye*, 305.

25. FBI notes shared with Sanders's defense team.

26. FBI press release, 5 December 1997.

27. James Sanders, *The Downing of TWA Flight 800*, 136.

28. FBI press release, 5 December 1997.

29. John McQuiston, "Couple Go on Trial in Theft of Piece of Crashed Jet," *New York Times*, 7 April 1999.

30. Robert Kessler, "TWA Theft Charges," Newsday.com, 6 December 1997—this and quotes that follow.

31. James Kallstrom, letter to Jim Hall, 3 December 1997. This letter was widely reported, and, given Hall's immediate compliance, became an enduring source of controversy.

32. Andrew Metz, "Eyewitness Accounts Shelved," Newsday.com, 5 December 1997.

33. Consider the *Newsday* headline from March 11, 1997: "Theory Discounted: Investigators debunk reports of TWA missile."

34. This detail and those that follow come from the accounts of the Sanderses, much of it captured on videotape for the documentary *Silenced*.

9. The Big Lie

1. FBI press conference, 18 November 1997.

2. Lawrence Wright, "The Counter-Terrorist," *New Yorker*, 14 January 2002.

3. Patricia Milton, *In the Blink of an Eye*, 333.

4. The CIA briefed the NTSB on April 30, 1999. This is documented in the National Transportation Safety Board Docket Materials for Investigation DCA96MA070, TWA Flight 800, 17 July 1996, Appendix FF.

5. NTSB Docket Materials, Appendix FF. The CIA analysts did, however, accompany the FBI "on one occasion" when the FBI "reinterviewed two eyewitnesses," neither specified.

6. NTSB Docket Materials, Witnesses, Appendix B.
7. NTSB Docket Materials, Witnesses, Appendix B.
8. Cmdr. William Donaldson, letter to FBI Director Louis Freeh, 3 December 1997.
9. NTSB Docket Materials, Appendix FF.
10. The video is officially titled, *TWA Flight 800: What Did the Witnesses See?* It is available for purchase through the NTSB. All future references to "the CIA video" will be to this. It originally aired November 18, 1997.
11. All of the following accounts, including Dwight Brumley's, come from the FBI 302s as posted with the NTSB Docket Materials for Investigation DCA96MA070, TWA Flight 800, 17 July 1996, under the "Witnesses" appendices.
12. Mike Wire, telephone interview by authors, January 2002.
13. "FBI Concludes No Criminal Evidence in TWA 800 Crash," CNN.com, 18 November 1997.
14. NTSB Docket Materials, Witnesses, Appendix B.
15. Maj. Fritz Meyer, interview by authors, videotape, August 2000.
16. NTSB Docket Materials, Witnesses, Appendix G. Mike Wire is Witness 571. He was interviewed by phone on July 23, 1996, and in person on July 30, 1996. The following quotes come from the July 30 interview.
17. Mike Wire, interview by authors, videotape, on-site, April 2001.
18. Mike Wire, telephone interview by authors, July 2001.
19. Reed Irvine documents his first conversations with Wire in a letter to the Justice Department from August 15, 2001, published as a Special Report by Accuracy in Media.
20. Dwight Brumley, interview by authors, videotape, September 2001. Subsequent information is from this interview. Brumley's interview varies only minimally from his FBI interview.
21. Brumley, interview, September 2001; also repeated publicly at an Accuracy in Media forum.
22. NTSB briefing of the CIA, 30 April 1999.
23. Milton, 334.
24. Benjamin Weiser, "In Graphic Simulation, F.B.I. Tries to Show Jet's Fiery End," *New York Times*, 19 November 1997.
25. Andrew Revkin, "To T.W.A. Crash Investigators Not All Eyewitnesses Are Equal," *New York Times*, 17 August 1996.
26. Don Van Natta Jr., "Fuel Tank's Condition Makes Malfunction Seem Less Likely," *New York Times*, 14 August 1996.
27. Christine Negroni, *Deadly Departure*, 136.
28. Weiser, "Graphic Simulation," *New York Times*, 19 November 1997.
29. Donaldson, letter to Freeh.
30. E-mail to authors, 20 June 2001; name withheld at authors' discretion.
31. From Boeing's press release, 18 November 1997, the day the video first aired.
32. Meyer, interview; also reproduced in authors' documentary, *Silenced*.
33. Paul Angelides, interview by authors, videotape, August 2000; also reproduced in authors' documentary, *Silenced*.
34. NTSB Docket Materials, Witnesses, Appendix Z.
35. NTSB Docket Materials, Appendix FF.
36. Wire, interview, videotape, and later e-mail correspondence.
37. Ray Lahr, interview by authors, videotape, April 2001—this and information that follows.
38. Cmdr. William Donaldson, videotaped presentation at the Granada Forum in California, 12 March 1998.
39. Ray Lahr, correspondence to the NTSB, shared with the authors. This one dates from 26 October 2001.
40. Lahr, interview; reproduced in authors' documentary, *Silenced*.
41. Ray Lahr, letter to NTSB Acting Director Carol Carmody, 24 September 2001.
42. Dr. Thomas Stalcup, interview by authors, videotape, April 2001; reproduced in authors' documentary, *Silenced*.
43. Petition for the Reconsideration and Modification of the National Transportation Safety Board's Findings and Determinations of the Probable Cause for the Crash of TWA 800, submitted 20 May 2002, by Dr. Thomas Stalcup, Flight 800 Independent Research Organization.
44. Ray Lahr, letter to NTSB Acting Director Carol Carmody, 21 June 2001.
45. Ray Lahr, letter to the NTSB general counsel, 4 August 2001. Subsequent information from this letter.

10. BLACK BOXES

1. The TWA Flight 800 CVR transcript is available through the Aviation Safety Network (aviation-safety.net) among other Internet sites.

2. Reuters, 19 July 1996, and elsewhere. The comment was widely reported.

3. The Turkish 757 recovery was widely reported. The U.S. Navy Public Affairs Service confirmed the find in its Navy Wire Service release, 26 July 1996.

4. The reports by pleasure boaters are widely reported on Internet sites dealing with TWA 800. The major media are oddly silent on the subject. The *New York Times* makes no reference to the Forbes incident or the search for the black boxes.

5. "What Happened to Flight 800?" CNN.com, 19 July 1996.

6. Kelly O'Meara, telephone interview by authors, December 2001. O'Meara also notes that the *Juniper* was first ship at the site of the crash, also sensitive, of EgyptAir 990.

7. The U.S. Navy Public Affairs Library can be accessed on-line, via www.chinfo.navy.mil/navpalib.

8. Pierre Salinger and Mike Sommer, *Paris Match*, 12 March 1997.

9. This executive order is widely posted on the Internet, including government sites. On February 11, 1998, Steven Honigman, the general counsel of the Navy, responded to Congressman Traficant's request for an explanation. He claimed that the order came in response to a request initiated by Local 22 of the AFL-CIO to represent this group. The request was allegedly made on June 10, 1996—nine months earlier—coincidentally the same day that the infamous dog-training exercise was alleged to have taken place.

10. Jerry Marken et al., "Divers Wait As Devices Scan Ocean," Newsday.com, 22 July 1996.

11. Marken et al., "Divers Wait," Newsday.com, 22 July 1996.

12. White House press conference, 25 July 1996.

13. Marken et al., "Divers Wait," Newsday.com, 22 July 1996.

14. Marken et al., "Divers Wait," Newsday.com, 22 July 1996.

15. All future references refer to this video. James Sanders, who has seen the video several times, says, "It's a hoot."

16. Milton, *In the Blink of an Eye*, 160.

17. Robert Francis, diver Kevin Gelhafen, interview by Betty Bowser, PBS *NewsHour* Online, 25 July 1996.

18. "The Fate of Flight 800: The President's Remarks," *New York Times*, 26 July 1996.

19. TWA Flight 800 public hearing, 8 December 1997.

20. Christine Negroni, *Deadly Departure*, 119.

21. Robert Francis, interview by Betty Bowser, PBS *NewsHour* Online, 25 July 1996.

22. Negroni, 119.

23. Milton, 161.

24. NTSB Group Chairman's Factual Report of Accident Investigation, 16 October 1997.

25. The video is officially titled, *TWA Flight 800: What Did the Witnesses See?*

26. TWA Flight 800 public hearing, 8 December 1997.

27. Air Line Pilots Association submission to the NTSB, 30 April 2000.

28. Interview by James Sanders, February 1997; name withheld upon request.

29. NTSB Group Chairman's Factual Report.

30. The narrative account comes from a word-for-word transcript of Donaldson's radio interview by Art Bell on *Coast to Coast*, 23 December 1997. Bell does occasionally deal with real events. Hard data can be found on Donaldson's Web site, TWA800.com.

31. David Hendrix, "Pilots Find Evidence of TWA 800 Missile," *Riverside (California) Press-Enterprise*, 9 January 1998.

32. Hendrix, "Pilots Find Evidence," *Riverside (California) Press-Enterprise*, 9 January 1998.

33. NTSB public hearing on TWA Flight 800, 22 August 2000.

34. Audio expert Glenn Schulze, telephone interview by Jack Cashill, February 2002. Following quotes from Schulze come from this interview unless otherwise noted.

35. Schulze, interview.

36. Don Nibert, interview by authors, videotape, August 2001. Following quotes from Nibert come from same interview.

37. Immediately after the December 12, 2000, meeting at the NTSB, Glenn Schulze wrote up a comprehensive five pages of minutes, sent them to the Niberts for confirmation, and then shared them with the authors.

38. As documented in Schulze's contemporaneous notes.

39. Schulze's notes.

40. "Briefs," AVWeb News Wire, 26 March 2001.

11. Exploding Hypotheses

1. Don Van Natta Jr., "Fuel Tank's Condition Makes Malfunction Less Likely," *New York Times*, 14 August 1996—this quote and those that follow.
2. Andrew Revkin, "Fuel Tank Crucial to All Crash Theories," *New York Times*, 19 September 1996.
3. Revkin, "Fuel Tank Crucial to All Crash Theories," *New York Times*, 19 September 1996.
4. Earl Lane et al., "Missing Fuel Pump May Hold Answers," Newsday.com, 24 October 1996.
5. FBI photos of the engineer's board, eventually released by the NTSB, show the switch in the off position. The NTSB acknowledged as much.
6. The document notes the following: "40 39 46.40 [latitude] 72 37 26.80 [longitude] scavenge pump." The NTSB log number, FBI log number, and hangar location are blank.
7. NTSB hearing, 22 August 2000.
8. Patricia Milton, *In the Blink of an Eye*, 259.
9. Milton, 339.
10. "Jet A Explosions—Field Test Plan," presented by NTSB and Explosion Dynamics Laboratory, 27 June 1997.
11. *Handbook of Aviation Fuels Properties*, (CRC Report 530, 1988), 71, table 8.
12. Cmdr. William Donaldson, letter to Jim Hall, 18 September 1997.
13. Cmdr. William Donaldson, letter to Louis Freeh, 3 December 1997.
14. NTSB final report, "In-flight Breakup Over the Atlantic Ocean, Trans World Airlines Flight 800," 10 August 2000 (hereafter, NTSB final report)—this and information following.
15. Milton, 327.
16. Jim Speer, interview by authors, videotape, September 2001.
17. "Extended Modeling Studies of the TWA 800 Center-Wing Fuel Tank Explosion," Sandia Labs, March 2000.
18. NTSB final report, 10 August 2000.
19. Milton, 328—this and Milton citations that follow.
20. Donaldson, letter to Freeh.
21. "Test Called Key Step in Study of Flight 800," *New York Times*, 29 August 1997.
22. Milton, 329.
23. "Test Called Key," *New York Times*, 29 August 1997.
24. Future references to "the report" will be to this NTSB report, "Factors Suggesting the Likelihood that a Short-Circuit Event Occurred on TWA Flight 800," as of 10 August 2000.
25. NTSB hearing, 22 August 2000.
26. "IAMAW Analysis and Recommendations," 10 August 2000—this citation and those that follow.
27. Don Van Natta Jr., "Fuel Tank's Condition Makes Malfunction Less Likely," *New York Times*, 14 August 1996.
28. NTSB Public Hearing, 8 December 1997.
29. NTSB hearing, 22 August 2000.
30. James Sanders has some 250 35mm photos from this occasion.
31. Boeing drawings are part of the NTSB CD-ROM containing all documents and photos related to this case released by the NTSB. Sanders also possesses the pool footage. The visual re-creation of this damage can best be viewed in the authors' documentary, *Silenced*.
32. Hearing of the Senate Judiciary Subcommittee on Administrative Oversight and the Courts, 10 May 1999.
33. NTSB hearing, 22 August 2000.
34. Joseph Fried, "T.W.A. Pilot Stole a Piece of Flight 800," *New York Times*, 6 December 1997.
35. Milton, 338.
36. Kristina Borjesson, *Into the Buzzsaw: Leading Journalists Expose the Myth of a Free Press*, 130–31.
37. Milton, 111.
38. Borjesson, 131. Borjesson asks the question. The quoted answer appears in her unpublished manuscript but not in the published text.
39. Medical/Forensic, Group Chairman Factual Report, NTSB final report, 10 August 2000.
40. Borjesson, 130.
41. NTSB final report, 10 August 2000.
42. "Bomb Still Leading Theory in TWA Crash," CNN.com, 1 August 1996.
43. Van Natta, "Fuel Tank's Condition Makes Malfunction Less Likely," *New York Times*, 14 August 1996, and elsewhere.
44. Milton, 167.
45. McCrone Lab, Chicago, Illinois, did the testing. Initial testing indicated a TNT presence.

Additional testing could not confirm or eliminate the presence of explosive residue. The family chooses not to be identified.

46. Philip Weiss, "Prosecuted for Criticism of Feds' Investigation?" *Jewish World Review*, 15 April 1999.

47. This and following notes comes from a report prepared by Graeme Sephton on January 4, 2002, and released to the authors on January 14, 2002.

48. FBI press release, 18 November 1997.

49. Yousef was on trial in New York the summer of 1996 for plotting to blow up a dozen jumbo jets. According to federal prosecutors, as related in the Newsday.com of September 4, 1996, "Yousef planted his bomb on Flight 434 in a life jacket pouch underneath seat 26K, a window seat off the wing near the center fuel tank. The explosion severely crippled the plane steering systems but the pilot was able to turn around and land safely in Okinawa."

50. This and the following citations were reported by the Associated Press, 3 March 2001.

51. "Thai Blast May Have Been Set for Premier," *New York Times*, 5 March 2001.

52. "Bomb Wrecked Thai PM's Plane," CNN.com, 4 March 2001.

53. This explosion was widely reported. A good account can be found in the *Japan Lawletter*, January 1987.

54. NTSB press release, 11 April 2001. On the following day, it was disseminated by the American Embassy in Thailand.

55. "A Similarity Is Seen in 2 Plane Explosions," *New York Times*, 11 April 2001.

56. "Thai 737 Explosion Prompts FAA Rule on Fuel Pumps," CNN.com, 26 April 2001.

12. SHOW TRIAL

1. Federal court transcript of Stacey allocution. Unless otherwise noted, all quotes in this chapter are from documents filed during the criminal proceedings, and/or transcripts of hearings and the Sanderses' trial.

2. FBI press release, 5 December 1997.

3. *NBC NightlyNews*, 5 December 1997.

4. Gutman was here referring to *Grosjean v. American Press Co.*, 56 S. Ct. 444, 449 (1936).

5. Grand Jury "overt act" description, contained in indictment against James and Elizabeth Sanders.

6. James Sanders filed a civil suit under Title 42, section 2000aa, which prohibits federal seizure of a journalist's work product. It should be noted that shortly after the FBI stole Sanders's computer and illegally entered the hard drive to seize the contents within, FBI senior management refused to allow FBI field officers to enter the hard drive of a computer owned by a man now under indictment for conspiring to destroy the World Trade Center on September 11, 2001.

7. John McQuiston, "Couple Go on Trial in Theft of Piece of Crashed Jet," *New York Times*, 7 April 1999.

8. McQuiston, "Couple Go On Trial," *New York Times*, 7 April 1999.

9. Associated Press, 12 April 1999.

10. On several occasions, various media reported the FBI as being on the verge of declaring the crash site a crime scene, but it never did so.

11. James Sanders's attorney still has this tape. Sanders has the official transcript.

12. John McQuiston, "Couple Convicted of Trying to Steal Wreckage From Flight 800 as Part of Research," *New York Times*, 14 April 1999.

13. John McQuiston, "Jury at Conspiracy Trial Shown Flight 800 Seats," *New York Times*, 8 April 1999.

14. Phillip Weiss, *Jewish World Review*, 15 April 1999.

15. McQuiston, "Couple Convicted," *New York Times*, 14 April 1999.

16. McQuiston, "Couple Convicted," *New York Times*, 14 April 1999.

13. IMAGINARY FLAGPOLES

1. NTSB public hearing, 8 December 1997.

2. NTSB hearing, 23 August 2000. Unless cited otherwise, all David Mayer quotes will be from this source, as will those by Bernard Loeb, Jim Hall, and George Black.

3. NTSB Group Chairman's Factual Report of Accident Investigation, 16 October 1997. This is covered in chapter 3.

4. NTSB public hearing, 8 December 1997.

5. *TWA Flight 800: What Did the Witnesses See?* aired on November 18, 1997.

6. CIA briefing of the NTSB, 30 April 1999, documented in the National Transportation Safety Board Docket Materials for Investigation DCA96MA070, TWA Flight 800, 17 July 1996, Appendix FF.

7. Paul Angelides's written account, 12 July 1998.

8. The authors summarize this account in the documentary *Silenced*. Channel 8 of West Hartford, Connecticut, would not give permission to show the actual footage, which the authors had in their possession.
9. CIA briefing, NTSB Docket Materials, Appendix FF.
10. Mike Wire is FBI Witness 571, documented in the NTSB Docket Materials, Witness Appendix G. He was interviewed by phone on July 23, 1996, and in person on July 30, 1996.
11. Wire, NTSB Docket Materials, Witness Appendix G.
12. CIA briefing, NTSB Docket Materials, Appendix FF.
13. Dwight Brumley, interview by authors, videotape, September 2001.
14. From Dwight Brumley's 302, documented in the NTSB Docket Materials, Witnesses, Appendix B.
15. Patricia Milton, *In the Blink of an Eye*, 79.
16. David Mayer, Witness Group Chairman's Factual Report: Appendix EE, NTSB Public Docket, 10 August 2000.
17. From Joseph Delgado's 302, documented in the NTSB Docket Materials, Witness 649, Appendix B.
18. This visual image is confirmed in the documentary *Silenced*.

14. FIRST STRIKE

1. NTSB hearing, 23 August 2000.
2. NTSB hearing, 22 August 2000.
3. As told to Andrea Stassau of Channel 8 in West Hartford, Connecticut, November 2000. Kallstrom had been using the "scintilla of evidence" phrase repeatedly since November 18, 1997, when the FBI withdrew from the case.
4. Patricia Milton, *In the Blink of an Eye*, 262.
5. Hank Hughes, response to the Senate Judiciary Subcommittee on Administrative Oversight and the Courts, 14 June 1999.
6. Donald Kerr, testimony before the Senate Judiciary Subcommittee on Administrative Oversight and the Courts, 10 May 1999.
7. NTSB hearing, 22 August 2000.
8. NTSB hearing, 22 August 2000. Only new references will be cited in this section, as most have been previously cited.
9. NTSB public hearing, 8 December 1997. This alteration was graphically shown in the authors' documentary, *Silenced*.
10. "IAMAW Analysis and Recommendations," 10 August 2000.
11. An otherwise abusive letter to the editor sent to *Ingram's Magazine*, of which Jack Cashill is the executive editor.
12. Lewis Schiliro, testimony before the Senate Judiciary Subcommittee on Administrative Oversight and the Courts, 10 May 1999.
13. Cmdr. William Donaldson, letter to Louis Freeh, 24 September 1998.
14. Milton, 333.
15. John Bacon, "Relatives of Flight 800 Victims to Gather Today," *USA Today*, 17 July 1997.
16. David Hendrix, "Military Exercises Stoke Theory on TWA Crash," *Riverside (California) Press-Enterprise*, 18 July 1998.
17. Yossef Bodansky, *Bin Laden: The Man Who Declared War on America* (Roseville, CA: Prima, [1999] 2001), 180.
18. According to CNN, 18 July 1996, "Attorney General Janet Reno said that two calls claiming responsibility had been received after the crash, adding that there are 'no indications' of terrorism at this time."
19. Bodansky, 182.
20. Bodansky, 182.
21. Simon Reeve, who investigated the 1993 World Trade Center attack and is the author of *The New Jackals: Ramzi Yousef, Osama bin Laden and the Future of Terrorism* (London: Andre Deutsch, 1999), tied the plots together in the September 12, 1999, *Guardian* with Giles Foden.
22. Republic of the Philippines intelligence report, 9 January 1995, reproduced in Bill Gertz, *Breakdown* (Washington: Regnery, 2002), Appendix A.
23. Johnelle Bryant, interview with Brian Ross, *ABC News*, 6 June 2002.
24. John Sugg, writing in the January/February 1999 issue of *Extra! Magazine*, approvingly documents the many news media that turned against Emerson, including those cited.

25. This shameful episode is well documented in Jonathan Tobin's September 4, 1998, column in *Jewish World Review.*

26. Sugg reports this.

27. CIA briefing of the NTSB, 30 April 1999, documented in the National Transportation Safety Board Docket Materials for Investigation DCA96MA070, TWA Flight 800, 17 July 1996—this and following CIA quotes.

28. Milton, 334.

29. NTSB hearing, 23 August 2000.

30. Anthony Curreri was interviewed on July 19, John Riley on July 20. The Suffolk County summaries are all available on the Internet, among other sites, at www.accessone.com/~rivero/CRASH/TWA/WIT/wit.

31. FBI Witness 24, documented in the NTSB Docket Materials for Investigation DCA96MA070, TWA Flight 800, 17 July 1996, Witness Appendix G.

32. Robert Kessler, "Streak ID'd As Plane, Not Missile," Newsday.com, 21 March 1997.

33. Kessler, "Streak ID'd As Plane," Newsday.com, 21 March 1997.

34. Hendrix, "Military Exercises Stoke Theory," *Riverside (California) Press-Enterprise*, 18 July 1998.

35. Dick Russell, interview by authors, videotape, September 2001.

36. Maj. Fritz Meyer, videotaped presentation at the Granada Forum in California, 12 March 1998.

37. Dr. Thomas Stalcup, interview by authors, videotape, April 2001. The Flight 800 Independent Researcher's Organization Web site, flight800.org, also presents a wealth of visual imagery on the radar sightings.

38. Stalcup, interview.

39. This is inferred from Meyer's statements made at the Granada Forum, 12 March 1988.

40. Accuracy in Media press conference, 8 January 1998; widely reported.

41. "IAMAW Analysis and Recommendations," 10 August 2000.

42. Dick Morris, interview by Greta Van Susteren, *On the Record with Greta Van Susteren*, FOXNews, 2 February 2002.

ACKNOWLEDGMENTS

This book could not have been written without the help of those many souls who braved scorn and fear of retribution to share their stories with us. Foremost among them are the family members of Flight 800's victims: Don Nibert, father of Cheryl; Flora Headley, mother of Captain Ralph Kevorkian; and Marge Gross, sister of Andy Krukar.

We thank, too, those key eyewitnesses to the tragedy who refused to be silenced: Major Fritz Meyer, Dwight Brumley, Mike Wire, Lisa Perry, and Paul Angelides among others.

We have the greatest respect for those involved with the investigation who dared to come forward and tell us what they knew—most notably Jim Speer, Kelly O'Meara, Herman Burnett, Victoria Cummock, and several more who understandably chose to remain anonymous.

Essential, too, were those reporters and independent investigators who insisted on the truth, often at great risk to their own careers, and upon whose work we built our case: Glena Schulze, Howard Mann, John Stankard, Robert Davey, Ray Lahr, Dave Hendrix, Kristina Borjesson, Dick Russell, Reed Irvine, Dr. Thomas Stalcup, Graeme Sephton, Ian Goddard, Michael Rivero, Marilyn Brady, Michael Hull, Tom Shoemaker, and, of course, Cmdr. Bill Donaldson and his brother, Bob Donaldson.

Kudos also to Joseph Farah of WorldNetDaily, who encouraged us from the beginning; Janis Reed, who introduced us to the Farahs; and Joel Miller, who graciously edited the book.

Thanks to Jack's wife, Joan, for her forbearance. And the greatest of all thanks to Elizabeth Sanders, whose grace and decency first attracted Jack to the story and whose courage and resolve sustained Jim through the story and beyond.

ABOUT THE AUTHORS

JACK CASHILL, Emmy award–winning writer and producer and the executive editor of *Ingram's* (Kansas City's leading business magazine), has produced documentaries for regional PBS and national cable channels. His writing has also appeared in *Fortune, Wall Street Journal, Washington Post, Weekly Standard,* and on WorldNetDaily.com.

JAMES SANDERS, a police officer turned investigative reporter, has written two prior books on this subject, *The Downing of TWA Flight 800* and *Altered Evidence.* In December of 1997, he and his wife, Elizabeth, a TWA flight attendant and trainer, were arrested for conspiracy to steal government property after receiving material from a whistle-blower within the Flight 800 investigation.

WND BOOKS

A DIVISION OF THOMAS NELSON, INC.

The pen is indeed mightier than the sword. In an age where swords are being rattled all over the world, a new voice has emerged. An unprecedented partnership between WorldNetDaily, the leading independent Internet news site, and Thomas Nelson, Inc., one of the leading publishers in America, has brought about a new book-publishing venture—WND Books.

You can find WND Books at your favorite bookstore, or by visiting the Web site www.WorldNetDaily.com.

In *Center of the Storm: Practicing Principled Leadership in Times of Crisis,* former Florida Secretary of State Katherine Harris discusses the behind-the-scenes negotiations and backroom bartering that everyone suspected, but no one dared to disclose, during the infamous 2000 presidential election vote recount. Through never-before-revealed anecdotes, she explains twelve essential principles that helped her not just survive but thrive. She clearly illustrates how we, too, can learn these skills that help us in times of crisis. ISBN 0-7852-6443-4

The Savage Nation: Saving America from the Liberal Assault on our Borders, Language, and Culture warns that our country is losing its identity and becoming a victim of political correctness, unmonitored immigration, and socialistic ideals. Michael Savage, whose program is the fourth largest radio talk show and is heard on more than three hundred stations coast to coast, uses bold, biting, and hilarious straight talk to take aim at the sacred cows of our ever-eroding culture and wages war against the "group of psychopaths" known as PETA, the ACLU, and the liberal media. ISBN 0-7852-6353-5

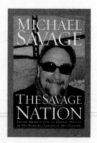

Taking America Back
ISBN 0-7852-6392-6

"Joseph Farah has written a thought-provoking recipe for reclaiming America's heritage of liberty and self-governance. I don't agree with all the solutions proposed here, but Farah definitely nails the problems."

—**Rush Limbaugh**
Host of America's #1 Talk Program,
The Rush Limbaugh Show

"I don't agree with everything Joseph Farah says in *Taking America Back,* but he has written a provocative, from-the-heart call to action. It's a must-read for anyone who wonders how we can expand liberty and reclaim the vision of our founders."

—**Sean Hannity**
Author of *Let Freedom Ring* and Cohost of *Hannity and Colmes* on FOX News

"Joseph Farah and I share a fierce passion for protecting children and a belief that without the Ten Commandments there would be no U.S. Constitution or Bill of Rights. Every American who shares our convictions should read this book."

—**Dr. Laura C. Schlessinger**
Author of *The Ten Commandments*

Available April 2003 from WND BOOKS

Patricia Roush's girls were kidnapped more than sixteen years ago and taken by their Saudi father, whom they hardly knew, to the kingdom of Saudi Arabia. *At Any Price* is the story of her fight to get them back from a father with a documented history of severe mental illnesses and violent tendencies. In the midst of this tragic set of circumstances was a bigger problem—an ongoing, demoralizing struggle with the U.S. government and the Saudi kingdom to reunite her with her children. This personal story of bravery, courage, and faith will warm and inspire readers. ISBN 0-7852-6365-9

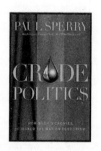